A HISTORY OF ARABIAN MUSIC

A HISTORY OF ARABIAN MUSIC

TO THE XIIIth CENTURY

BY

HENRY GEORGE FARMER

M.A., Ph.D., M.R.A.S.

AUTHOR OF

" *The Arabian Influence on Musical Theory.*"

" *The Arabic Musical Manuscripts in the Bodleian Library.*"

" *The Influence of Music: From Arabic Sources.*"

Goodword

BOOKS

First published in London 1929
First published by Goodword Books 2001

GOODWORD BOOKS
1, Nizamuddin West Market,
New Delhi 110 013
Tel. 462 5454, 462 6666
Fax 469 7333, 464 7980
e-mail: skhan@vsnl.com
website: http://www.alrisala.org

Printed in India

To the Memory of my
MU'ALLIM,
the late
Rev. Dr. T. H. Weir,
M.A., B.D., D.D.,
lecturer in arabic in
the university of glasgow (1902-28),
this volume is dedicated
in token of gratitude.

" I regard it as a high compliment having been invited to write the Preface to a treatise which is the fruit of so much research, and which displays so much industry and accuracy. It is, however, certain that you require no introduction from me to the Orientalist public, and none from anyone to the musical. I might, therefore, be charged with presumption if I accepted your invitation.

" Further, I find a fair number of propositions in the work which differ seriously from my own conclusions ; the latter may certainly be erroneous, and I am most willing and even anxious that such as differ from them should be put before the world. . . . I am sure therefore that bearing in mind these considerations, you will accept my cordial thanks for your proposal while excusing me for declining it."
—PROFESSOR D. S. MARGOLIOUTH, Oxford University.

PREFACE

Although this work was commenced fifteen years ago, it was not until 1919–25, whilst I was fulfilling a Research Studentship at the University of Glasgow that it assumed its present form. During this period I had the benefit of the teaching, on the linguistical and historical side, of the late Rev. Dr. T. H. Weir, a scholar of rare ability,[1] as well as the occasional guidance, in matters relating to the science of music, of the late Dr. H. J. Watt.[2] Death has claimed both of these savants. Nevertheless, I take this opportunity of acknowledging, more especially to the former, my deep appreciation of their advice and help, always given ungrudgingly.

In this work I have observed the conventional chronological method because it was best suited to my purpose. Only by adopting this system could I have conveniently demonstrated how culture stood in relation to the social and political regimen. Each chapter is divided into three sections. The *first* deals with the social and political factors which determined the general musical culture. The *second* describes the musical life of the period, together with details of the theory and practice of music. This has been kept free, as far as was possible, from technicalities, although the author hopes to deal with the theory and science of Arabian music in detail, from an historical standpoint, in a companion volume. The *third* section is devoted to biographies of all the celebrated composers, singers, instrumentalists, theorists, scientists, and *littérateurs*.

In the transliteration of Arabic and Persian words I have adopted the system approved by the International Congress of Orientalists (1894), and recommended by the

[1] The Lecturer in Arabic.
[2] The Lecturer on Psychology.

Royal Asiatic Society, with but slight modifications, notably in the non-observance of the ligature or logotype in *th*, *dh*, etc. In regard to proper names, I have kept to Arabic forms so far as I have considered reasonable. For instance, I have written Al-Mauṣil rather than Mosul, but with Mecca, Damascus, Cordova, I have fallen back on conventional usage, although I have only made a half-concession in Al-Medīna. In dispensing with the forms *Caliph* and *Caliphate* in favour of *Khalif* and *Khalifate*, rather than the more proper *Khalīfa* and *Khilāfat*, I sincerely trust that I have not committed too serious a breach of convention. In the question of the use of the Arabic definite article, I probably have not always been consistent. A similar criticism may also be urged against my transliteration of the *hamza*. As for any inconsistency in plural forms, I have, generally speaking, only used Arabic plurals in words of non-European usage.

The work has been planned to satisfy both the orientalist and the musician, and in spite of the reputed fate of those who attempt to serve two masters, I can only hope that in this case the exception proves the rule.

My sincere thanks are due to Professor Dr. D. S. Margoliouth, of Oxford, and to Professor Dr. W. B. Stevenson, of Glasgow, for useful hints. To Dr. Richard Bell, of Edinburgh, and Mr. John Walker, M.A., I owe an acknowledgment for having read the proof sheets of this work.

Glasgow, 1928

CONTENTS

DESCRIPTION OF THE PLATES.

Frontispiece.

From the *Kitāb al-mūsīqī* of Al-Fārābī (d. 950) in the Bibliotheca Nacionale at Madrid.[1] This copy dates from the 12th century, and it is claimed that it was made for Ibn Bājja or Avenpace (d. 1138).[2] Whether this design of the *shāhrūd* appeared in the original work of Al-Fārābī, or whether it is an addition by a later copyist, we have no evidence. The design does not appear in the Leyden copy.[3] Whilst its zither-like form agrees with the 11th century descriptions of Ibn Sīnā[4] and Ibn Zaila,[5] its lute-like structure is vouched for by Ibn Ghaibī in the 15th century.[6]

To face page 108.

From the *Risāla fī khubr ta'līf al-alḥān* of Al-Kindī (d. 874) in the British Museum.[7] This transcript was made in the year 1661, and the scribe informs us that it was copied from a "defective" and "unreliable" exemplar which had been written in the city of Damascus in the year 1224. In this treatise, Al-Kindī deals with the theory of music almost entirely as he had learned it from the Greek treatises, and his system of notation was probably influenced by these.

To face page 202.

From the *Kitāb al-adwār* of Ṣafī al-Dīn 'Abd al-Mu'min (d. 1294) in the British Museum.[8] The MS. was copied in the year 1390. This folio gives a phonetic notation of a song in the *Naurūz* melodic mode (*awāz*) and the *Ramal* rhythmic mode (*ḍarb*). This scheme of notation, which may be found as early as Ibn Zaila (d. 1048),[9] was probably borrowed from Nikomachos.

[1] No. 602, fol. 18, v.
[2] Cf. Robles, *Catálago*, p. 249.
[3] Or. 651.
[4] *India Office MS.*, No. 1811, fol. 173
[5] *Brit. Mus. MS.*, Or. 2361, fol. 235.
[6] *Bodleian MS.*, Marsh, 282, fol. 79.
[7] No. 2361, fol. 167, v.
[8] Or. 136, fol. 38, v.
[9] *Brit. Mus. MS.*, Or. 2361, fol. 226. See my *Facts for the Arabian Musical Influence*, p. 92, and *Studies in Oriental Musical Instruments*, pp. 34-5.

INTRODUCTION

" We must cease to regard Arabia as a land of deserts and barbarism ; it was, on the contrary, a trading centre of the ancient world, and the Muslims who went forth from it to conquer Christendom and found empires, were but the successors of those who, in earlier times, had exercised a profound influence upon the destinies of the East."

Professor A. H. Sayce, *Early Israel*, p. 128.

ALMOST everyone who has written on the subject of the music of the Arabs has looked, in the matter of origins, to either Greece or Persia. Much of this is perhaps excusable, seeing that until recent years we knew next to nothing of pre-Islāmic Arabia save what could be gleaned from Greek and Latin authors or the legendary material handed down from pre-Islāmic Arabic sources. Thus the temptation to look towards Greece and Persia in this question was considerable, especially when we consider the position of Arabia and the outside civilizations which came in culture-contact with it. Yet the truth is that Arabian culture did not originate in that shadowy period of the so-called " Days of Idolatry " when Greek, Roman, Byzantine, or Persian hegemonies were at their height, any more than it began with Islām, but dates back to a period long anterior to them all.

The excavations made in recent years on the sites of ancient Semitic civilizations, have wrought wondrous changes in our notions of the world's culture-history. The earliest reference to Arabia reaches at present to the third millennium B.C., when we have cuneiform inscriptions which mention lands identified as being situated in Arabia. Under the Babylonian ruler Narām-Sin (*ca.* 2600 B.C.) a king of Magan or Makkan was conquered. In the time of Gudea (*ca.* 2400 B.C.) we read of a kingdom called Kimash or Māshu, as well as a place named Khakhu, and a land of Malukhkha. Finally, an inscription of

Arad-Nannar (*ca.* 2300 B.C.) mentions a region known as Sabu. Although the precise location of these lands has been the subject of controversy, yet there is general agreement that they were situated in Arabia. Both Magan and Sabu have been identified with the South Arabian kingdoms of Ma'ān (Ma'īn) and Sabā'. Kimash or Māshu has been located in Central Arabia, whilst Khaḳhu and Malukhkha are said to have been in Western Arabia, the latter being considered the land of the Banū 'Amālīq.

At the beginning of the first millennium B.C., we certainly have definite evidence of some of these Arab kingdoms. The South Arabian monuments reveal two important kingdoms, Ma'īn with its capitals at Qarnāwu and Yathil, and Sabā' with its capital at Ma'rib. They each had their turn at dominion apparently, and both extended their power as far north as the Gulf of 'Aqaba, where we read of an Arab territory called Muṣrān. About the sixth century B.C., the latter country fell to the Arab Liḥyānids, who made their capital at Al-Ḥijr. The Arab Nabaṭæans, about the fourth century B.C., then took the political lead in these parts, with their capital at Petra. They continued their dominion until Trajan subdued them in 106 A.D. Meanwhile, other Arab kingdoms had sprung up further south. From Theophrastos (fourth cent. B.C.) we learn that there were four kingdoms south of the Gulf of 'Aqaba. These were Sabā', Ḥaḍramaut, Qatabān, and *Mamali* (*Mali*). Eratosthenēs (third cent. B.C.) mentions Ma'īn with Qarnāwu as capital, Sabā' with Ma'rib, Qatabān with Tamna', and Ḥaḍramaut with Shabwat.

Thanks to the labours of travellers, excavators, and scholars, we are able to appreciate that these ancient Arab kingdoms were in possession of a civilization quite as important in its way as that of Babylonia-Assyria. "In South Arabia," says Dr. Fritz Hommel, "we come upon traces of a high civilization at a very early period."[1] Later research has enabled this scholar to say almost definitely that "South Arabian civilization with its

[1] Hommel, *Ancient Hebrew Tradition*, 77.

gods, incense altars, inscriptions, forts and castles, must have been in a flourishing condition as early as the beginning of the first millennium B.C."[1] The greatness of these civilizations is testified not only by the monuments themselves, but by the Babylonian-Assyrian cuneiform inscriptions, the Old Testament, and classical authors. Whilst admitting the all-pervading influence of Babylonian-Assyrian culture, it must also be allowed that Arabia itself played no small part in determining this culture. Hommel has pointed out that the great importance of the Arabs for the ancient East lies in the domain of *civilization* and *religion*, and if we mention but two words, *incense* and *moon-worship*, we can realize how the Arabs influenced their nearer neighbours, especially the Hebrews and Greeks.[2]

Yet scarcely a line has come down to us concerning the music of the ancient Arabs. That their music was appreciated is borne out by an inscription of Ashurbānipal (seventh cent. B.C.), where Arab prisoners toiling for their Assyrian masters whiled away their hours in singing (*alili*) and music (*ninguti*), which so delighted the Assyrians that they begged for more.[3] This need not, however, preclude us from surmising what the musical culture of the ancient Arab kingdoms was like, because in view of the definite similarity in general culture between all the Semitic groups, especially in religion, with which music was so closely associated, it could scarcely have been otherwise than that a certain level of musical culture was maintained among the Assyrians, Phœnicians, Hebrews, and Arabs, who were connected by political and commercial ties, and above all, speaking practically the same language. In all the other groups we see the inordinate elevation to which music had been raised, and if we take into consideration the accounts of the Greeks and Romans concerning the Arab kingdoms whose luxurious living was the envy of their neighbours, and whose wealth exceeded that of all other nations,

[1] *Encyclopædia of Islām*, i, 380.
[2] *Ibid.*, i, 379.
[3] Schrader, *Keilinschriftliche Bibliothek*, ii, 234.

one can only assume that they must have been as well served in matters musical as the other Semites.

Professor Stephen Langdon, the eminent Assyriologist, has demonstrated the close connection between the music of the Assyrian and Hebrew cults. If names can tell us anything, this relationship can be extended to the Arabs. The *sharrū* or precentor in Assyria can be traced in the *shā'ir* or poet-soothsayer of the Arabs. The Assyrian hymn was the *shīru,* and in it we recognize the Hebrew *shīr* (song) and the Arabic *shi'r* (verse, knowledge). The psalm in Assyrian was the *zamāru,* which equates with the Hebrew *zimrāh* (song) and *mizmōr* (psalm). Certainly the Assyrian *shigū* or penitential psalm is identical with the *shiggāiōn* of the Hebrews and the *shajan* of the Arabs in origin. In a like way the *allū* or wail in Assyrian may be linked up with the Hebrew and Arabic *elal* and *wilwāl.* Indeed, the Assyrian *shidru* or recitation may find its cognate in the *inshād* of the Arabs.

The generic term for music in Assyrian was *nigūtu* or *ningūtu,* the root being *nagū* ("to sound"). Hebrew furnishes its like in *nāgan* ("to play a stringed instrument"), hence *negīnāh* (music, stringed instruments). In Assyrian the word *'an* stood for song. It is the Hebrew *'ānāh* and the Arabic *ghinā'.* Scholars have even identified the Assyrian *alalu* with the noisy *tehillāh* of the Hebrews and the *tahlīl* of the Arabs. The word *nāqu* in Assyrian means "to lament." and this must surely be connected with the Hebrew *nehī* and the Arabic *nauḥ* (lamentory song).

As for musical instruments, the Babylonian-Assyrian *ṭabbalu* (drum) and *adapu* (tambourine) can be matched by the Aramaic-Hebrew *ṭibela* and *toph* and the Arabic *ṭabl* and *duff.* The Hebrew reed-pipe called *zemer* and the Arabic *zamr,* are manifestly identical, just as the Assyrian *qarnu,* the Hebrew *qeren,* and the Arabic *qarn* (horn), and the Assyrian *ibbubu* or *imbubu,* the Aramaic *abūbā,* and the Arabic *unbūb* (pipe) are connected. These very striking similarities in nomenclature would not, however, be of such import if we did not know of the close cultural connection between all these Semites.

About the opening of the Christian era, powerful forces came into operation which were to change the entire political and economic life of the peninsula. The decay and final extinction of the great cities of the Mesopotamian plains in the fall of Babylonia and Assyria must already have reacted on the Arab kingdoms who, from time immemorial, had controlled the great trade routes. Then came the decline of the Phœnician markets, which was a further setback. More serious still was the opening of the sea-trade route up the Red Sea by the Romans about the first century A.D. This completely ruined the southern overland caravan trade which had been the mainstay of the Arab kingdoms of the south. Political events made matters worse. In the north, where the Nabaṭæans held the northern caravan entrepôts, the end came swifter still when the Romans put Palmyra to the sword in 272 A.D. The Arab kingdoms never recovered from the economic pressure and political stress. Migrations became the order of the day. The mighty cities were deserted and left to crumble. Yet Arabia was not smitten with sterility. From this womb of the Semites was to issue one more child which was to become the progenitor of the Islāmic civilization of the Khalifate, a worthy successor of the great Semitic civilizations of the past. Just as the latter had been built up by successive migrations from the heart of Arabia, so the former was to receive a similar impulse. This time, however, it is more clearly defined, and it is here that we take up our story of the History of Arabian Music.

CHAPTER I

THE DAYS OF IDOLATRY

(From the First to the Sixth Century)

"Be content to listen to the singing-girl who delights us on a cloudy day."

'Abd al-Masīḥ ibn 'Asala (6th century ?), *Al-mufaḍḍaliyyāt.*

THIS is the period which Muslims have called the *jāhiliyya* or "Days of Ignorance," meaning by that, ignorance of the revelations of the Prophet Muḥammad.[1] In truth, these were days of ignorance, since not only had political, economic, and cultural decay set in, but all knowledge of the old Arab civilizations which had flourished for two millenniums was practically lost. When the Islāmic historians came to deal with this period they could only fill their pages with legendary genealogies, vague traditions, heroic epics, and sundry folk-lore, such as had been handed down by poet and minstrel, much of it of small historical value, but sufficient to enable later writers to build some sort of edifice on the foundations afforded by the monuments and inscriptions.

Of those Arab kingdoms of antiquity which began with Magan, Sabu, Malukhkha, and others in Babylonian-Assyrian times, the Arabs of the Days of Idolatry knew but little. The nearest that they got was in an occasional line in proverb, song, or story, about the people of 'Ād, 'Amālīq, Thamūd, Ṭasm and Jadīs, whom the *Qur'ān* holds before the eyes of those who say—"There is no God but God," as a perpetual warning against the fate of their proud, pleasure-loving ancestors, who were humbled to the dust and brought to destruction.[2] But the fall

[1] The *jāhiliyya* properly refers to the period from the "creation of the world" to the birth of Muḥammad.

[2] *Qur'ān*, vii, xi, xxvi, xlvi.

of the ancient Arab kingdoms was due, as has already been pointed out, to political and economic forces, speeded up by subsequent migrations.

Historians are in common agreement that the first line of the migratory Arabs from South Arabia began to move northwards about the second century A.D.[1] This was the migration of the Banū Azd, connected in legend with the bursting of the famous Dyke of Ma'rib.[2] The movement soon extended, and fresh Arab blood was introduced not only into Al-Ḥijāz, Al-Yamāma, 'Umān, Hajar, and Al-Baḥrain, but also into Mesopotamia and Syria, where there were still to be found the descendants of those Semitic peoples whose culture had been of such immense value to civilization. Much of this culture had been preserved (with the help of Greece and Persia) by Arab Chaldæans, Nabaṭæans and Palmyrenes, and by Aramæans, Jews, and Syrians, who formed the bulk of the population. This culture came to the new Arab settlers, although it only blossomed into luxuriance in the days of Islām.

§ I

South Arabia, the most ancient of the Arab kingdoms, despite the political and commercial decline, still echoed some of the old culture. At the opening of the Christian era there were Sabæan rulers at Mā'rib from the Banū Hamdān. In the fourth century the "Kings of Sabā'" belonged to the Banū Ḥimyar, a dynasty which lasted until the year 525. Music and poetry flourished, and although none of the authors of the *Mu'allaqāt* came from these parts (Al-A'shā lived in Najrān), many of those in the *Mufaḍḍaliyyāt* and the *Ḥamāsa* were of southern blood. We read of a *tubba'* ruler named Ibn Alīshra who was surnamed Dhū Jadan (Owner of the Beautiful Voice).[3] The last *tubba'* ruler, 'Als ibn Zaid (d. 525) also bore this *laqab* or nickname, and Al-Iṣfahānī says

[1] Muir, *Moḥammad*, xc. Cf. Nicholson, *Literary History of the Arabs*, 15, 17.
[2] Al-Mas'ūdī, iii, 378.
[3] Caussin de Perceval, *Hist. Arabes*, i, 75-6.

that he was the first [?among princes] to sing in Al-Yaman.[1] The pre-Islāmic song of Al-Yaman is mentioned as late as the ninth century, since Al-Mas'ūdī quotes Ibn Khurdādhbih to the effect that the people of Al-Yaman practised two kinds of music: the *ḥimyarī* and the *ḥanafī*.[2] The former was evidently the music of the Ḥimyarites and the latter perhaps that of more recent adoption. Several musical instruments used in Islāmic times were of South Arabian provenance and among them the *mi'zaf* (? barbiton) and the *kūs* (large kettledrum). Even to-day, the Arabs of Al-Ḥijāz say that the best and real Arabian music comes from Al-Yaman, whilst the Ḥaḍramī minstrels are always considered to be superior *artistes*.[3]

Al-Ḥijāz was a land of some commercial importance even in these days. At the opening of the Christian era, Mecca, which was then known as Makuraba, was under the dominion of the Banū Jurhum, who, tradition says, succeeded the shadowy Banū 'Amālīq. Al-Medīna, or as it was then called Yathrib, was practically in the hands of the Banū Naḍīr, Banū Quraiẓa, and other tribes who professed the Jewish faith.[4] In the waves of migration from the south already adverted to, clans of the Banū Azd became masters of these two important towns in Al-Ḥijāz and their surrounding territory. Under the rule of the Quraish at Mecca, its *ka'ba* together with the fair at 'Ukāẓ, made these parts a sort of national rendezvous which neither the ancient renown of Al-Yaman nor the brilliant culture of Al-Ḥīra and Ghassān could ever hope to rival. It became the centre of the indigenous arts. At 'Ukāẓ, the poets and minstrels from all parts of the peninsula vied with each other for supremacy in their art. It was here that the famous *Mu'allaqāt* were recited or sung.[5] Singing Girls (*qainät* or *qiyān*) were famous in these days,[6] and legend takes them back

[1] *Aghānī*, iv, 37.
[2] Al-Mas'ūdī, viii, 93.
[3] Personal information from Professor Snouck Hurgronje.
[4] *Aghānī*, xiii, 110. Caussin de Perceval, *op. cit.*, i, 214, 644.
[5] *Encyclopædia of Islām*, i, 403. Entire *qaṣīdas* are still sung by the *badawī* Arabs. Burckhardt, *Bedouins and Wahabys*, i, 75, 253.
[6] *Aghānī*, viii, 2. Cf. the Assyrian *qinītu*.

to the time of the Banū 'Amālīq.[1] Musicians from Al-Ḥijāz found favour even at other courts.[2] Among the musical instruments in use we read of the *mizhar* (lute), *mi'zafa* (? psaltery), *quṣṣāba* (flute), *mizmār* (reed-pipe) and *duff* (tambourine). Al-Ḥijāz even claims to be the fount of music, and we have the author of the *'Iqd al-farīd* saying that it is clear and evident that the origin and source of music (*ghinā'*) are to be traced to the slaves in the market towns of the Arabs such as Al-Medīna, Al-Ṭā'if, Khaibar, Wādī al-Qura, and others.[3]

Al-Ḥīra was another important culture centre. Mesopotamia, in spite of the disappearance of the great Babylonian-Assyrian cities, could still boast of large towns peopled by Chaldæans, Aramæans, and Jews, and, in spite of foreign domination, still carried on much of the old Semitic culture.[4] As a result of the Arab migration from South Arabia, a group of tribes, confederated under the title of the Tanūkh,[5] settled in Hajar and Al-Baḥrain, after subduing the older population who were Aramæans and Chaldæans.[6] About the third century they moved northwards into Mesopotamia, establishing themselves in the land called 'Irāq 'Arabī, making Al-Anbār, and later Al-Ḥīra (close by ancient Babylon) their chief town. Under a later dynasty, the Lakhmids, Al-Ḥīra became one of the celebrated cities of the East, and although to some extent impressed by Persian influences,[7] it deviated but little from Semitic ideals. It was to Al-Ḥīra that Bahrām Ghūr (430-8), the Persian monarch, was sent, as a prince, to be educated. Here, he was taught music among other Arab accomplishments.[8] When he ascended the throne, one of his first edicts was to improve the status of the musicians

[1] Al-Mas'ūdī, iii, 157. [2] *Aghānī*, xvi, 15. [3] *'Iqd al-farīd*, iii, 186.

[4] King, *Babylon*, 284-7. Greek culture was certainly felt, but this only made headway on the lower Tigris which had become the political and industrial centre instead of on the Euphrates as formerly. King, *op. cit.*, 287-8.

[5] *Aghānī*, xi, 161.

[6] In the *Aghānī* they are called Nabaṭæans, but the Aramæans are intended. See Nicholson, *Lit. Hist. of the Arabs*, xxv.

[7] Persia herself was more influenced by the Semites. Browne, *Lit. Hist. of Persia*, i, 65-6.

[8] Al-Ṭabarī, i, 185. Mīrkhwānd, i (2), 356.

at the Persian court.[1] Al-Ṭabarī tells us about the last Lakhmid king of Al-Ḥīra, Al-Nu'mān III (*ca.* 580-602), that among his shortcomings was an extraordinary passion for music.

The influence of Al-Ḥīra on the culture of Arabia generally was considerable. It was the literary centre from whence poetry radiated to all parts.[2] It was at the Lakhmid court that the poets Al-Nābigha, Ṭarafa, 'Amr ibn Kulthūm, and 'Adī ibn Zaid were treated with princely munificence. Seeing how closely music was allied to poetry, it may be conjectured that the former was equally favoured. It was from Al-Ḥīra that Al-Ḥijāz borrowed a more artistic song than the *naṣb* hitherto used, and also, it would seem, the wooden-bellied *'ūd* (lute) in the place of the skin-bellied *mizhar.*[3] It was here, too, that the *ṣanj* or *jank* (harp) and *ṭunbūr* (pandore) were countenanced.

Syria, at the time that we are dealing with, was also populated by a considerable Arabian element. The Arab Nabaṭæans of the north-west had extended their influence as far north as Palmyra (Tadmor), including Damascus and Boṣrā. When Trajan broke up the Nabaṭæan kingdom of Petra in 106 A.D., the political and commercial leadership of the Nabaṭæan communities passed to Palmyra. This remained an important culture centre until the *débâcle* of 272 A.D., when its inhabitants were put to the sword. Of the specific culture of the Nabaṭæans we have a reliable index in the art remains of Petra, Boṣrā, and Palmyra. Whilst we see plainly the impress of Greece and Rome, there is still the clearest evidence that the older Semitic ideals still pervaded the social and religious life. We know little of the musical culture of the Nabaṭæans. Strabo tells us that they employed musicians at their entertainments.[4] At Palmyra we read of the *kinōrā* (= Heb. *kinnōr*).[5]

[1] Al-Mas'ūdī, iii, 157.
[2] Huart, *Arabic Literature,* 12. Nicholson, *op. cit.,* 37.
[3] Al-Mas'ūdī, viii, 94.
[4] Strabo, xvi, iv, 27.
[5] *Zeitschrift d. Deutschen Morgenländischen Gesellschaft,* xviii, 105. See also the *Corpus Inscriptionum Semiticarum,* ii, No. 268, and the *Mission archéologique en Arabie* by Jaussen and Savignac, p. 217.

After the fall of Palmyra, the territory hitherto controlled by the Nabaṭæans came under the jurisdiction of the Ghassānids, who had just then migrated from the south. The shaikhs of the Ghassānids became phylarchs of the Byzantine Emperors for the old Provincia Arabia as well as Syria, and with them the influence of Byzantium was probably considerable. On this account perhaps, it is said that the culture of the Ghassānids was the most advanced among the Arab kingdoms of the Days of Idolatry.[1] Both Al-Nābigha and Ḥassān ibn Thābit have given glowing accounts of the Ghassānid court, where not only Arab musicians from Mecca and elsewhere were favoured, but singing-girls from Al-Ḥīra and Byzantium.[2] We are told that they played on the *barbaṭ*, which was either a lute or a barbiton.

On the plains of upper Mesopotamia were the Jarmaqs, (Jarāmiqa), who, together with the Nabaṭæans, are said to have used a stringed instrument, the playing of which was similar to that of the *ṭunbūr*.[3] Even among the *badawī* Arabs of the interior we find that music was appreciated. We read not only of the professional singing-girl, but of the matrons of the tribe playing and singing. Musical instruments are frequently mentioned among them, such as the *mizhar* (lute), *kirān* (lute), *muwattar* (*lit.* " a stringed instrument")[4]; *mizmār* (reed-pipe), *duff* (tambourine), *jalājil* (bells), and *nāqūs* (clapper).

§ II

With the Arabs, whose strong point is genealogy, music is given its appropriate family tree. Jubal the son of Cain (Qain) is credited with the first song, which

[1] *Encyclopædia of Islām*, ii, 142.

[2] *Aghānī*, xvi, 15.

[3] Al-Mas'ūdī, viii, 91. The text has *ghīrwāra* but it is corrupt, and Barbier de Meynard thinks that the word *kinnāra* is intended. On the other hand a MS. in the Berlin Staatsbibliothek (Pet. ii, 173) has *qundhūra*. cf. the Arabic *qunbūz* and Persian *qupūz*. See my *Studies in Oriental Musical Instruments*, p. 59.

[4] It has been identified with the lute, being played with the thumb. Lane, *Lexicon*, i, 126, b.

was an elegy on the death of Abel.[1] Bar Hebræus the Syrian (d. 1289) tells us that the inventors of musical instruments were the daughters of Cain, hence the name for a singing-girl, which was *qaina*! It will be recalled that the Hebrews make Jubal, the son of Lamech, "the father of all such as handle the *kinnōr* and *'ugāb*."[2] The latter, as Lamak, also has a place in Arabic musical tradition as the "inventor" of the *'ūd* (lute). His son Tūbal is credited with having introduced the *ṭabl* (drum) and *duff* (tambourine), whilst his daughter Ḍilāl is claimed to have been responsible for the *ma'āzif* (instruments with open strings).[3] From the same Arabic source we learn that the *ṭunbūr* (pandore) came from the people of Sodom (Lūṭ), although others say the Sabæans.[4] At any rate, since both of these people were probably of Arab blood, the statements agree with the account of Julius Pollux, who attributes the instrument to the Arabs.[5] The Persians are allowed the *nāy* (vertical flute), the *suryānai* (flute or reed-pipe), the *diyānai* (double reed-pipe)[6] and the *jank* (harp).[7] Many of the above instruments are depicted in Persian art remains.[8]

As with all the Semites, music played an important part in the mysteries of the Arab soothsayer, enchanter, and prophet. The *jinn* (genii) were evidently conjured by means of music, and the later notion that it was the *jinn* who prompted the verses of the poet and the melodies of the musician, was a survival of this belief.[9] The *Qur'ān* hands down some interesting conceptions which

[1] Al-Mas'ūdī, i, 65. Al-Ṭabarī, i, 146. Mīrkhwānd, i (1), 53. Al-Jundī, *Risāla rauḍ al-masarrāt.*

[2] *Genesis*, iv. 21.

[3] As a generic term the *ma'āzif* were instruments whose strings gave open notes like the harp, psaltery, or barbiton.

[4] *Huth MS.* in the author's possession.

[5] Julius Pollux, iv, 9, 60.

[6] Barbier de Meynard, the editor, adopts the forms *surnāy* and *dūnāy*. See my *Studies in Oriental Musical Instruments*, p. 57.

[7] The text has *ṣanj*.

[8] See Flandrin et Coste, *Voyage en Perse*, pl. x and xii, for musical instruments *temp.* Shāpūr II (309-79 A.D.), and Dalton's *Treasures of the Oxus*, 211.

[9] Musicians in the days of Islām, such as Ibrāhīm al-Mauṣilī, his son Isḥāq, and Ziryāb, all claimed to have been taught melodies by the *jinn*.

relate to music and magic.[1] The intimate connection between these two is borne out by philology. In Arabic, the voice of the *jinn* is termed the *'azf*, which is also the name for a certain musical instrument.[2] When the Jews likened "God's Holy Spirit" to the sounds of the *kithara*, as we find in *Odes of Solomon* (iv, xiv), the apparent symbolism seems to have its origin in primitive culture.

What part music played in the Pagan worship of the Days of Idolatry we know but little. The *ḥajj* or pilgrimage to the various *ka'bāt* was practised,[3] although Mecca was evidently the chief attraction. During the *ḥajj*, the pilgrims appear to have indulged in those primitive musical chantings which still exist in the *tahlīl* and *talbiyya*. Perhaps we may even look for some sort of ritual and even hymns.[4] One fragment of the ritual performed during the *ḥajj* has been preserved in the words *ashriq thabīr kaimā nughīr*, said to have been sung during the *ifāḍa* to Mina.[5] St. Nilus tells us of the Arabs of the north, who chanted a hymn whilst encircling the sacrificial stone.[6] Noeldeke likens it to the *tahlīl*. Doughty saw a stone (*nuṣb*) at Al-Ṭā'if in Al-Ḥijāz which was dedicated to Al-Lāt the goddess.[7] It was upon such stones that sacrifices were offered,[8] and it is not improbable that the song called the *naṣb*, may have been connected originally with the cult. Both Imru'u'l-Qais and Labīd, the pre-Islāmic poets, speak of "maidens circling a pillar," which would most likely be performed in a dance, accompanied by music or song, as with the Phœnico-Cyprian maidens that the art remains have revealed.[9]

Yet in spite of idols and temples, the Arabs of the

[1] *Sūras*, xxi, 79. xxxiv, 10. xxxviii, 17-18. *Kashf al-maḥjūb*, 402-3. Al-Ṭabarī (Zotenberg Edit.), i, 426.

[2] *'Azf = mi'zaf*. Lane, *Lexicon*. See *Bibliotheca Geographorum Arabicorum*, vi, 68 (text).

[3] Syed Aḥmed Khan, *Manners and Customs of the Pre-Islāmic Arabians*, 15.

[4] Nicholson, *Lit. Hist. of the Arabs*, 73. *Encyclopædia of Religion and Ethics*, x, 883.

[5] *Encyclopædia of Islām*, ii, 200.

[6] Migne, *Pat. Lat.*, lxxi, 612.

[7] Doughty, *Travels in Arabia Deserta*, ii, 511.

[8] Lyall, *Ancient Arabian Poetry*, xxviii.

[9] Rawlinson, *History of Phœnicia*, 187.

jāhiliyya interested themselves but little in religion of any sort.[1] The *badawī* view of life, which was thoroughly secular, and quite hedonistic, dominated even the cities and towns. To the *badawī* Arab, " love, wine, gambling, hunting, the pleasures of song and romance, the brief, pointed and elegant expression of wit and wisdom," alone came to be the affairs that mattered. " These things he knew to be good. Beyond them he only saw the grave."[2] We see these thoughts in a poem by Sulmī ibn Rabī'a, who lived in the century before Islām. It is given in the *Ḥamāsa*. The poet tells us how death comes to all and sundry, but meanwhile, there are " life's joys," and among them the pleasure of listening to the music of the *mizhar* (lute).

Everywhere the *shā'ir* or poet-soothsayer possessed high social prestige, alike at the courts of Al-Ḥīra and Ghassān, the fair at 'Ukāẓ, and the *badawī* encampment.[3] The *hijā* or satire (originally an incantation) was held in the utmost veneration. It was delivered in rhymed prose called *saj'*, or else in unrhymed poetry known as *rajaz*. The *shā'ir* was doubtless often as much a musician as a poet, although it would seem that he sometimes engaged a musician (*mughann, mughannī*) to chant his verses for him, in the same way as he would employ a reciter (*rāwī*) to recite them. This idea persisted even unto the days of Islām, when we find a poet like A'shā Hamdān and a musician like Aḥmad al-Naṣībī in this kind of partnership.[4]

How highly the *shā'ir* was esteemed we have evidence from the *Muzhir* of Al-Suyūṭī[5]:

> " When there appeared a poet in a family of the Arabs, the other tribes round about would gather together to that family and wish them joy in their good luck. Feasts would be got ready, the women

[1] Lyall, *op. cit.*, xxvii. Nicholson, *op. cit.*, 135.
[2] Nicholson, *op. cit.*, 136.
[3] That a number of kings and chiefs during the *jāhiliyya* were poets and musicians is significant.
[4] *Aghānī*, v, 162.
[5] Al-Suyūṭī, *Muzhir*, ii, 236. The translation is from Lyall's *Ancient Arabian Poetry*, xvii. See Sale's *Koran*, 20.

of the tribes would join together in bands, playing upon their lutes (*mazāhir*, sing. *mizhar*), as they were wont to do at bridals . . . for a poet was a defence to the honour of them all, a weapon to ward off insult from their good name, and a means of perpetuating their glorious deeds and of establishing their fame for ever."

There was also the female musician (*mughanniya*), who played no inconsiderable part in the musical and literary life. The *ḥarīm* was unknown, and women appear to have enjoyed almost as much liberty as men.[1] It was the women of the tribes who joined in the music of the family or tribal festivities with their instruments, a custom which continued down to the time of Muḥammad, whose nuptials with Khadīja were "celebrated with great festivity, mirth, music, and dancing." At Uḥud (625) the journey of the Quraish was enlivened by the women led by Hind bint 'Utba singing war songs and laments for the slain at Badr, and playing their tambourines (*dufūf*, sing. *duff*).[2] At the onset to battle, they were still singing and playing.[3] What the women generally excelled in was the *marthiya* or lament, and the *nauḥ* or elegy.[4]

Side by side with these matrons we find a class known as the *qaināt* or *qiyān* (sing. *qaina*). These were the singing-girls, who were invariably found in the household of every Arab of social standing. Singing-girls appear in the old story of the destruction of the people of 'Ād as told by Al-Ṭabarī and Al-Mas'ūdī.[5] The people of 'Ād are said to have belonged to South Arabia,[6] and when a lengthy drought afflicted this land, suppliants were sent to the temple at Makuraba (Mecca) to beseech divine aid for rain. At Makuraba the deputation was received by the amīr of the Banū 'Amālīq, Mu'āwiya

[1] Lyall, *op. cit.*, xxxi.
[2] Caussin de Perceval, *Hist. Arabes*, iii, 91.
[3] *Ibid.*, iii, 99. Muir, *Moḥammad*, 259.
[4] *Mufaḍḍaliyyāt*, ii, 215. *Aghānī*, xix, 87.
[5] Al-Ṭabarī, i, 231. Al-Mas'ūdī, iii, 296-7, and *L'abrégé des Merveilles*, 134.
[6] *Encyclopædia of Islām*, i, 121.

ibn Bakr, who entertained them suitably, especially with the music of his two famous singing-girls known as the *jarādatān* (the two grasshoppers). These pleasantries continued for a month, and meanwhile the suppliants were neglecting their mission. Finally, supplications were begun, but the deity was so wroth with the people of 'Ād on account of their sins, that a storm cloud was sent over the land which, bursting, destroyed the whole race.[1] At a period just prior to the dawn of Islām, a Quraish chief, 'Abdallāh ibn Jud'ān, possessed two singing-girls called the *jarādatān* of 'Ād, and while he had them they were such an attraction at Mecca that he was compelled to keep an " open house." He then presented them to his friend Umayya ibn Abī'l-Ṣalt (d. 630), the Pagan poet of Mecca.[2]

How much the singing-girls had become an integral part of social life may be seen in the early struggles of Muḥammad himself. When the Meccans were marching to Badr in 624, they took with them " all the instruments and appurtenances of pleasure, and singing-girls; the latter performing on musical instruments, singing near every water, where a halt was made, and lengthening their tongues with reproaches against the professors of Islām."[3] When Muḥammad was known to be approaching, the Meccan chief was counselled to retire rather than risk a battle, but he replied: " No. I will not return to Mecca until we have refreshed ourselves at Badr, and spent three days in feasting and listening to the singing and playing of the singing-girls."[4]

At the court of the Ghassānid monarch, Jabala ibn al-Aiham (*ca.* 623-37), ten or more of these singing-

[1] The *jarādatān* passed into proverb. See Freytag, *Arabum Proverbia.* iii, 49. xxiii, 517.

[2] *Aghānī*, viii, 3.

[3] Mīrkhwānd, II (I), 291.

[4] Al-Ṭabarī, i, 1307. The singing-girl is sometimes called a *karīna.* (*'Iqd al-farīd*, iii, 186. Al-Mas'ūdī, viii, 419. Al-Tibrīzī, 83). *Dājina* or *mudjina* was also given her, and the name has particular interest from a point of view of etymology. The words are derived from the verbal root *dajana* = " to be cloudy." (Cf. *Mufaḍḍaliyyāt*, ii, 89, 221.) It was customary for the *dājina* to sing and play when the skies were overcast so as to conjure rain. (See my *Influence of Music; From Arabic Sources*, 9.) One of the *jarādatān* was named Thamād (= preserver of water). Cf. the name of the tribe Thamūd.

girls were in evidence.[1] Ḥassan ibn Thābit (*ca.* 563-683) says[2]:

"I saw ten singing-girls, five of them Byzantines, singing the songs of their country to the accompaniment of the *barbaṭ* (lute or barbiton), and five others from Al-Ḥīra, who had been given to King Jabala by Iyās ibn Qabīsa, singing the songs of their country. Arab singers also came from Mecca and elsewhere for his [Jabala's] pleasure."

At Al-Ḥīra,[3] and at the Persian court,[4] we see these singing-girls, and even with the *badawī* Arabs. It was the antiphonal chanting of the singing-girls (*dājināt*) that Bishr ibn 'Amr praised.[5] One of the singing-girls of this old pre-Islāmic poet, who was named Huraira, led the more famous poet-minstrel Al-A'shā Maimūn ibn Qais to declare his love.[6] The valiant poet-shaikh of the Banū'l-Ḥārith, 'Abd Yaghūth ibn Waqqāṣ (d. *ca.* 612), could not forget the delights of the singing-girls even in his death-song.[7]

Singing-girls were also attached to the taverns for the entertainment of visitors. Al-A'shā Maimūn ibn Qais sings of the bitter-sweet joys of the tavern, not merely of the "flowing bowl," but of the alluring *jank* (harp) and the refrain (*tarjī'*) of thé singing-girl.[8] Ṭarafa,[9] Labīd,[10] and 'Abd al-Masīḥ ibn 'Asala,[11] all praised the good-cheer of the tavern singing-girl.[12]

Lyall was of opinion that these singing-girls "were all foreigners, either Persians or Greeks from Syria; they sang, however, at any rate sometimes, poems in Arabic, though probably to foreign airs."[13] Von Kremer goes further and says: "It is clear beyond doubt that these female singers originally sang in their own tongue:

[1] Professor Nicholson points out that this reference really belongs to an earlier period.
[2] *Aghānī*, xvi, 15. [3] *Mufaḍḍaliyyāt*, xxx. [4] *Ibid.*, lxxii, xxvi.
[5] *Ibid.*, lxxi. [6] *Aghānī*, viii, 79. [7] *Mufaḍḍaliyyāt*, xxx.
[8] Al-Tibrīzī, 146. The text has *ṣanj*, a word sometimes used instead of *jank* to represent the Persian *chang*.
[9] *Mu'allaqāt*. [10] Al-Tibrīzī, 73. [11] *Mufaḍḍaliyyāt*, lxxii.
[12] For the particular character of these singing girls see Al-Tirmidhī, ii, 33. *Tāj al-'arūs*, sub "Zammār.
[13] Lyall, *op. cit.*, xxvi, 87. Cf. Clouston, *Arabian Poetry* . . . 377.

Greek or Persian and not Arabic. . . . Ṭuwais is the first who sang in Arabic with the accompaniment of the hand drum." I do not know of any authority for these statements. That *all* the singing-girls were "foreigners" can scarcely be true, unless we are to discredit the great *Kitāb al-aghānī* and the poets of the *jāhiliyya,* who most certainly tell us about Arab singing-girls, who sang in their native tongue.[1] The *qaina* who sang the verses of Al-Nābigha, and made the poet realize for the first time that his poetry contained faulty rhymes (*iqwā'*), must have spoken Arabic well, and was assuredly an Arab by education.[2] Indeed, one can scarcely imagine that the Arabs would have listened for one moment to Arabic poetry from the mouth of a "foreigner," who could rarely have been able to apportion the vocalic and consonantal values which are inseparable from the poetic art, especially when sung. That Ṭuwais was the first to sing in Arabic, is certainly not the case. What has been claimed for him in this respect by Arab historians is something quite different, as we shall see later.

"Before Islām," says Perron, "music was little else than unpretentious psalming,[3] varied and embroidered by the singer, male or female, according to the taste, emotion, or effect desired. These variations, or rather caprices, were prolonged interminably on a syllable, word or hemistich, in such a way that the singing of a *cantilena* of two or three verses might be prolonged for hours. . . . The timbre of the voice, its mobility and vibrations, the feeling which made it sound or quaver, determined the merit of the singer."[4] Everyone sang in unison or octave, as harmony in our acceptation of the term in music, was quite unknown. The only "harmony," if such it could be called, was that supplied by the various instruments of percussion such as the *ṭabl* (drum), *duff* (tambourine), or *qaḍīb* (wand), and the

[1] *Mufaḍḍaliyyāt,* xv.

[2] *Aghānī,* ix, 164. For the importance of correct pronunciation in the song see also *Aghānī,* v, 57.

[3] *Tarannum* was the Arabic word for this. Ibn Khaldūn says that the young men of the *jāhiliyya* passed their idle hours away by indulging in this "psalming."

[4] Perron, *Femmes arabes avant l'Islamisme.*

figuration of the melody by means of ornaments in the shape of trills or turns which were called *zawā'id*.

Bisbr ibn 'Amr tells us about a skilful songstress (*dājina*) who "sang antiphonally with another like her, and struck the resounding lute."[1] Ṭarafa, describing a scene "where men tap the wine skins," speaks of the "low note" upon which the song began. Again we are told in a poem by 'Abda ibn al-Ṭabīb that "the singer prolonged the final vowels with a high trill (*tudrī*) and clearly enunciated the syllables (*tartīl*) giving each its due measure and value."[2]

Arab historians like to expatiate upon the origin of the song. The first song is claimed to have been the *ḥudā'* or caravan song, and its origin is traced to Muḍar ibn Nizār ibn Ma'add,[3] who is the Almodad of the *Old Testament*.[4] It was in the *rajaz* metre, a measure said to correspond with the lifting and lowering of the camel's feet.[5] From the *ḥudā'* there issued the *naṣb*, which is expressly stated to be no more than an improved *ḥudā'*. With the folk, the *ḥudā'*, sometimes called the *rakbānī*, was the "muse populaire."[6] Being in the simple *rajaz* metre it was pre-eminently suitable for the extemporaneous song known as the *ghinā' murtajal*, which we frequently read of among the earlier untutored minstrels, who used a *qaḍīb* or wand to mark the measure of the song. The later Al-Aṣma'ī objected to this type of music, probably because it savoured of Paganism.

In Al-Ḥijāz, which was not so advanced musically as either Al-Ḥīra or Ghassān perhaps, the *naṣb* and the *nauḥ* were the only types of songs practised until the close of the sixth century or beginning of the seventh, when the poet-minstrel Al-Naḍr ibn al-Ḥārith (d. 624) introduced several innovations from Al-Ḥīra, and among them the

[1] *Mufaḍḍaliyyāt*, lxxi.
[2] *Ibid.*, xxvi, p. 101.
[3] Al-Mas'ūdī, viii, 92. Ibn Khaldūn, ii, 359. The story runs that Muḍar fell from his camel and fractured his hand. In his pain he cried out: "*Yā yadāh, yadāh*" ("O my hand"), which gave birth to the *rajaz* metre.
[4] 1 *Chronicles*, i, 20.
[5] See my *Influence of Music; From Arabic Sources*, 9.
[6] *Encyclopædia of Islām*, i, 466.

more advanced song (*ghinā'*), which supplanted the *naṣb*, and the wooden-bellied *'ūd*, which seemingly took the place of the skin-bellied *mizhar*.[1] Rhythm (*īqā'*), such as we read of in the *sinād* and *hazaj* types of song in the late seventh century, appears not to have been practised in these days,[2] for although we are told that the *ḥudā'* and the *naṣb* (by inference) were made up of measured melodies (*alḥān mauzūna*),[3] the musical measure was evidently determined by the prosodical feet of the verse, and was not independent of the verse metre as was the later rhythm called *īqā'*.

In Al-Yaman there were two kinds of song practised, the *ḥimyarī* and the *ḥanafī*, the latter being considered the better.[4] Here we are clearly introduced to a Pre-Islāmic type in the *ḥimyarī*, i.e., the music of the Ḥimyarites, and a more recent type, the *ḥanafī*. There is a passage in the *Qur'ān* (liii, 61), which is claimed to refer to pre-Islāmic music. The passage runs—"Ye laugh and do not weep and ye are *sāmidūn*." Abū'l-'Abbās 'Abdallāh ibn al-'Abbās ibn al-Muṭṭalib (d. 688) said that the *sāmidūn* were those who indulged in the singing of the Ḥimyarites.[5]

In the Days of Idolatry we do not find the mention of the *ṭunbūr* (pandore), although it most certainly existed. Al-Fārābī (d. 950) tells us that the *ṭunbūr al-baghdādī* or *ṭunbūr al-mīzānī* of his day was fretted in accordance with a pre-Islāmic scale which was arrived at by dividing a string into forty parts.[6] The lute was quite common it would seem. It was known variously as the *mizhar*, *kirān*, *barbaṭ*, *muwattar*, and *'ūd*.[7] The earlier instrument was a skin-bellied contrivance, and this we imagine to have been the *mizhar*.[8] The *kirān*, which is stated to have been not absolutely identical with the *'ūd*,[9] may

[1] Al-Mas'ūdī, viii, 93-94. [3] *'Iqd al-farīd*, iii, 186.
[2] Al-Ghazālī, *Iḥyā 'ulūm al-dīn*, in *J.R.A.S.* (1901), p. 217.
[4] Al-Mas'ūdī, viii, 93. [5] Al-Ghazālī, *loc. cit.*
[6] Land, *Recherches*, 140-49. Kosegarten, *Lib. Cant.*, 89. *Mafātīḥ al-'ulūm*, 237.
[7] *'Iqd al-farīd*, iii, 186. Lane, *Lexicon*, p. 1262.
[8] The verbal root *zahara* = "to shine brightly" produces *mizhar* = "a thing that brightens."
[9] *Madrid MS.*, No. 603. *Kitāb al-imtā'*.

have been a name derived through Syriac-Hebrew sources, being a metathesis of *kinār* or *kinnār* (= Hebrew *kinnōr*, Nabaṭæan *kinōrā*).[1] *Barbaṭ* was the Persian name apparently for the wooden-bellied lute adopted by the Arabs as the *'ūd* (= wood).[2] *Muwattar* means literally "an instrument of strings," but it is identified by the old Arabic lexicographers with the lute, and it would seem that it was played with the thumb.[3] Finally, there were the *jank* (= Persian *chang*), also called the *ṣanj*, which was a harp, the *mi'zafa*, which may have been a kind of psaltery,[4] and the *murabba'*, most probably the flat-chested quadrangular guitar.[5] So far the stringed instruments.

Among wind instruments and the percussion group there are not many to record. The term *mizmār* stood for any wood-wind instrument in general, although in particular it was used for a reed-pipe.[6] The *quṣṣāba* (= *qaṣaba*) was the vertical flute.[7] It was this long type which gave the Greeks the prompting for a proverb.[8] The *Qur'ān* mentions the *ṣūr* and *nāqūr* as the instruments upon which "the last trump" will sound.[9] The *ṭabl* (drum) and *duff* (tambourine), as well as the more primitive *qaḍīb* (wand), were the instruments for determining the measure. *Ṣunūj* (sing. *ṣinj*) or metal castanets and *jalājil* (sing. *juljul*) or sonnettes were also favoured.[10] Cymbals were used in battle as Clement of

[1] *Cf.* Forbes, *Dict. of the Hindūstānī Language*, sub "karān."

[2] Persian lexicographers derive the word from *bar* (= "breast") and *baṭ* (= "duck"), because its shape was like the breast of a duck. The Greeks borrowed both word and instrument in the *βαρβιτος*. That the *barbaṭ* and *'ūd* were synonymous in the 11th century is apparent from the *Shifā'* of Ibn Sīnā (d. 1037). The *barbaṭ* had four strings in the time of Khusrau Parwīż (7th cent.) if we are to accept the authority of Khālid al-Fayyāḍ (d. *ca.* 718). *J.R.A.S.* (1899), p. 59.

[3] Lane, *Lexicon*, sub *āl*.

[4] See ante pp. 4, 7, and my *Studies in Oriental Musical Instruments* p. 7-8.

[5] See the instrument depicted in the frescoes of the Quṣair 'Amra palace. *Ḳuṣejr 'Amra*, ii, pl. 34. (Published by the *Kais. Akad. der Wissenschaften*, Vienna, 1907.)

[6] *Aghānī*, ii, 175. The *mizmār* and *duff* were the martial instruments of the tribes.

[7] *Mufaḍḍaliyyāt*, xvii.

[8] Suidas, *Lexicon*, sub *'Αράβιος*.

[9] *Sūras*, vi, 73. lxxiv, 8.

[10] Lane, *Lexicon*.

Alexandria tells us, while *jalājil* were part of the impedimenta of dancers.

During the Days of Ignorance as to-day[1] music was to be found in the private, public, and religious life of the Arabs. Just as they toiled for their Assyrian taskmasters in ancient times to the joy of their songs,[2] so the Arabs of Al-Medīna sang as they dug the fosse around the city when the Meccans threatened them.[3] Just as the Israelites sang their "Well Song,"[4] so did the fifth century Arabs.[5] Just as the ancients entered battle to music,[6] so did the Arabs of the *jāhiliyya*.[7] Just as Sargon sang of the exploits of his Assyrian warriors, so did the fourth-century Arabs recount their victory over the Romans in song.[8] Just as the temples of Ishtar and Yahweh resounded with music and song, so possibly did the temples and shrines of the Arabs.[9] When the Hebrews said, "A concert of music at a banquet of wine is as a signet of carbuncle set in gold,"[10] the Arabs were not far behind when their poet, 'Abda ibn al-Ṭabīb, who lived during the *jāhiliyya*, spoke of music at a festive gathering as being like "painters' work set off with gold."[11] If the harvesters of Israel had their songs, so had the Arab workers in the palm-tree oases.[12] Music and song were with the Arabs from the lullaby at the cradle[13] to the elegy at the bier.[14]

§ III

Of the musicians of the Days of Idolatry but few names have been preserved for us. We are told, however, that "the singers in the Days of Idolatry were many,"[15] and one of the writers mentioned in the *Fihrist* (tenth century) wrote a *Kitāb al-aghānī 'alā ḥurūf* which con-

[1] Parisot, *Musique Orientale*, 5.
[2] Schrader, *Keil. Bibl.*, ii, 234.
[3] Ibn Sa'd, ii/i, 50. [4] *Numbers*, xxi, 17.
[5] *Pat. Lat.* lxxi, 612. [6] *Ezekiel*, xxxiii, 3. [7] *Hamāsa*, 254.
[8] Sozomen, *Hist. Eccles.*, vi, 38.
[9] Nicholson, *Lit. Hist. of the Arabs*, 73.
[10] *Ecclesiasticus*, xxxii, 5-6.
[11] *Mufaḍḍaliyyāt*, xxvi.
[12] *Encyclopædia of Islām*, i, 402.
[13] *'Iqd al-farīd*, iii, 176. [14] *Aghānī*, xix, 87.
[15] *Huth MS.* In the author's possession.

tained the names of the male and female singers *in the Days of Idolatry* as well as in the Days of Islām.[1] It seems highly probable, as Brockelmann says, that the poems of the *jāhiliyya* were meant to be chanted to a simple musical accompaniment.[2] Indeed the *laḥn* (melody) to which *shi'r* (verse) was set was a survival of the more primitive chanting (*talḥīn*) of the *shā'ir* when he was a soothsayer pure and simple. It is significant that the more primitive meanings of *laḥan* and *shi'r* are " intelligence " and " knowledge." In the days that we are concerned with it was perhaps the fact that a poet had a good voice that soon marked him out as being the superior of another.

'Adī ibn al-Rabī'a (d. *ca.* 495), the famous poet of the Banū Taghlib, is said to have been surnamed Muhalhil on account of his voice.[3] Some writers, however, attribute other promptings for this name.[4]

'Alqama ibn 'Abda (sixth century) was one of the poets sometimes included in the *Mu'allaqāt*. That he was a singer is evident from a statement made by Al-Fārābī, who tells us 'Alqama was refused a hearing by the Ghassānid king Al-Ḥārith ibn Abī Shamir (529-69) until he had melodized (*laḥḥana*) his verse and sung (*ghanna*) it to him.[5]

Al-A'shā Maimūn ibn Qais (d. *ca.* 629) belonged to Al-Yamāma, although he had travelled the whole Peninsula " harp in hand," as Professor Nicholson says, singing the wonderful verses that gave him a place in the *Mu'allaqāt*. He was called " the *ṣannājat al-'arab*," i.e., " the ṣanjist of the Arabs." It is on this account that it has been presumed that he played the harp (*ṣanj* = *jank*),[6] although it is quite likely that the name meant " the measurer [in poetry] of the Arabs," having the clashing idea of the cymbals (*ṣinjān*) in mind.[7]

Al-Naḍr ibn al-Ḥārith (d. 624), a descendant of the

[1] *Fihrist*, 145. [2] *Encyclopædia of Islām*, i, 403.
[3] Caussin de Perceval, *Hist. Arabes*, ii, 280.
[4] Huart, *Arab. Lit.*, 12. *J.R.A.S.* (1925), 422.
[5] Al-Fārābī, *Leyden MS.*, Or. 651, fol. 7. Kosegarten, *Lib. Cant.*, 200.
[6] Nicholson, *Lit. Hist. of the Arabs*, 123. *Aghānī* (Sāsī Edit.), i, 146.
[7] See below p. 79.

famous Quṣaiy and a cousin of the Prophet Muḥammad, was certainly one of the poet-minstrels of the *jāhiliyya.* He became one of the Prophet's rivals in a professional as well as in a political sense,[1] since they both desired the ear of the public, the one with "song and story," and the other with "Revelations." It was Al-Naḍr whom the Prophet pilloried in the *Qur'ān* (xxxi, 5-6). At the Arab court of Al-Ḥīra, Al-Naḍr had learned to play the new type of lute called the *'ūd*, which apparently superseded the old *mizhar* and its congeners,[2] as well as to sing the more artistic *ghinā'*, which ousted the *naṣb.* These innovations he introduced into Mecca.[3]

Outside of those in personal contact with Muḥammad after the *Hijra,* who will be mentioned later, only one other male musician can be traced, and that is Mālik ibn Jubair al-Mughannī, who formed one of the deputation of the Banū Ṭai' to the Prophet in the year 630.[4]

Among the songstresses many names have been preserved. The legendary period supplies four at least. The famous *jarādatān* of the Banū 'Ād were named Qu'ād and Thamād.[5] Hazīla and 'Afīra were singing-girls of the Banū Jadīs, the tribe which utterly destroyed the Banū Ṭasm.[6]

The mother of the celebrated poet Ḥātim al-Ṭā'ī was probably a musician, and Al-Khansā the exquisite elegaist sang her laments (*marāthī*) to music.[7] Hind bint 'Utba, a representative matron of the Arabs of the *jāhiliyya,* was both a poet and musician. Bint 'Afzar was a songstress who kept or was employed at a house of entertainment where the renowned Al-Ḥārith ibn Ẓālim and Khālid ibn Ja'far met.[8] Huraira and Khulaida were singing-girls of Bishr ibn 'Amr a grandee of Al-Ḥīra in the days of Al-Nu'mān III (d. *ca.* 602).[9] It was in praise of the first of these that Al-A'shā Maimūn ibn Qais sang.[10]

[1] Huart, *op. cit.*, 32. [2] See *ante* p. 15. [3] Al-Mas'ūdī, viii, 93-4.
[4] *Aghānī*, xvi, 48, xxi, 191. Al-Ṭabarī calls him Mālik ibn 'Abdallāh ibn Khaibarī. See also Ḥājiz ibn 'Awf al-Azdī in the *Aghānī.*
[5] Al-Mas'ūdī, iii, 296. Ibn Badrūn, 53. *Aghānī*, x, 48.
[6] Al-Mas'ūdī, iii, 29. Ibn Badrūn, 65. [7] *Aghānī*, xiii, 140.
[8] *Aghānī*, x, 18. A wife of Ḥātim al-Ṭā'ī was named Māwiya bint 'Afzar.
[9] *Aghānī*, viii, 79. [10] See *ante* p. 12.

CHAPTER II

ISLĀM AND MUSIC

"To listen to music is to transgress the law: To make music is to transgress religion: To take pleasure in music is to transgress the faith and renders you an infidel."

D'Ohsson, *Tableau général de l'Empire Othoman*, ii, 188.

ABOUT the year 571 a child was born at Mecca who was destined to change the entire fortunes of Arabia and the Arabs. This was Muḥammad "the Prophet of Allāh." He belonged to the famous tribe of the Quraish, which had been masters of Mecca since the fifth century, and he was a grandson of one of its most eminent shaikhs, 'Abd al-Muṭṭalib, himself the great-grandson of the famous Quṣaiy, who created the hegemony of the Quraish in Mecca.[1] When nearly forty years of age (610), Muḥammad began to receive his "Revelations," which later became the foundation of the *Qur'ān*.

The Quraish, however, would have none of these "Revelations" and vigorously opposed Muḥammad. At first they thought him a *shā'ir* (poet-soothsayer) or a *kāhin* (magician), for, indeed, his "Revelations" showed the style of the *saj'* or rhymed prose, such as the

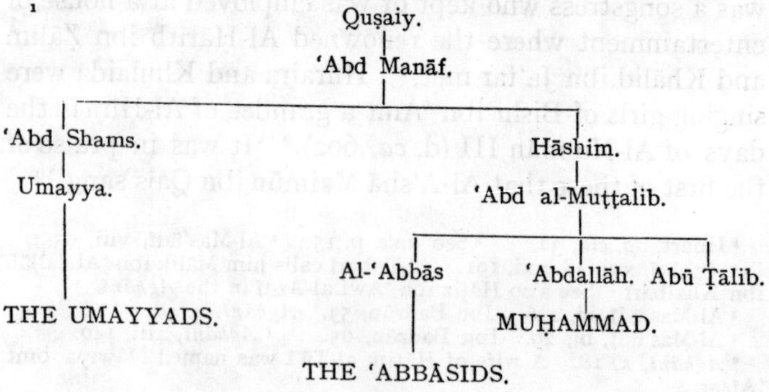

shā'ir used. He was in fact called a *shā'ir majnūn,* i.e., a poet-soothsayer possessed of the *jinn* (*genii*), and was looked upon as an ordinary augur.[1] The Prophet indignantly repudiated the title of soothsayer in *Sūra* lxix, although one can scarcely read *Sūras* cxiii and cxiv without feeling that they are no more than what could be expected from a *kāhin,* whilst *Sūra* cxi is a typical *hijā* or curse of a soothsayer.[2]

In the course of time Muḥammad's teaching bore fruit, and although his disciples were few, yet they included some of the most influential men of the Quraish. Indeed, his influence at Mecca became so commanding that the Umayya branch of the Quraish actually proscribed him, and later (622) he was compelled to seek refuge in the city of Yathrib. This was the "Year of the *Hijra* (migration)," and Muḥammad gave to his city of refuge the name of *Al-Medīna* ("The City"), whilst its two tribes which formed the bulk of the population, the Banū'l-Aws and Banū'l-Khazraj, had the title of *Al-Anṣār* ("The Helpers") bestowed on them. With the armed forces of Al-Medīna at his back, Muḥammad unsheathed the sword of Islām against the unbelievers.

Muḥammad died in 632, but he had witnessed the triumph of his mission in Arabia—even as far afield as Al-Baḥrain—*the preaching of Islām.* Al-Ḥijāz was now the centre of attraction for the peninsula. The ancient renown of Al-Yaman, the culture of Al-'Irāq, the puissance of Ghassān, counted for naught in the face of the new spirit cradled in Al-Ḥijāz, which, within a century, was to hold the minds of all peoples from the confines of China and the banks of the Indus to the shores of Morocco and the peaks of the Pyrenees.

[1] Hirschfeld, *New Researches into the Composition and Exegesis of the Qoran,* 10.

[2] Two of these *Sūras* are "charms" against bewitchery and *jinn* (*genii*), and to this very day they are engraved on amulets for this purpose. There is little difference between these *Sūras* and the charms or denunciations of the ancient Babylonian-Assyrian *ashshipu.*

§ I

One of the most perplexing points in Islām is its attitude towards music, and for centuries its legists have argued the question whether listening to music (*al-samā'*) is lawful or not. It is not easy to comprehend how the question arose, seeing that there is not a word of direct censure against music in the *Qur'ān*, and above all, in face of the fact that music was almost an indispensable item in the social life of the Arabs. Where then did the "authority" come from for this opposition to music? The censure of "wine, woman, and song" was certainly nothing new to Semitic peoples, for the Hebrews, and apparently the Phœnicians also, had their puritans who cried out against these things.[1] Something of this spirit seems to have pervaded even Pagan Arabia, and the heathen poet Umayya ibn Abī'l-Ṣalt was quite a puritan in some respects, although he never breathed a word against music.

Orientalists are divided on the question of the origin of the Islāmic censure of "listening to music." One group attributes it directly to the Prophet Muḥammad himself, whilst the other holds that it was manufactured by the theologians of the 'Abbāsid era, who were jealous of the inordinate attention paid to music and musicians. At first sight it would appear to be an easy matter to settle this question by an appeal to the *Qur'ān* and the *Ḥadīth*. Yet the former is interpreted according to the particular view of the exegete, whilst the latter has definite statements which support both sides.

It is claimed by Muslim exegetes that the verse (*Sūra*, xxxv, 1), which says,—"He increases in His creatures that which he wills," refers to the "Beautiful Voice."[2] Again they say that where the text (*Sūra*, xxxi, 18) says,—"Verily, the worse liked of voices is the voice of the ass," we have a negative praise of the "Beautiful Voice."[3] Then it is argued from *Sūra*, vii, 30, that singing

[1] *Isaiah*, v, 12 *Amos*, vi, 5. xxiii, 15, 16. Jesus ben Sirach says: "Use not much the company of a woman that is a singer." *Ecclus.*, ix, 4.

[2] This was the view of Al-Zuhrī. Cf. Al-Baiḍāwī, ii, 148.

[3] *'Iqd al-farīd*, iii, 177. Al-Ghazālī, *op. cit.*, 209.

is allowable since it is laid down,—"Say, who hath forbidden the adornment of Allāh which he hath provided for His creatures."[1] On the other hand, the objectors aver that singing is "unlawful" because it employs poetry, and they point to the Prophet's denunciation of poets in *Sūra*, xxxi, 5-6, where he says,—"There is one who purchases a ludicrous story, that he may seduce men from the way of Allāh, without knowledge, and may laugh the same to scorn: these shall suffer a shameful punishment." This *anathema* was hurled directly at the poet-minstrel Al-Naḍr ibn al-Ḥārith, whose Pagan song and story were being more readily listened to at first than were the "Revelations" of the Prophet Muḥammad. Indeed, several of the early Muslims considered that the "ludicrous story" meant "singing," and among them Abū 'Abd al-Raḥmān ibn Mas'ūd (d. 653), Ibrāhīm ibn Yazīd al-Nakha'ī (d. 715), and Abū Sa'īd al-Ḥasan al-Baṣrī (d. 728). Then again, we see Muḥammad condemning the poet in *Sūra*, xxvi, 224-26, saying,—"And the poets do those follow who go astray. Dost thou not see that they wander distraught in every vale?" Yet this, too, was probably not directed against poetry as such, but simply against the poet who in the eyes of the Prophet was the incarnation of Pagan ideals, and who, moreover, was pouring out satires and invective against him.[2] There can be little doubt but that Muḥammad feared the poets and minstrels, and stopped at nothing to accomplish their discredit and even destruction, as we know in the case of Ka'b ibn al-Ashraf, Ka'b ibn Zuhair, and Al-Naḍr ibn al-Ḥārith. All that savoured of the old religion was treated contumeliously by Muḥammad. Note how scornful he is of whistling and hand-clapping in *Sūra*, viii, 35.[3] On the whole, however, it was not in the *Qur'ān* that the contemners of music found any real basis for their

[1] Al-Ghazālī, *op. cit.*, 214.

[2] Muḥammad himself employed an official poet in Ḥassān ibn Thābit to denounce his enemies. "Pour out the raid against them," he says to Ḥassān, "for by Allāh, your poetry is more potent than the falling of arrows in the darkness of dawn." *'Iqd al-farīd*, iii, 178.

[3] That is why whistling is still considered a prompting of the Devil by the Arabs.

strictures, and they were compelled therefore to turn to the only other "authority",—the *Ḥadīth.*

Ḥadīth was the name given to a saying or story of Muḥammad which acquired "the force of law and some of the authority of inspiration,"[1] and it was looked upon as second only to the *Qur'ān.* Which *Ḥadīth* is to be implicitly accepted, which is only a partial truth, and which is to be totally rejected, is determined by rules drawn up by Muslim legists, which cannot be dealt with here. Suffice it to say that no *Ḥadīth* can be accepted that is at variance with the *Qur'ān.* Of the "traditions" which deal with the question of "listening to music" there are many, and first of all we may consider those which consider it "unlawful."

'Ā'isha the wife of the Prophet has handed down a tradition that Muḥammad once said,—"Verily, Allāh hath made the singing-girl (*qaina*) unlawful, and the selling of her and her price and teaching her." Al-Ghazālī says that this *Ḥadīth* only refers to the singing-girl of the taverns.[2] A tradition of Jābir ibn 'Abdallāh makes the Prophet say,—"Iblīs (Satan) was the first who wailed and the first who sang." Another *Ḥadīth* from Abū Umāma runs,—"No one lifts up his voice in singing, but Allāh sends to him two devils to his shoulders, beating with their heels on his breast until he refrains."[3] Muḥammad is also credited with having said,—"Music and singing cause hypocrisy to grow in the heart as water makes corn grow,"[4] whilst others attribute the origin of this *Ḥadīth* to Ibn Mas'ūd.[5]

In the *Ṣaḥīḥ* of Al-Tirmidhī (d. 892), the Prophet is said to have cursed both singing and the singer,[6] although the truth of this *Ḥadīth* has been questioned.[7] In another tradition the singing-girls and stringed instruments (*ma'āzif*) are given as signs of the end of the world.[8]

[1] Nicholson, *Lit. Hist. of the Arabs*, 144.
[2] Al-Ghazālī, *op. cit.*, 244-5.
[3] *Ibid.*, 246.
[4] *Mishkāt al-maṣābīḥ*, ii, 425.
[5] Al-Ghazālī, *op. cit.*, 248.
[6] Al-Tirmidhī, i, 241.
[7] Lammens, *Mélanges de la Faculté Orientale* (*Beyrouth*), iii, 233.
[8] Al-Tirmidhī, ii, 33.

Musical instruments are declared to be among the most powerful means by which the devil seduces men. An instrument of music is the devil's *mu'adhdhin* (caller to prayer) serving to call man to the devil's worship.[1]

The legists even brought the testimony of the "Companions of the Prophet" and other illustrious men of Islām against "listening to music." 'Abdallāh ibn 'Umar is said to have heard a pilgrim singing and rebuked him saying,—"I do not hear Allāh from you." This same worthy, hearing the playing of a *mizmār* (reed-pipe), stopped his ears, saying,—"Thus I saw the Apostle of Allāh do."[2] Singing was as bad as lying, for 'Uthmān said,—"I have not sung and I have not lied."[3] Other contemners quote the Prophet's rebuke to Shīrīn, the singing-girl of Ḥassān ibn Thābit, whom he forbade to sing; and 'Umar's flogging the "Companions" who used to listen to music; and 'Alī's finding fault with Mu'āwiya for keeping singing-girls; and his not allowing Al-Ḥasan to look at the Abyssinian women who used to sing.[4]

The traditions in favour of "listening to music" are however almost as weighty, although not as numerous, as those against it. There are two which attribute to Muḥammad the following sayings: "Allāh has not sent a Prophet except with a Beautiful Voice," and, "Allāh listens more intently to a man with a Beautiful Voice reading the *Qur'ān* than does a master of a singing-girl to her singing.[5] It is related of Anas ibn Mālik (d. 715) that Muḥammad "used to make him sing the *ḥudā'* (caravan song) when travelling, and that Anjusha used to sing it for the women and Al-Barā ibn Mālik (the brother of Anas) for the men.[6] Al-Ghazālī testifies that the *ḥudā'* "did not cease to be one of the customs of the Arabs in the time of the Apostle of Allāh, and in the time of the 'Companions,' and that it is nothing but poems

[1] Lane, *Arabian Nights*, i, 200.
[2] Al-Ghazālī, *op. cit.*, 248. Ibn Khallikān, *Biog. Dict.*, iii, 521.
[3] *Lisān al-'arab*, s.v.
[4] *Kashf al-maḥjūb*, 411.
[5] Al-Ghazālī, *op. cit.*, 209.
[6] *Ibid.*, 217.

equipped with agreeable sounds (*ṣawāt ṭayyiba*) and measured melodies (*alḥān mauzūna*)."[1]

As for the singing-girls which a previous *Ḥadīth* proscribes, there seems to be overwhelming evidence that the Prophet considered them " allowable." First there is the *Ḥadīth* concerning the Prophet who heard the voice of the singing-girl when passing the abode of Ḥassān ibn Thābit. Asked by the poet if it were sinful to sing, Muḥammad replied,—" Certainly not!"[2]

Two traditions of 'Ā'isha on this question are of interest. The first runs,—" Abū Bakr came in to her ['Ā'isha] in the Days of Minā, and with her were two girls playing tambourines and beating time while the Prophet was wrapped in his robe. And Abū Bakr rebuked them, but the Prophet uncovered his face and said, ' Let them alone, Abū Bakr, for it is the time of the Festivals.' "[3] The second runs, " The Apostle of Allāh came in to me ['Ā'isha] while two girls were with me singing a song (*ghinā'*) of the Day of Bu'āth, and lay down on his side on the bed and turned away his face. Then Abū Bakr entered and rebuked me, and said, ' The pipe of the Devil (*mizmār al-shaiṭān*) in the presence of the Apostle of Allāh!', but the Apostle of Allāh turned to him and said,—' Let them alone.' "[4]

Another story of 'Ā'isha is told as follows, " 'Ā'isha said, ' A slave-girl was singing in my house when 'Umar asked leave to enter. As soon as she [the slave-girl] heard his steps she ran away. He came in and the Apostle smiled. ' O Apostle of Allāh,' said 'Umar, ' what hath made thee smile?' The Apostle answered, ' A slave-girl was singing here, but she ran away as soon as she heard thy step!' ' I will not depart,' said 'Umar, ' until I hear what the Apostle heard.' So the Apostle called the girl back and she began to sing, the Apostle listening to her."[5]

On another occasion, Muḥammad entered the house of

[1] Al-Ghazālī, *op. cit.*, 217.
[2] *Usd al-ghāba*, v, 496. Cf. ii, 127. iv, 126.
[3] Al-Ghazālī, *op. cit.*, 224-5.
[4] Al-Ghazālī, *op. cit.*, 226.
[5] *Kashf al-maḥjūb*, 401.

Al-Rubayyi' bint Mu'awwidh, when singing-girls were singing, and one of them remarked as the Prophet entered,—" And with us is a Prophet who knoweth what shall be to-morrow." Muḥammad replied,—" Leave off that and say what thou wast saying (singing)."[1]

We also read that the women greeted Muḥammad's arrival from the housetops with recitation (*inshād*) set to melody (*laḥn*), and accompanied by the beating of tambourines (*dufūf*).[2] Finally, there is the story of 'Ā'isha who took to one of the Anṣār his bride. When she returned, Muḥammad said to her,—" Did you lead the girl to her husband ? " and 'Ā'isha answered,—" Yes." He then said,—" And did you not send someone who could sing ? " and 'Ā'isha answered—" No." Then the Prophet said,—" Surely you knew that the Anṣār are people who delight in the *ghazal* (love song)."[3]

Although some legists imagined that the Qur'ānic condemnation of poets and poetry was directed equally against music, others held the view that poetry was " allowable," and since the song issued from poetry, this, too, must be lawful. The author of the *'Iqd al-farīd* says,—" People differ in regard to the song (*ghinā'*). Most of the people of Al-Ḥijāz permit it, but most of those of Al-'Irāq dislike it. A part of the proof of those who allow it is that its origin is poetry, which the Prophet commanded. He incited to it, urged his ' Companions ' to it, and found help in it against the Unbelievers."[4] 'Ā'isha, too, had said,—" Teach your children poetry which will sweeten their tongue."[5] It is also recorded that Muḥammad was riding one day with some friends when he asked one of them to recite the poetry of Umayya. A hundred lines were recited for him, and Muḥammad said at the finish,—"Well done ! " "And when the satire in the poetry and the talking about it wearied them," says the tradition, " it was said, ' The poetry is good, and we do not see any harm in a beautiful melody (*laḥn*).' "[6]

[1] Al-Ghazālī, *op. cit.*, 743.
[2] Al-Ghazālī, *op. cit.*, 224.
[3] *'Iqd al-farīd*, iii, 178.
[4] *Ibid.* [5] *Ibid.*
[6] *Ibid.* The poetry was sung evidently.

On another occasion Muḥammad passed by a slave-girl and she immediately sang aloud:

> "Is there upon me (Woe to you)
> Any crime if I am gay?"

Muḥammad answered her,—"There will be no crime, please Allāh."[1] Considerable importance was claimed for the testimony of al-Dīnawarī (d. 895), who said that he had seen Muḥammad in a vision, and that he had asked him specially whether he blamed music and singing, and that the Prophet replied,—"I do not blame anything in it, but say to them (who resort to music and singing) that they open before it with the *Qur'ān*, and close after it with the *Qur'ān*."[2]

One of the stories in the great *Kitāb al-aghānī* (tenth cent.) seems to show that there was no specific ban on music at the dawn of Islām. The Quraish had heard that the famous poet-minstrel, Al-A'shā Maimūn ibn Qais, was on his way to meet Muḥammad, and they decided to intercept him. This they did and they endeavoured to dissuade him from his project by pointing out that Muḥammad had made "unlawful" many things to which Al-A'shā was strongly addicted. "And what are these?" enquired the poet-minstrel. "They are fornication, gambling, usury, and wine," answered Abū Sufyān, the chief of the Quraish. Had music been among the "unlawful" things, it would assuredly have been mentioned, seeing that Al-A'shā was interested in the art.[3]

Tradition is fairly persistent that Muḥammad tolerated instrumental music.[4] He had said, "Publish the marriage, and beat the *ghirbāl* (round tambourine)."[5] His own nuptials with Khadīja were celebrated with music, and so were those of his daughter Fāṭima.[6] Popular legend mentions many musicians among his personal friends and supporters.[7]

[1] *Ibid.* [2] Al-Ghazālī, *op. cit.*, 206. [3] *Aghānī*, viii, 85-6.
[4] Important passages on Muḥammad and music may be found also in Ibn Ḥajar, iii, 20. Ibn Sa'd, *Ṭabaqāt*, iv (i), 120.
[5] Al-Ghazālī, *op. cit.*, 743. *Lisān al-'arab*, s. "ghirbāl."
[6] Evliyā Chelebī, *Travels*, i, (ii), 226. [7] *Ibid.*

Out of this maze of "tradition" or "testimony," Islām has endeavoured to formulate a law on "listening to music." The four great legal schools, the Ḥanafī, the Mālikī, the Shāfi'ī, and the Ḥanbalī, broadly decided against its legality, although hundreds of treatises have been written by both legists and laymen to prove the opposite.

Abū Ḥanīfa (699-767) is said to have "disliked singing (*ghinā'*), and made listening to it a sin,"[1] although he appears to have looked upon musical instruments as lawful.[2] Mālik ibn Anas (715-95) also forbade singing and said,—"When a man buys a slave-girl and finds that she is a singer, then it is his duty to send her back."[3] The Imām al-Shāfi'ī (767-820) said, "Singing (*ghinā'*) is a sport which is disliked and which resembles what is false; he who meddles much with it is light of understanding, you shall reject his testimony."[4] Aḥmad ibn Ḥanbal (780-855) disliked listening to music (*al-samā'*).[5] Thus we see that the very founders of the four great sects were opposed to music, although their views differed considerably.

In spite of the foregoing censure of Al-Shāfi'ī, it would appear that he held that music in itself was "lawful." The legist himself said,—"I do not know one of the learned in Al-Ḥijāz who disliked music and singing except what consisted in amatory descriptions; as for the *ḥudā'* (caravan song) and the mention of the traces of the encampment and of the spring pastures,[6] and the making beautiful of the voice in singing poems, they are permitted."[7] His school holds therefore that it is lawful to sing and to listen to the *ḥudā'* and the like, but interdicts all other singing that is not accompanied by musical instruments. Yet, even these latter are banned if they tend to excite unlawful desires, and among the instruments so banned are the *'ūd, ṣanj, nāy al-'irāqī, barbaṭ, rabāb*, etc. These were instruments used by professional

[1] Al-Ghazālī, *op. cit.*, 202. [2] *Hidāya*, iii, 558.
[3] Al-Ghazālī, *op. cit.*, 201. [4] *Ibid.*, 201. [5] *Ibid.*, 204.
[6] This refers to the prelude (*nasīb*) of the *qaṣīda*, which, when used by itself, is called a *qiṭ'a*.
[7] Al-Ghazālī, *op. cit.*, 242-3.

musicians, and their employment being for mere æsthetic or illicit pleasure they were condemned.[1] Al-Ghazālī himself says that the objection to these instruments is "in so far as they are badges of people who drink and of the *mukhannathūn*."[2] On the other hand, the *ṭabl*, *shāhīn*, *qaḍīb*, *ghirbāl* (or *duff*) were "permissible" instruments, because they were used by pilgrims.[3]

According to the general reading of the Shāfi'ī law, any of the "unlawful" instruments can be broken or destroyed (under certain conditions) without the breaker or destroyer incurring any liability.[4] The legal question turns, it would seem, on whether the instruments are "property" or not. If these instruments are "unlawful" they cannot be owned by a Muslim, and therefore cannot be property. Thus a Muslim could destroy them. So far the Shāfi'ī school.

The Ḥanafī school argue that these musical instruments are "property" and in consequence are "capable of yielding a lawful advantage."[5] The fact that they are used for "unlawful" purposes does not alter their value as property. It is laid down therefore by this school that,—"If a person break a *barbaṭ*, *ṭabl*, *mizmār*, or *duff* of a Muslim . . . he is responsible, the sale of such articles being lawful." Some say that the difference between the two schools obtains only in regard to such instruments as are used merely for amusement.[6]

There were certain classes of theft which were punishable by amputation of the hand, but the Shāfi'ī school said,—"The hand of the thief is not cut off according to the two disciples for stealing a *duff*, *ṭabl*, or *mizmār*, because, in their opinion, these articles bear no price." The Ḥanafī school point out, however, that the thief could say that he stole them to destroy them.[7] The

[1] *Ibid.*, 214. Al-Nawawī, 515.
[2] The drum called the *kūba* was condemned on account of its use by the *mukhannathūn*.
[3] Al-Ghazālī, *op. cit.*, 214, 237, 743.
[4] Al-Nawawī, 200.
[5] Abū Ḥanīfa had a neighbour who sang, and he once bailed him out of jail, because he "missed his voice." *'Iqd al-farīd*, iii, 181.
[6] *Hidāya*, iii, 558-9.
[7] *Hidāya*, ii, 92.

same law applies to the *ṭunbūr* or other stringed instruments (*ma'āzif*).[1]

The actual purveyor of music also felt the hand of the legists. At the time of Hārūn al-Rashīd (786-809) a musician was denied ordinary justice in the courts. The Imām al-Shāfi'ī had laid it down that the testimony of a person who indulged in music was untrustworthy. According to the *Hidāya*, "the testimony of women that lament or sing is not admissible, because they are guilty of forbidden actions, inasmuch as the Prophet has prohibited those two species of noise."[2] In the *Tanbīh* of Abū Isḥāq al-Shīrāzī (d. 1083), singers in general were included in this law.[3] The *Hidāya* also stipulates that "It is not lawful to give a pledge for the wages either of a mourner or of a singer."[4]

When one views all these pains and penalties which had been directed against music, it is a wonder that the art thrived at all under Islām. But the truth is that in spite of the rigours of the legists and theologians, the law concerning "listening to music" has been honoured more in the breach than in the observance. Sinners in this respect always had some sort of back-door of escape, which is well illustrated by a story in the *'Iqd al-farīd*. A certain prominent man of Al-Ḥijāz was making the pilgrimage to Mecca and was found lying on his prayer-mat singing. A kinsman who passed by reproved him saying,—"Allāh forbid that I should hear you do the like of this, and you a pilgrim." The offending one replied, "O son of my brother, and are *you* not *listening* to me?"[5] The law condemns not only the singer or player, but also the listener![6]

Islām never really eradicated the Pagan ideals of the Arab so far as music is concerned. Although the charge that the opposition to "listening" (*al-samā'*) was fabricated by the 'Abbāsid theologians may have much to support it, yet there can be little doubt that Muḥammad

[1] *Ibid.*, II, 89. [2] *Ibid.*, ii, 687. [3] *Tanbīh*, 336.
[4] *Hidāya*, iv, 212.
[5] *'Iqd al-farīd*, iii, 178.
[6] D'Ohsson, *Tab. Gén.*, ii, 188.

was indirectly responsible for the germ of the opposition.[1]

There are some writers who account for Muḥammad's attitude on purely physiological grounds. In him, the senses appear to have been quite abnormally developed. His sense of smell was a veritable burden to him. He was hypersensitive in the matter of touch. Gastronomic affairs almost became a mania with him. He had visions. He was afflicted with hummings in the ears, and heard the sounds of cats, hares, and bells, which caused him much annoyance, if not suffering. Even the jingling of the caravan bells troubled him. In such an extraordinary structure, a veritable slave to hyperæsthesia, one might reasonably expect to find a mind temperamentally averse to music, or at least, insensible to its charms and beauties. To the same cause has been attributed his lack of rhythmic instinct.[2] It is very easy, however, to overstate the physical and psychical reflexes in Muḥammad, and there is, in fact, many a *Ḥadīth* to counter objections on these lines. It has been shown by Dr. Hartwig Hirschfeld that this so-called "lack of rhythmic instinct" was really a deliberate attempt by Muḥammad to ignore prosodical forms lest he should be taken for a mere soothsayer or magician. "The general form of any sort of public announcement being poetic, Muḥammad had to avoid all imitation of it, and this gave him immense trouble." Yet although he only just managed to escape from the "ditty" form of the *urjuza* (verses in *rajaz*), he could not evade the *saj*ʿ (rhymed prose).[3]

Muḥammad's attitude towards music might perhaps be explained on somewhat similar lines. The kind of music that accompanied the poetry which glorified in

[1] A Muslim has said,—"Nowhere do we see pious men more given to falsehood than in tradition" (Noeldeke, *Gesch. des Qorans*, 22). It does not follow however, that all were conscious frauds, for we must remember Muḥammad's saying,—"Whatever good saying has been said, I myself have said it." And again :—"You must compare the sayings attributed to the *Qur'ān* ; what agrees therewith is from me, whether I actually said it or no." See Goldziher, *Muh. Stud.*, 48.

[2] Lammens, *Mélanges de la Faculté Orientale* (*Beyrouth*), iii, 230-3.

[3] Hirschfeld, 37.

the ideals of Paganism he had to avoid. He may not have been blessed with the "Beautiful Voice" himself with which to deliver his "Revelations," but he certainly realized the value of it. He favoured Abū Mahdura on account of his "Beautiful Voice," whilst he likened the chanting (*qarā'a*) of Abū Mūsā al-Ash'arī to "a pipe (*mizmār*) from the pipes of David."[1] Yet this chanting of the *Qur'ān* would have to be different from the singing of poetry if Muḥammad would keep his hearers' minds away from thoughts of Paganism, and so a legal fiction arose which determined that the cantilation (*taghbīr*)[2] of the *Qur'ān* and the *tahlīl*, was merely a modulation of the voice which could be grasped by the learned and unlearned in music alike, it being of a different genre (so it was said) from the *ghinā'* or song proper, which belonged to the professional musician.[3] The cantilation of the *Qur'ān* is said to have been introduced by 'Ubaidallāh ibn Abī Bakr, the governor of Sijistān (appointed 697), but it evidently had an earlier existence.

The *adhān* (call to prayer) was instituted by the Prophet himself in the first or second year of the *Hijra*, and Bilāl the Abyssinian was the first *mu'adhdhin* (caller to prayer).[4] The *adhān*, too, is considered a cantilation of a like nature to that of the *Qur'ān*, but in spite of the legal distinction between "cantilation" and "singing," we are assured by Ibn Qutaiba (d. *ca.* 889) that the *Qur'ān* was sung to no different rules than those of the ordinary artistic songs (*alḥān al-ghinā'*), and the caravan song (*ḥudā'*).[5] Indeed, it was openly said that if melodies (*alḥān*) were to be considered "unlawful" then the cantilations of the *Qur'ān* and the *adhān* were equally so and had better be dispensed with.[6] The cantilation of the *Qur'ān* was in fact actually pro-

[1] *'Iqd al-farīd*, iii, 176. Al-Ghazālī, *op. cit.*, 209.

[2] Professor D. B. Macdonald, quoting Sayyid Murtaḍa's *Itḥāf al-sāda*, writes *ta'bīr* ("expression"), but Ibn Khaldūn, both in Quatremère's text and in Von Hammer's translation has *taghbīr*. Cf. Dozy, *Glossaire*, 13. Abū Isḥāq al-Zajjāj (d. 922) makes it *taghbīr* and explains its derivation from *ghabīr*.

[3] Ibn Khaldūn, ii, 359.

[4] Al-Bukhārī, i, 209. *Mishkāt al-maṣābīḥ*, i, 141.

[5] Ibn Qutaiba, 265.

[6] *'Iqd al-farīd*, iii, 178.

scribed by the Mālikī school, although allowed by the Shāfi'ī.[1] All the schools, except the Hanbalī, permitted the *adhān*.

Besides these "allowable" musical customs there were those of Pagan Arabia, which Islām was impotent in restricting, as in many other of the moving social Semitic forces.[2] Like the Christian Roman emperors, Muḥammad had to adapt himself to the social resistance when he found that he could not mould it to his wishes, and in this way the Pagan festivals, even with their *malāhī* or "forbidden pleasures," came into acceptance under fresh sanctions.

First there were the old Pagan chantings of the pilgrimage, the *tahlīl* and *talbiyya*, which were turned favourably to the account of Islām and became "lawful," even to the allowability of the *ṭabl* (drum) and *shāhīn* (fife) as an accompaniment.[3] Music for the pilgrimage became a necessity.[4]

The song of war, i.e., of inciting to war against the infidel, was allowable because it "summons a man to warfare by inciting courage and by moving wrath and anger against the unbelievers." The actual battle-song, such as that in the *rajaz* verses, was allowed on the same grounds. The legists allowed what they could not prevent in most cases, because many of these customs were too deeply ingrained in the Semite to be plucked out by a fiat. It had been the custom of 'Alī and Khālid, and other valiant "Companions of the Prophet."[5] Yet the *shāhīn* was forbidden in the camp lest its plaintive sound should "soften the heart."[6]

The *nauḥ* or elegy was lawful, for this was too valuable an asset to Islām, despite its pagan character, to be set aside. The *wilwāl* or wailing, however, was forbidden (save in certain cases), but in spite of all the penalties, and all the centuries, it still remains.[7]

[1] Ibn Khaldūn, ii, 357.
[2] Abū'l-Fidā' says: "The Arabs of the Days of Idolatry did things which Islām has accepted."
[3] Al-Ghazālī, 220. [4] Al-Ghazālī, 221. [5] Al-Ghazālī, 222.
[6] *Ibid.* In one of the Arabic chronicles of the Crusades the Muslims are made to banish flutes from their camp for this reason.
[7] 'Alī Bey, i, 183.

Then there was the music of the feast and festival such as abounded in Pagan Arabia. This, too, found a place in the public festivals connected with Islām, such as exists to-day in the *'īd al-aḍḥa*, the *'īd al-fiṭr*, the *yaum 'ashūra*, and the various *mawālid*.[1] Music was allowed when joy was allowed, such as on the days of private festivals like betrothals, weddings, births, and circumcisions. Finally, the love-song was allowable.

Yet there was something that even the legists had not taken into account, and that was the spiritual effects of music. It was this that had given the soothsayer and magician of old that wonderful power over the people, and strange to say the legists did not apprehend it. Arabic tradition had it that the Prophet David brought the birds and beasts to listen by means of his voice, and the two-and-seventy different notes of his "blessed throat."[2] People that heard his voice died of rapture.[3] The mysterious power of music was something that the Arabs could see for themselves in every-day life. They saw the camel alter its pace according to a change of rhythm or measure[4]; deer were rendered docile by melody[5]; snakes were charmed, bees made to alight,[6] and birds actually dropped dead at the sound of music.[7] There is an abundant literature which tells us of people who have been deeply influenced by the "Beautiful Voice."[8] Yet what connection has this "spiritual" music to that which the legists said was the procurer of drunkenness and fornication? The *ṣūfī* shall answer.

"Music and singing do not produce in the heart that which is not in it," says Abū Sulaimān al-Dārānī (d. *ca.* 820),[9] and so those who are affected by music can be divided into two classes as has been done by Al-Hujwīrī (eleventh cent.), the author of the *Kashf al-maḥjūb*, as

[1] The *'īd al-aḍḥa* (sacrificial feast) is held on the 10th *dhū'l-ḥijja*, and it is the actual day that the Pagan Arabs sacrificed in the Vale of Minā.

[2] Mīrkhwānd, ii (1), 57.

[3] *'Iqd al-farīd*, iii, 179. *Kashf al-maḥjūb*, 402.

[4] *'Iqd al-farīd*, iii, 177. Al-Ghazālī, 219.

[5] *Kashf al-maḥjūb*, 400.

[6] *'Iqd al-farīd*, iii, 177.

[7] *Aghānī*, v, 52. Al-Ghazālī, 219. Sa'dī, *Gulistān*, ii, 27. iii, 28.

[8] *'Iqd al-farīd*, iii, 198. Al-Ghazālī, 715. *Kash al-maḥjūb*, 407.

[9] Al-Ghazālī, 220.

follows: (1) *Those who hear the spiritual meaning*, and (2) *Those who hear the material sound.* "There are good and evil results in each case," says this author. "Listening to sweet sounds produces an effervescence of the substance moulded in man; true, if the substance be true, false, if the substance be false. When the stuff of man's temperament is evil, that which he hears will be evil, too."[1] Then he goes on to quote Muḥammad in the saying,—"O Allāh, let us see things as they are." So, says our author, "right audition consists in hearing everything as it is in quality and predicament." Thus the *ṣūfī* looked upon music as a means of revelation attained through ecstasy.

Dhū'l-Nūn says,—"Listening (*al-samā'*) is a divine influence which stirs the heart to see Allāh; those who listen to it spiritually attain to Allāh, and those who listen to it sensually fall into heresy." Another *ṣūfī*, Al-Shiblī, says,—"Listening to music is outwardly a temptation and inwardly an admonition." Says Abū'l-Ḥusain al-Darrāj,—"Listening . . . causes me to find the existence of the Truth beside the Veil."

In the *ṣūfī* conception of music, such as we have in Al-Hujwīrī and Al-Ghazālī,[2] we see much of what the modern Schopenhauer taught. To the latter, music is the eternal will itself, and through it one can pierce the Veil, witness the Watcher, and behold the Unseen.[3] Thus was music called in as a handmaid to Islām after all, and as such it is recognized in every Islāmic land in spite of Islām.

§ II

Of the musicians contemporary with Muḥammad, several have been mentioned in the preceding chapter. Besides these there were a few who came in personal contact with the Prophet and Islām, and on that account are mentioned here.

[1] *Kashf al-maḥjūb*, 402-3.
[2] Both the *Kashf al-maḥjūb* of Al-Hujwīrī and the section on music in the *Iḥyā 'ulūm al-dīn* of Al-Ghazālī have been translated into English. See Bibliography.
[3] Al-Ghazālī, 720.

Bilāl ibn Riyāḥ (Rabāḥ, Ribāb) al-Ḥabashī (d. 641) was the son of an Abyssinian slave-girl who had been ransomed by Abū Bakr. He was one of the first converts to Islām, and suffered for it. Muḥammad called him "The First-Fruits of Abyssinia," and made him his purse-bearer. To him the Prophet is claimed to have said, "O Bilāl, sing us a *ghazal*." He was the first *mu'adhdhin* (caller to prayer) in Islām, and is nowadays considered the patron saint of those who follow this calling. Bilāl died at Damascus, where his tomb may be seen.[1]

Shīrīn is the name of the singing-girl of Ḥassān ibn Thābit the Prophet's panegyrist.[2] It is not improbable that she is the slave-girl Sīrīn who, with her sister Māriya the Copt was sent to the Prophet by Al-Muqauqis, the governor of Egypt in 630. Sīrīn was handed over to Ḥassān, whilst Māriya became one of the Prophet's wives.[3] During the "Orthodox" khalifate we read that the famous songstress, 'Azza al-Mailā', sang the songs of an early singing-girl (*qaina*) named Sīrīn, who may have been identical with the Sīrīn or Shīrīn of Ḥassān ibn Thābit.[4]

The names of three other singing-girls have come down to us from this period in consequence of their being doomed for destruction by the Prophet just prior to his entrance into Mecca as conqueror in 630. Their sole "crime" was that they had sung satirical songs against him. The first of these singing girls was Sāra, who belonged to 'Amr ibn Hāshim (or Hishām) ibn 'Abd al-Muṭṭalib. She escaped death by "opportunate submission."[5] Qurainā (or Kurinnā, Fartanā) and Qarība (or Arnab), who were in the service of 'Abdallāh [ibn Hilāl] ibn Khaṭal al-Adramī, were also proscribed. Only Qurainā suffered the death penalty.[6]

[1] Ibn Hishām, 205. Caetani, iii, 99. Evliyā Chelebī, i, (ii), 91, 111. Al-Nawawī, 176.
[2] *Kashf al-maḥjūb*, 411.
[3] Al-Ṭabarī, cf. Index.
[4] *Aghānī*, iv, 14. Guidi looks upon them as separate individuals.
[5] Muir, *Moḥammad*, 411.
[6] Al-Ṭabarī, i, 1626, 1640-2. Al-Wāqidī, 343. Caetani, ii, (1), 134.

From a comparatively modern Turkish authority, Evliyā Chelebī (d. *ca.* 1680), we learn the names of three male musicians who are said to have performed before the Prophet. Only one of these names has a classical attestation, and that is 'Amr ibn Umayya, although we get no mention of his musical accomplishments from the latter source.[1] Yet the tradition can scarcely be of late origin, seeing that two of these individuals are claimed as patron saints of musical fraternities. The three musicians mentioned by Evliyā Chelebī are:

'Amr ibn Umayya Dhamīrī, also called Bābā 'Amr, or 'Amr 'Iyār, is said to have played the *dā'ira* (round tambourine) at the wedding of 'Alī and Fāṭima, and all tambourine players look upon him as their patron saint.[2] He was one of the "Companions of the Prophet."

Ḥamza ibn Yatīm (or Yatīma) is said to have sung with Bilāl in the presence of the Prophet, and to have been girded by 'Alī (or Salmān al-Fārisī). He is also said to to have sung at the wedding of 'Alī and Fāṭima. He is the patron saint of all singers, and his tomb is pointed out at Al-Ṭā'if.[3]

Bābā Sawandīk was an Indian who is credited with having played the kettledrum called *kūs* in the Prophet's military expeditions. He is said to have been buried at Al-Mauṣil, near Jarjīsh.[4]

[1] Caetani, i, 283.
[2] Evliyā Chelebī, i, (ii), 226, 234.
[3] Evliyā Chelebī, i, (ii), 113, 226, 233, 234.
[4] *Ibid.*, i, (ii), 226.

CHAPTER III

THE ORTHODOX KHALIFS

(A.D. 632-661)

"And the first of those who sang the graceful music (*ghinā' al-raqīq*) in Islām was Ṭuwais."

Ibn 'Abd Rabbihi, *'Iqd al-farīd* (10th century).

UPON the death of the Prophet in 632, the Faithful elected a successor in the person of Abū Bakr, whom they saluted as *Khalīfa* ("Successor"). Three succeeding khalifs were also elected by the suffrages of the Muslims, and these "Successors" were 'Umar (634), 'Uthmān (644), and 'Alī (656). No sooner had the Prophet passed away than Arabia was torn asunder by dissension. False prophets arose on every side, and the tribes from distant 'Umān to the very threshold of Al-Medīna the capital were in open revolt against the Khalifate and in avowed apostasy from Islām. Yet within a year the dissident crowd was brought back to the political and religious fold. To effect this, however, huge armies had been set in motion, and the spirit of warfare against the infidel in general was roused to its highest pitch. Babylonia, Mesopotamia, Syria, and Egypt, were invaded and conquered (633-43), a circumstance which was of great cultural significance to the coming Muslim civilization.

The days of the four *Rāshidūn* or "Orthodox" khalifs were the strict days of Islām, when the letter of the law as laid down or implied by the Prophet, or such interpretations of it as the "Companions of the Prophet" thought it their duty to declare, were rigidly enforced. *Music was banned.* Ibn Khaldūn, the greatest of Muslim historians, avers that at the beginning of Islām everything that did not fall in with the teachings of the *Qur'ān* was scorned, whilst the song and pantomime were forbidden. On the other hand, a modern Muslim historian, Sayyid Amīr 'Alī, is of opinion that music was not proscribed until the later legists came on the scene.[1]

The first two khalifs had, possibly, little love for, nor any interest in, music. They were certainly too busy with the sword in consolidating Islām to dally much with the arts. They practised the utmost simplicity of life themselves, and they expected it in others. They knew that the arts could not be indulged in without ostentation and even prodigality, both of which were frowned on by these khalifs. We know that one of the charges brought against the famous Arab general, Abū Mūsā, was that he had bestowed a thousand pieces of silver (*darāhim*)[2] upon a poet.[3]

Since general culture was primarily dependent upon the social and political regimen, and this is nowhere more conspicuously evident than in the Khalifate, it will be my plan in each chapter to deal with the individual khalifs and rulers first of all, so that we may apprehend the culture conditions at the outset.

§ I

Under Abū Bakr (632-34) it may be taken for granted that music as part and parcel of the *malāhī* or " forbidden pleasures " was interdicted. Precise evidence, however, is wanting. The singing-girls (*qaināt, qiyān*), who were slaves in the households of the noble and wealthy families, were possibly not interfered with, but it is fairly certain that those of the taverns, as well as public musicians in general were suppressed, or at least, dared not follow their vocation. The singer of elegies (*nā'iḥ*, fem. *nā'iḥa*) was probably tolerated for the reason that the elegy (*nauḥ*) was not considered music like the song called

[1] Syed Ameer Ali, *Short Hist. of the Saracens*, 457.

[2] A *dirham* (pl. *darāhim*) was a silver coin something like a sixpence, and twenty of them made a *dīnār* (pl. *danānīr*), a gold coin, not unlike a half-sovereign.

[3] Muir, *The Caliphate*, 180.

ghinā'. Al-Ṭabarī has recorded that two singing-girls named Thabjā al-Ḥaḍramiyya and Hind bint Yāmīn, had their hands cut off and their teeth pulled out, so that they could neither play nor sing. This was done by Al-Muhājir when he subdued Al-Yaman in 633, and it received the approbation of Abū Bakr. Yet this punishment was not necessarily occasioned by the fact that they were musicians, but merely because they had sung songs which had satirized the Muslims[1] to the accompaniment of a reed-pipe (*mizmār*).

In spite of the austere *régime* of Abū Bakr, there appear to have been a goodly few who indulged in the *malāhī*. " Nature is not to be for ever thus pent up ; the rebound too often comes ; and in casting off its shackles, humanity not seldom bursts likewise through the barriers of Faith. The gay youth of Islām, cloyed with the dull delights of the sequestered *ḥarīm*, were tempted thus when abroad to evade the restrictions of their creed, and seek in the cup, in music, games and dissipation, the excitement which the young and lighthearted will demand."[2] But there were days of greater freedom in store.

'Umar (634-44) seems to have been little different from his predecessor in this respect. According to a *Ḥadīth* of 'Ā'isha, 'Umar had heard a singing-girl in the very household of the Prophet.[3] This may have influenced him in favour of the singing-girls at least. It is also said that he trembled at the thought that the *Qur'ān* should be recited otherwise than in melodious tones.[4] 'Āṣim his son was particularly devoted to music, whilst one of the khalif's governors, Al-Nu'mān ibn 'Adī, who had charge of Maisān, was certainly a patron of the art.[5]

On the other hand there is a story told by Ibn al-Faqīh al-Hamadhānī (*fl.* 902) that on one occasion 'Umar heard slave-girls playing their tambourines (*dufūf*) and singing that " Life is made for pleasure," when he up-

[1] Al-Ṭabarī, i, 2014. Al-Balādhurī, 102. Caetani, ii (2), 802.
[2] Muir, *The Caliphate*, 185.
[3] *Kashf al-maḥjūb*, 401.
[4] Ibn Sa'd, *Ṭabaqāt al-kabīr*, v, 42.
[5] Ibn Hishām, 782.

braided and cudgelled them for this.[1] Yet one must ask whether his disapproval was on account of the song or of the sentiment. The latter is the more likely explanation, since we have the tradition that 'Umar was abroad one day when the sound of the tambourine reached his ears. 'Umar asked what it was, and when he was told that it was the merry-making at a circumcision, it is distinctly stated that the khalif held his peace.[2]

Several stories are told in the *'Iqd al-farīd* concerning 'Umar and music. In one of these, 'Umar, when asking a man to sing added,—"May Allāh forgive you for it." The remark clearly shows how he stood in regard to the conventional ban. Two nobles of the Quraish (one of them being 'Āṣim ibn 'Amr), whom 'Umar heard singing, were dubbed "asses" by the khalif. On both these occasions the singing was the *rakbānī* of the *naṣb*, which had tacitly been acknowledged to be "allowable."[3] 'Umar was wont to make a tour of Al-Medīna at night, so as to see that there were no infractions of the law.[4] On one occasion he came to a house where the master was listening to the voice of his singing-girl and was indulging in the wine-cup to boot. 'Umar burst in upon the scene crying,—"Shame on thee." The shamed one turned the tables on the khalif by retorting,—"Shame on thee for violating the sanctity of the household, which is forbidden by the word of Allāh."[5] The author of the *Kitāb al-aghānī* says,—"It has been said that Khalif 'Umar had composed a song, but nothing is less probable." Possibly, the historians had confused this khalif with the later 'Umar II (717-20), who was certainly a composer. Yet 'Umar I has been claimed as a poet by Ibn Ḥajar[6] and Ibn Duraid.[7]

'Uthmān (644-56) was the next khalif, and under his rule a great change came to the social and political life of the Arabs. Unlike his predecessor, 'Umar, who was

[1] Ibn al-Faqīh, *Bibl. Geog. Arab.*, v, 43.
[2] *Tāj al-'arūs*, sub *'azifa*. See also Ibn Khallikān, i, 359.
[3] *'Iqd al-farīd*, iii, 178-9.
[4] Cf. Syed Ameer Ali, *Short History*, 67.
[5] Lammens, iii, 275. Cf. Al-Ṭabarī, i, 2742.
[6] Ibn Ḥajar, ii, 21.
[7] Ibn Duraid, *Ishtiqāt*, 225. Cf. Al-Balādhurī, 99.

content to sit on the steps of the mosque at Al-Medīna eating his barley-bread and dates, 'Uthmān was fond of wealth and display. With the vast treasures and crowds of captives which kept pouring into Al-Ḥijāz from conquered lands, the Arabs were able to build up for themselves such glories as they had seen and envied in other Arabian lands, as well as in Persia and the Byzantine Empire, which had fallen to their swords. Gorgeous palaces, large retinues of slaves, brilliant equipages and sumptuous living became the order of the day not only in Al-'Irāq and Syria, which already knew of these things, but even in the holy cities of Al-Ḥijāz. In all the palaces and houses of the nobility and the wealthy, music and musicians came in for special indulgence, in spite of the averred ban of the Prophet, and the murmurs of the stricter Muslims.

'Alī (656-61) was himself a poet, and he was the first khalif who extended any open and real protection to the fine arts and letters by authorizing the study of the sciences, poetry and music.[1] From this date, the future of music was assured, and when the Khalifate passed from the *Rāshidūn* khalifs to the Umayyad dynasty, the art had practically become established in the court of the very "successor" of the Prophet.

§ II

The general position of music and musicians, together with considerable details of the theory and practice of the art in the early days of the Khalifate, seem fairly well defined by the annalists. In the first half-century of Islām, the conditions, as we have seen, were scarcely propitious for the arts. Not only were men's minds centred on the battle throng, but the austerity of life under the new *régime* left little room for these things. In Pagan days the tribes would dispute the pre-eminence of one poet over another, but now they squabbled over the precise way of reading the *Qur'ān*. Yet there were new social forces at work in Al-Ḥijāz. The propagation

[1] Salvador-Daniel, 20.

of Islām by the sword brought its own revenge. The Arab armies had reclaimed Babylonia and Mesopotamia from the Persians. Syria and Egypt had been wrested from Byzantium. Finally, the great land of Persia itself had been conquered. The banner of Islām had not only linked up the two extremes of Arab social life, the nomads of the desert and the cultured citizens of Al-Ḥīra, Al-Yaman and Ghassān, but it had brought them in touch with civilizations which were more cultured and refined than anything that Al-Ḥijāz, the political centre, had hitherto experienced. The result was that Al-Medīna, the seat of the Khalifate, became "the centre of attraction, not to the hosts of Arabia only, but also to enquirers from abroad. Here flocked the Persian, the Greek, the Syrian, the 'Irāqian, and the African."[1] The influence of these people cannot be ignored, although the induction of alien elements must not be overstated. Clearly, the Arabs were too jealous of encroachments upon that sacred and superior thing called Arab nationality to permit of "foreign" ways and customs to any great degree. Every word of 'Umar tells us that.[2] Islām meant much in these days, but the word "Arab" meant more.[3]

We have seen that during the "Days of Idolatry" music, as a profession, was in the hands of the women-folk and slave-girls for the greater part, at any rate in Al-Ḥijāz and the peninsula generally. This continued for the first decade of the Khalifate. During the reign of 'Uthmān (644-56), however, a new figure appears in Al-Ḥijāz—*the male professional musician.* He was quite common in Persia and Al-Ḥīra, whilst in Byzantium and Syria he had had a place from time immemorial. It is worthy of note from whence this innovation came. The first male professional musicians in Al-Ḥijāz belonged to a class known as the *mukhannathūn* (sing. *mukhannath*), who were evidently unknown in Pagan times.[4] These people were an effeminate class who dyed their hands and

[1] Syed Ameer Ali, *Moḥammad,* 531.
[2] Al-Ṭabarī, i, 2751.
[3] Jurjī Zaidān, 29-31.
[4] Lane, *Lexicon,* s.v.

affected the habits of women.[1] The first male professional musician in the days of Islām is generally acknowledged to have been Ṭuwais the *mukhannath*, and indeed, it is said that "in Al-Medīna, music (*ghinā'*) had its origin among the *mukhannathūn*."[2]

The circumstance scarcely augured well for music. Already the stricter Muslims had proscribed this art, or at any rate looked upon it as something disreputable. No wonder that it had become part and parcel of the *malāhī* or "forbidden pleasures," and linked up with wine-bibbing, gaming and fornication.[3] Indeed, the notoriety of the singing-girls of the taverns had led to such terms as *mughanniya* (female musician), *ṣannāja* (female *ṣanj* player), and *zammāra* (female *zamr* player) being considered as synonyms for courtesan and adulteress.[4] Now there was added the disrepute of the *mukhannathūn*. Yet in spite of these unpleasant associations, the art was able to throw off much of the anathema hurled against it. This was mainly owing to the interest displayed by the upper classes, and also perhaps to the old musical traditions of Al-Medīna, the city of the Anṣār who had always been keen lovers of the song, as even the Prophet himself had testified.

At first, all the professional musicians, male and female, came from the servile class, slaves or free-folk. These latter were called the *mawālī* (sing. *maulā*). Ibn Khaldūn has said that the Arabs, in their exercise of military command and government service, were led to look upon the arts as beneath their personal attention. The study and cultivation of such things were for the *mawālī*, who were, for the most part, Persians. That is substantially true. The Arabs looked upon themselves as the elect of Allāh, the aristocracy of nations, whose only "business" was that of the warrior. It does not mean,

[1] For these *mukhannathūn* see *Aghānī*, i, 97, 108. ii, 170-1. iv, 35, 59, 61. Abū'l-Fidā', *Annales Moslemici* (Reiske), i, 109. Ibn Khallikān, i, 438. Kosegarten, *Lib. Cant.*, 11. Burton, *Arabian Nights*, Terminal Essay. Caetani, ii (1), 175, and the *lexica* of Lane and Freytag.

[2] *Aghānī*, iv, 161. Probably a canard of the legists (*'ulamā'*).

[3] Abū Muslim, *Ṣaḥīḥ*, ii, 123.

[4] Al-'Askarī. (Quoted by Lammens iii, 235).

however, that they ceased to be interested in the arts, for never in the history of the East did they flourish as they did under the Khalifate. Nor does it mean, as so many have assumed, that the arts which were encouraged were wholly alien importations.[1] Nothing can be further from the truth. We may talk about music being an international language, but to the Arab it could not be divorced from song. He had his own national dispositions, and perhaps pre-dispositions, to be satisfied on the purely melodic and mensural or rhythmic side, which no alien music could satiate. He obviously had an indigenous musical system which was different to some extent from that of Persia and Byzantium.

The first male professional musician in Islām, Ṭuwais, was evidently an Arab, or at least he appears to have been born and educated in Arabia, and therefore had been schooled in the national music.[2] Sā'ib Khāthir, although the son of a Persian slave, was brought up to Arabian music, and only learned some of the tricks of the Persian art later. 'Azza al-Mailā', one of the first important female professional musicians in Islām, boasted that she carried on the musical traditions of the old Pagan songstresses of Arabia, Sīrīn, Zirnab, Khaula, Al-Rabāb, Salma and Rā'iqa, her own teacher. It was her renderings of the old Arabian music that brought her fame. That she also sang Persian melodies is merely incidental, as it was with other musicians.

What the music of the Arabs was like at this period we can conjecture from the names of their musical instruments and the various technical musical expressions. Among the stringed instruments we read of the *mi'zafa* (? psaltery) and *mi'zaf* (? barbiton).[3] The former was especially favoured in Al-Ḥijāz, and the latter in Al-Yaman.[4] The *mizhar* was a lute, apparently

[1] 'Umar detested the Persians and would have none of their refinements for his people. He had the palace of Sa'd ibn Abī Waqqāṣ at Al-Kūfa burned. It had been built by the Muslims in imitation of the Persian Ṭāq-i Khusrau, at Al-Madā'in.

[2] The date of his birth, 632, proves that to some extent.

[3] See my *Studies in Oriental Musical Instruments*, pp. 7-8.

[4] *Aghānī*, xvi, 13. Al-Mas'ūdī, viii, 93. Lane, *Lexicon*, s.v.

with a skin belly, which had considerable vogue,[1] although it had been superseded, to a considerable extent probably, by the *'ūd*, a wooden-bellied lute, introduced about the close of the previous century from Al-Ḥīra.[2] The *ṭunbūr* or pandore appears to have received greater appreciation in Al-'Irāq,[3] where the *jank* or harp was also afforded grace.

Among the wind instruments, the vertical flute was known as the *quṣṣāba* or *qaṣaba*,[4] whilst the reed-pipe was called the *mizmār*, a term also used for wood-wind instruments in general, as we have seen.[5] The horn or clarion was the *būq*,[6] although it was not yet a martial instrument.

First among the instruments of percussion was the *qaḍīb* or wand, which was popular with those who sang the improvisation (*murtajal*).[7] The *duff* or square tambourine was another favoured instrument for marking the rhythms or measures.[8] The *ṣunnūj ṣaghīra* were the small metal castanets which were part of the impedimenta of the dancers. Finally, the term *ṭabl* covered the drum family proper.

In chamber music we do not read of a combination of these different instruments in performance, although this does not preclude the possibility of it.[9] Ṭuwais, the first male professional musician in Islām, never accompanied himself with any other instrument save the *duff*. 'Azza al-Mailā' is usually represented playing on the old Arabian *mi'zafa* and *mizhar*, although she could also play the *'ūd*. Sā'ib Khāthir began his career with the *qaḍīb*, but later he took up the *'ūd*, and he is claimed to have been the first in Al-Medīna to accompany his singing with the *'ūd*, which looks as though the instrument had previously been used only for purely instrumental performances, or else that it had fallen into desuetude under early Islāmic rigours.

Considerable progress was made on the technical side of the art. This was due to a variety of causes.

[1] *Aghānī*, xvi, 13-14.
[2] Al-Mas'ūdī, viii, 93-4.
[3] *Aghānī*, v, 161.
[4] Lane, *Lexicon*, s.v.
[5] *Mufaḍḍaliyyāt*, xvii.
[6] Lane, *Lexicon*, s.v.
[7] *Aghānī*, vii, 188.
[8] *Aghānī*, ii, 174.
[9] *Ibid.*

First, there were the new ideas which came to the Arabs through the fresh culture contacts. Then there was the rise of a professional class of male musicians. Finally, the inordinate passion for music, which found its lead in the highest circles, gave an impetus to improvement on the technical side, so as to meet with the new demands that verse was making.

It was the patronage of the art and its professors by the nobility that put the hall-mark of "respectability" and "allowableness" upon music. 'Ā'isha, the favourite wife of the Prophet, Al-Ḥasan, the grandson of Khalif 'Alī, Sukaina, the daughter of Al-Ḥusain, Sa'd ibn Abī Waqqāṣ, 'Ā'isha bint Sa'd, Muṣ'ab ibn al-Zubair, 'Ā'isha bint Ṭalḥa, and 'Abdallāh ibn Ja'far, were all keen supporters of music and protectors of its professors. At a reception given by 'Ā'isha bint Ṭalḥa, the wife of Muṣ'ab ibn al-Zubair, a prominent professional songstress like 'Azza al-Mailā', who was engaged to entertain the guests, was treated on an equality with the noble dames of the Quraish. 'Abdallāh ibn Ja'far, himself a brilliant amateur, made his palace a veritable conservatory of music.[1] He was the patron of most of the eminent musicians of the day, and among them, Ṭuwais, Sā'ib Khāthir, Nashīṭ, Nāfi' al-Khair, Budaiḥ al-Malīḥ, Qand, and 'Azza al-Mailā'.

Fresh culture contacts found expression in new types of song or styles of singing. The prisoners captured in the Persian wars were toiling as slaves on the public works at Al-Medīna, and their national melodies began to attract considerable attention. Ṭuwais, the leading Arab musician of the day, found it profitable to imitate their style. Later, a Persian slave named Nashīṭ, became the rage on account of the vogue for Persian airs. Sā'ib Khāthir also realized that he had to fall in with the popular demand and supply his public with the latest craze. Even 'Azza al-Mailā', the conservatrix of the old Arabian art, had to go to Nashīṭ and Sā'ib Khāthir so as to learn these novel fancies. Yet, as I have pointed

[1] Al-Mas'ūdī, v, 385. Cf. De Meynard's translation of this passage. Jurjī Zaidān, 89. '*Iqd al-farīd*, iii, 198.

out elsewhere,[1] there is no question of any musical system or theory being borrowed from the Persians, since it was no more than one nationality borrowing from the other a particular type of song or style of singing, and the imitation is expressly mentioned in the *Kitāb al-aghānī* as being connected with the melody. Indeed, we know that Nashīṭ himself had to take lessons from Sā'ib Khāthir in the Arabian type of song or style of singing, so as to meet the demands of his patrons.

That progress was made in the art at this period is stressed by the historians. We have seen that in the "Days of Idolatry" there was only one type of song known in Al-Ḥijāz, and that was the *naṣb*, which was merely an improved *ḥudā'* or caravan song. This is said to have been made up of "measured melodies" (*alḥān mauzūna*), although we must not suppose that this measure referred to the *īqā'* or "rhythm" that we read of later, but rather that the melody was measured according to the prosodical feet (*'arūḍ*).

About the close of the "Orthodox" period, we read of the introduction of a more artistic genre of music called the *ghinā' al-mutqan*, whose special feature was the application of an *īqā'* or rhythm to the melody of the song, which was independent of the metre (*'arūḍ*) of the verse. Whatever may have prompted it, its production would appear to have been quite indigenous, and seemingly was an offshoot from metrical principles. At any rate it was scarcely borrowed from the Persians, who have been claimed as the inventors of *īqā'* or "rhythm" by Ibn Khurdādhbih,[2] if we are to credit the assertion that they were unacquainted with metre at this time.[3] We certainly know that subsequent to the introduction of the *ghinā al-mutqan*, with its rhythms into Al-Ḥijāz, the Persian-minded city of Al-Ḥīra was still using the older type of song of the genre of the *naṣb*.

The conflicting claims in the *Kitāb al-aghānī* make

[1] Farmer, *Facts for the Arabian Musical Influence*, p. 53

[2] Al-Mas'ūdī, viii, 90.

[3] Browne, *Sources of Dawlatshāh*, in *J.R.A.S.* (1899), pp. 56, 61, 62. Cf. his *Literary History of Persia*, i, 12-14.

it rather difficult to appreciate the actual innovations in the *ghinā' al-mutqan*. Ibn al-Kalbī (d. 819), a most reliable traditionist,[1] who passed on traditions from his father, who was a really scientific enquirer in his way, tells us something about the various genres of music. He says,—" Music (*ghinā'*) is in three styles (*awjuh*)—the *naṣb*, the *sinād*, and the *hazaj*. As for the *naṣb*, it is the music of the riders (*rukbān*) and the singing-girls (*qaināt*). As for the *sinād*, it is the heavy refrain, full of notes (*naghamāt*). And as for the *hazaj*, it is the light [song], all of it, and it is that which stirs the hearts and excites the forbearing."[2] Evidently it was the *sinād* and *hazaj* that were introduced in the *ghinā' al-mutqan* at the time that we are speaking of.

In the *Kitāb al-aghānī* we are informed through a long string of authorities ending with Al-Kalbī (d. 763) and Abū Miskīn, that " the first who sang in Arabic [?] in Al-Medīna was Ṭuwais," and again that " the first music (*ghinā'*) was his [Ṭuwais'] music, with the *hazaj* in it " :

" Love has so emaciated me,
That through it I am almost melting away."[3]

In another place in the same work (as though it were another Ṭuwais) we are told that Ṭuwais was " the first to sing the *ghinā' al-mutqan*," and that he was the foremost exponent of the *hazaj* rhythm.[4] The author (d. 940) of the '*Iqd al-farīd* says,—" The first of those who sang in the time of Islām the graceful music (*ghinā' al-raqīq*) was Ṭuwais."[5] Finally, the *Kitāb al-aghānī*

[1] *Encyclopædia of Islām*, ii, 689.
[2] '*Iqd al-farīd*, iii, 186. Al-Mas'ūdī (viii, 93) on the authority of Ibn Khurdādhbih (*ca.* 870-92) has a slightly different version. He says: " Music (*ghinā'*) is the *naṣb* which comprises three genres—the *rakbānī* (=*ghinā' al-rukbān*) the *sinād* or heavy, and the *hazaj* or light." The word *naṣb* appears to have got shifted from its place after genres.
The passage in the '*Iqd al-farīd* also occurs in the *Mustaṭraf* (15th cent.), ii, 134. Mitjana in *Le Monde Orientale* (1906, p. 205) attributes the tradition in the *Mustaṭraf* to Abū Muḥammad al-Mundhirī. This is an error. The author of the *Mustaṭraf* says that it is Abū Mundhir Hishām, *i.e.*, Ibn al-Kalbī. In fact, all of the chapters dealing with music in the *Mustaṭraf* appear to have been lifted from the '*Iqd al-farīd*.
[3] *Aghānī*, ii, 170. [4] *Aghānī*, iv, 38. [5] '*Iqd al-farīd*, iii, 187.

says,—"The first in Al-Medīna to sing the music introducing in it the *īqā'* (rhythm) was Ṭuwais."

It is this last tradition which appears to sum up the truth of all the others, and that is that the graceful music (*ghinā' al-raqīq*) or artistic music (*ghinā' al-mutqan*) was that which employed a new device of rhythmical symmetry quite independent of the metrical structure of the verse. The first *īqā'* (rhythm) introduced was the *hazaj*.

Another claimant for honours in introducing the "new music" is 'Azza al-Mailā', since it is said that "she was the first who sang the rhythmic song (*ghinā' al-mauqi'*) in Al-Ḥijāz."[1] Sā'ib Khāthir also contributed a share to this "new music," and Ibn al-Kalbī says that the song commencing:

> "Why are these homes desolated,
> The sport of wind and rain?"

which is in the *īqā'* (rhythm) called *thaqīl awwal*, was the first song in the music of the Arabs of artistic and savant composition in the days of Islām.[2] These rhythmic modes, which became a special feature in Arabian music, were soon extended, as we shall see. Meanwhile we turn to the melody.

Music was known by the generic term *ghinā'*, which primarily meant "song," hence *mughann* or *mughannī* stood generally for "musician," although in its specific sense it implied "singer." Music was also called *ṭarab*, hence *muṭrib* meant "musician," or from a point of view of the stricter Muslim, music was *lahw* (lit. "entertainment") and musical instruments were dubbed *malāhī*. Throughout the *Kitāb al-aghānī* we find the verses that were set to music superscribed with the term *ṣaut*, and the word was strictly confined to "vocal music," although later it came to be used by the theorists to mean "noise" in contradistinction to *ṭanīn* ("tone") and *naghma* ("musical note"). An interval was called a

[1] *Aghānī*, xvi, 13.
[2] *Aghānī*, vii. 188.

nabra in these days,[1] although there were no names for the specific intervals, save in the nomenclature of the finger-places on the lute, such as *muṭlaq* ("open string"), *sabbāba* ("first finger"), *wusṭā* ("second finger"), *binṣir* ("third finger"), and *khinṣir* ("fourth finger"). It is highly probable, however, that the terms for the tonic and octave at this period were *sajāḥ* (*shuḥāj*) and *ṣiyyāḥ*.[2]

The term for melody was *laḥn*, and all serious or artistic music was composed in certain melodic modal formulas called *aṣābi'* ("fingers," sing. *aṣba'*). At first we meet with these modes described merely according to their *majrā* or "course."[3] There were two "courses,"—the *binṣir* and *wusṭā*. Later, the *aṣābi'* are more clearly designated by their tonics.

§ III

Among the names of the great musicians of the first days of Islām are a few that have been preserved in song, story, verse and proverb among the Arabs, which show the high esteem in which they were held. Fortunately, we have precise details of their lives from other sources, for the most part from that mine of Arabian verse and history, the great *Kitāb al-aghānī*.

The first musician to make a name under Islām was Ṭuwais ("The Little Peacock"), whose full name was Abū 'Abd al-Muna''am 'Īsā ibn 'Abdallāh al-Dhā'ib (632-710)[4] He was a freeman (*maulā*) of the Banū Makhzūm and belonged to Al-Medīna, having been brought up in the household of Arwā', the mother of Khalif 'Uthmān. Whilst he was still young, he was

[1] See the definitions in the *Tāj al-'arūs*; Land, *Remarks, etc.*, p. 156. Ribera, *La música de las cantigas*, p. 23. Ḥasan Ḥusnī 'Abdulwahab, *Le Developpement de la Musique Arabe en Orient, Espagne et Tunisie* (Tunis, 1918), p. 5.

[2] See the *Mafātīḥ al-'ulūm*, 240, and Land, *Remarks*, 157.

[3] *Aghānī*, ii, 171. xvi, 16.

[4] Freytag, *Arab. Prov.*, xiii, 158. Ibn Khallikān, i, 438. The proverb,—"More unfortunate than Ṭuwais" was due to the fact that all the great events of his life,—his birth, circumcision, marriage, etc., happened to fall on the dates when one of the illustrious men of Islām died.

attracted by the melodies sung by the Persian slaves who were employed at Al-Medīna, and he imitated their style. According to Ibn Badrūn, it was in the later years of Khalif 'Uthmān (644-66) that Ṭuwais rose to fame.[1] He is highly esteemed in Arabian annals for his musical abilities. Ibn Suraij, his pupil, called him the finest singer of his day, whilst he was considered the greatest exponent in the *hazaj* rhythm. We have already seen that he is generally credited with being the first to sing the "new music" which was introduced in his time. According to the *Kitāb al-aghānī*, he only used the square tambourine called the *duff* in accompanying himself, which he carried in a bag,[2] or in his robe.[3]

Like the majority of the first male musicians in Al-Medīna at this period, he was socially an outcast, by reason of his being a *mukhannath*.[4] Yet he was highly esteemed by the nobility. When Mu'āwiya I (661-80) ascended to the Khalifate, Marwān ibn al-Ḥakam, the governor of Al-Medīna, offered a reward for every *mukhannath* that was delivered into his hands. One of these, Al-Naghāshī, was put to death.[5] Ṭuwais sought refuge at Suwaidā on the road to Syria. Here, the old musician remained until his death, full of bitterness that his musical reputation had not exempted him from the edict of Marwān the governor. Among his pupils were Ibn Suraij, Al-Dalāl Nāfidh, Nauma al-Ḍuḥā, and Fand.[6]

Sā'ib Khāthir (d. 683) or more properly, Abū Ja'far Sā'ib ibn Yassār, was the son of a Persian slave in the service of the Laith family of Al-Medīna. Given his freedom, he entered commercial life, and in his leisure hours he attended the weekly concerts of the *nā'iḥāt* (female singers of elegies), which gave him an ambition

[1] Ibn Badrūn, 64.
[2] *'Iqd al-farīd*, iii, 186. [3] *Aghānī* ii, 174.
[4] Hence the proverb, "More effeminate than Ṭuwais." Freytag, *Arab. Prov.*, vii, 124.
[5] *Aghānī*, ii, 171. Ṭuwais was scarcely the first *mukhannath* in Al-Medīna as this author says. Cf. Al-Bukhārī, iv, 32. Al-Tirmidhī, i, 271. Ibn al-Athīr, *Usd al-ghāba*, iv, 268.
[6] *Aghānī*, ii, 170-76. iv, 38-9. *'Iqd al-farīd*, iii, 186. Ibn Khallikān, ii, 438. Guidi makes out that there were two musicians named Ṭuwais.

to be a singer. Devoting himself to the art, he made such progress that one day, a noble of the Quraish, ʻAbdallāh ibn Jaʻfar, hearing him sing, took him into his service. At this time, following the practice of untutored musicians, he merely accompanied himself with the *qaḍīb* or wand, but he soon abandoned this for the *ʻūd* (lute), and he is credited with being the first in Al-Medīna to accompany his songs with this instrument. When Nashīṭ the Persian became the rage on account of his national airs, Sā'ib showed that he could sing the same to Arabic verse. He is also reputed to have been the originator of the *thaqīl awwal* rhythm, and the first song in which he used it is esteemed to be the first song in Arabian music of artistic composition.

When his protector, ʻAbdallāh ibn Jaʻfar, visited Khalif Muʻāwiya I (661-80) at Damascus, he took Sā'ib with him. As this khalif was influenced by the conventional ban on music, ʻAbdallāh had to introduce this musician to court as a poet who " embellished " his verse. After Sā'ib had given a display of his singing, which his protector had called " embellished verse," the khalif rewarded Sā'ib with a present. During the reign of Yazīd I, the people of Al-Medīna revolted, and an army was sent against the rebels. One of the first innocent victims of the soldiery after the battle of Al-Ḥarra (683) was the musician Sā'ib Khāthir. Sā'ib had four eminent pupils—ʻAzza al Mailā', Ibn Suraij, Jamīla, and Maʻbad.[1]

ʻAzza al-Mailā' (d. *ca.* 705) received her cognomen on account of her figure. She was a handsome half-caste of Al-Medīna, and was a pupil of an old songstress named Rā'iqa, who taught her the music of olden days, such as had been sung or played by Sīrīn, Zirnab, Khaula, Al-Rabāb and Salma. Later she learned some of the Persian airs from Nashīṭ and Sā'ib Khāthir. As a young woman, we find her with her teacher, Rā'iqa, and the poet Ḥassān ibn Thābit (d. *ca.* 674) at the best festivities in Al-Medīna. This was in the reign of ʻUthmān. The weekly concerts at her house attracted a throng of

[1] *Aghānī*, vii, 188-90.

dilettanti, and her influence was felt even at Mecca.[1] Ṭuwais, who attended these concerts, testified that "the most complete propriety was observed at them." Strict silence was demanded from the audience, and the slightest misbehaviour was reproved by a stroke with a stick.[2]

The extraordinary popularity of 'Azza al-Mailā' scandalized the stricter Muslims, and during the reign of Mu'āwiya I (661-80) they complained to Sa'īd ibn al-'Āṣ, the governor of Al-Medīna, who would have upheld their grievance had not the great art patron, 'Abdallāh ibn Ja'far intervened. Many poets and musicians sang her praises. Ḥassān ibn Thābit said that her performances reminded him of the artistic music at the Ghassānid court in the "Days of Idolatry." Ṭuwais said that she was the "Queen of Singers." Although she made a speciality of playing the *mizhar* and *mi'zafa*, which were the instruments of the olden days, we have it on the authority of Ma'bad that she excelled in playing the *'ūd*. The date of her death has not been recorded, but she died before 710.[3] There was a later songstress named Nā'ila bint al-Mailā', who was probably her daughter.[4]

Nashīṭ was a Persian slave in the service of 'Abdallāh ibn Ja'far, who freed him later. He created a *furore* in Al-Medīna on account of his Persian melodies, and Arab singers were compelled to adopt Persian airs for their repertory in consequence. At the same time, Nashīṭ had to take lessons from Sā'ib Khāthir in order to learn the Arabian melodies, so as to keep pace with his rivals. Nashīṭ had the honour of being one of the teachers of 'Azza al-Mailā' and Ma'bad.[5] We read of a Ḥammād ibn Nashīṭ, who appears to have been his son.[6]

Ḥunain al-Ḥīrī was the usual name given to Abū Ka'b Ḥunain ibn Ballū' al-Ḥīrī (d. *ca.* 718). As his name implies, he was a native of Al-Ḥīra, and he appears to have been an Arab of the Banū'l-Ḥārith ibn Ka'b, and

[1] *Aghānī*, x, 55.
[2] *Aghānī*, xvi, 14. We read of the same custom in Plato's *Laws*, 700.
[3] *Aghānī*, xvi, 13-20.
[4] *Aghānī*, v, 176.
[5] *Aghānī*, vii, 188.
[6] *Aghānī*, iv, 61.

a Christian, which partly explains why he, an Arab, is to be found among the purveyors of this illicit calling of music. As a young man he followed the employment of a flower-seller, and this took him to the houses of the nobility and wealthy classes, where he became infatuated with the performances of the singing-girls, until one day he decided to become a musician. After studying under good masters,[1] he became a first-rate performer on the *'ūd*, an excellent singer, and a composer of repute. He was the first in Al-'Irāq in the time of Islām, to cultivate the artistic song in the *sinād* genre, his predecessors, we are told, having been satisfied with the *hazaj*, which was, at this time, little different from the *naṣb* in Al-'Irāq.

Ḥunain must have started his career in the time of 'Uthmān (644-56) at least. During the reign of 'Abd al-Malik (685-705), the governor of Al-'Irāq, Khālid ibn 'Abdallāh al-Qasrī, interdicted music and musicians, but owing to the reputation of Ḥunain, the latter was permitted to follow his avocation, provided that no bad or dissolute characters were admitted to audition. When Bishr ibn Marwān, the brother of Khalif 'Abd al-Malik, became governor, the edict was rescinded and Ḥunain was summoned to his palace at Al-Kūfa, where he remained in constant attendance on this prince.

About the year 718, the *virtuosi* of Al-Ḥijāz, desiring to pay their respects to their venerable *confrère* of Al-'Irāq, invited him to Mecca. Here, an illustrious gathering of musicians, poets and *dilettanti* received him with pomp and ceremony. At the residence of Sukaina bint al-Ḥusain, a liberal patroness of music, a grand musical *fête* was prepared, and during its progress a gallery which had become overcrowded with the audience collapsed, and the aged Ḥunain was killed. On the authority of his son 'Ubaidallāh, Ḥunain al-Ḥīrī is to be ranked among "the four great singers" of Islām.[2]

Aḥmad al-Naṣībī, or Aḥmad ibn Usāma al-Hamdānī, belonged to Al-Kūfa. It seems that he began his musical

[1] 'Umar al-Wādī and Ḥakam al-Wādī are mentioned as the teachers of Ḥunain, but their dates preclude the possibility of this.
[2] *Aghānī*, ii, 120-27. Cf. *post.* p. 80.

career during the "Orthodox" Khalifate. He was an Arab, and a kinsman of the poet A'sha Hamdān (d. 702), whose companion he was. His singing of the poet's verses brought him fame. He was a master of the type of song called the *naṣb*, and it was due to him that it was introduced into serious music. Apparently, he was the first in the days of Islām to make a name as a performer on the *ṭunbūr* (pandore). He became the minstrel and boon companion of 'Ubaidallāh ibn Ziyād (d. 685), who was governor of Al-Kūfa. Although Jaḥẓa al-Barmakī the author of the *Kitāb al-ṭunbūriyyīn* speaks of him with contempt, the author of the *Kitāb al-aghānī* says that he was unrivalled as a composer and performer on the *ṭunbūr*.[1]

Qand of Al-Medīna was another of the musicians of the "first period," says the *'Iqd al-farīd*. He was a freeman of Sa'd ibn Abī Waqqāṣ (d. 670) and 'Ā'isha the "Mother of the Faithful," was particularly attached to him. Sa'd once thrashed Qand, and this so enraged 'Ā'isha that she refused to speak to the noble Quraishite until he had begged the musician's pardon. Qand was alive as late as the appointment of Sa'īd ibn al-'Āṣ (d. 672-78) to the governorship of Al-Medīna.[2]

Fand or Find, sometimes called Abū Zaid, was a freeman of 'Ā'isha bint Sa'd. He was a man of debauched character, although a fine musician. His remissness passed into the proverb, "More delaying than Fand."[3] He lived to take part in the famous Jamīla pilgrimage in the days of the Umayyads.[4]

Al-Dalāl Nāfidh[5] Abū Yazīd belonged to Al-Medīna and was a freeman of the Banū Fahm. He was also in the service of 'Ā'isha bint Sa'd. Khalif 'Abd al-Malik (685-705) favoured him, for he was a fine musician and

[1] *Aghānī*, v, 161-4.

[2] *Aghānī*, vii, 135. *'Iqd al-farīd*, iii, 189. Cf. Qa'īd mentioned by Von Hammer, *Lit. der Arab.*, ii, 705.

[3] Freytag, *Arab. Prov.*, ii, 159. iii, 81.

[4] *Aghānī*, xvi, 60-1. vii, 135. Fand and the preceding Qand would appear to be the same person.

[5] Written Al-Dallāl by De Meynard and Freytag. Cf. Kosegarten *Lib. Cant.*, and Lane, *Lexicon*, sub "khanatha." The Sāsī edition of the *Aghānī* has Nāfid, and Von Hammer says Nāqid.

had studied under Ṭuwais. Like his teacher, he was a *mukhannath*, and he is pilloried by Al-Maidānī in the proverb,—" More effeminate than Al-Dalāl." His melodies were imitated a century later by one of the most famous of Arab musicians—Ibrāhīm al-Mauṣilī.[1]

Budaiḥ al-Malīḥ was a freeman of 'Abdallāh ibn Ja'far (d. 699) together with Nāfi' al-Khair and Nauma al-Ḍuḥā. All of these musicians took part in the Jamīla pilgrimage. Nauma al-Ḍuḥā was taught by Ṭuwais, and Nāfi' al-Khair was at the courts of Mu'āwiya I (661-80) and Yazīd I (680-3).[2]

In Al-'Irāq were some lesser known musicians—Zaid ibn al-Ṭalīs, Zaid ibn Ka'b and Mālik ibn Ḥamama.[3]

[1] *Aghānī*, iv, 59-73. vii, 137. *'Iqd al-farīd*, iii, 187. Freytag, *Arab. Prov.*, vii, 96.

[2] *Aghānī*, xiv, 9-11. iii, 86. vii, 103, 104, 135. Cf. iv, 61, 129 (Ḥabīb Nauma al Ḍuḥā). *'Iqd al-farīd*, iii, 186.

[3] *Aghānī*, ii, 125.

CHAPTER IV

THE UMAYYADS

(A.D. 661-750)

"There is no true joy but in lending ear to music."[1]
Khalif Al-Walīd II.

THE Khalifate fell to the house of Umayya on the death of 'Alī (661). Although the Umayyads ruled for nearly a century, the stricter Muslims looked upon them as usurpers, not merely because they came of the Pagan aristocracy of "unbelieving Mecca" that had withstood the Prophet, but on account of their worldly ways. Yet it was under this dynasty that the Arabian empire and Muslim civilization entered upon a path of glory. The Khalifate extended its dominions eastward as far as the Oxus and Indus, and westward as far as the Atlantic and the Pyrenees. Indeed, it has well been said that where the Orthodox khalifs had made Islām a religion, the Umayyads had created it an empire.[2]

The removal of the capital from Al-Medīna to Damascus, where it remained practically for the whole of the Umayyad period, was not an auspicious event politically, although culturally it made for progress. The wider influence brought to intellectual life by closer contact with Byzantium and Persia, lifted the people beyond the confines of Islām and the insularity of Arabia. The circumstance eventually re-acted on European culture generally, for the Arabs became the pioneers of that regeneration of culture which led to the Renaissance.[3]

[1] Nicholson, *Risālat al-ghufrān* (*J.R.A.S.*, 1902), and *Literary History of the Arabs*, 206.
[2] Jurjī Zaidān, 74.
[3] See my *Arabian Influence on Musical Theory* (1925).

§ I

Mu'āwiya I (661-80) was a ruler of literary and artistic tastes.[1] "He assembled at his court all who were most distinguished by scientific acquirements; he surrounded himself with poets; and as he had subjected to his dominion many of the Grecian isles and provinces, the sciences of Greece first began, under him, to obtain an influence over the Arabs."[2] Yet although the khalif was susceptible to the charms of poetry, and his *badawī* wife Maisūn was an accomplished poetess, he appears to have been swayed by the conventional ban against artistic music.[3] His governors frequently interdicted the art, and we know that when 'Abdallāh ibn Ja'far wished to introduce a certain musician at court, he had to plead that the latter was a "poet," because the khalif pretended that he had no idea of music and had never admitted a musician into his presence.[4] Yet the khalif was pleased with the performance of the so-called "poet," who happened to be Sā'ib Khāthir, one of the foremost musicians of his day, who did not deliver "poetry" but sang before the khalif! Towards the end of his reign, Mu'āwiya heard this musician once more in Al-Medīna, and rewarded him with a present.

Yazīd I (680-83) was the son of Maisūn, and it is no wonder therefore that he had such inordinate tastes for poetry and music. He was himself a poet of no mean order,[5] and Al-Mas'ūdī says that he was "appassioned for music (*ṭarab*),"[6] whilst in the *Kitāb al-aghānī* we read that he was "the first to introduce musical instruments (*malāhī*) and singers into the court."[7] The strict Muslims

[1] Al-Mas'ūdī, v, 77.
[2] Sismondi, i, 50.
[3] Al-Ṭabarī, ii, 214. There was music of a kind at court, such as the singing-girls provided. This we know from the pathetic song of the khalif's wife Maisūn who longed for the desert tent instead of the gilded court,—

"The wind's voice where the hill-path went
Was more than tambourine[s] can be."
(Quoted by Nicholson, *Lit. Hist. of the Arabs*, 195.)

[4] Cf. *'Iqd al-farīd*, i, 318. iii, 238.
[5] Lammens, iii, 193.
[6] Al-Mas'ūdī, v, 156.
[7] *Aghānī*, xvi, 70.

were scandalized at the "ungodliness of the court—wine and music, singing-men and singing-women, cock-fighting and hounds."[1]

Mu'āwiya II (683-84) and Marwān (684-85) only occupied the throne for a year, too brief a space to have any appreciable influence on the culture of the period. The latter, however, banished all the *mukhannathūn* from Al-Medīna when he was its governor as a prince, including the famous musician Ṭuwais.

'Abd al-Malik (685-705) gave general encouragement to music and letters. He was "a composer of no mean merit," and he "encouraged poets with a princely liberality."[2] Both Ibn Misjaḥ and Budaiḥ al-Malīḥ, the best known musicians of the time, were patronized by him. At the same time, so as to display some appearance of "orthodoxy," he appears to have made a pretence not only to be ignorant of music, but even to disapprove of it. Before his courtiers, he censured music as "debasing to manliness, and ruinous to dignity and honour," but he was taken to task by 'Abdallāh ibn Ja'far for this opinion.[3] Again, in the *Ḥalbat al-kumait*, it is said that 'Abd al-Malik once simulated unacquaintance with the purpose of the *'ūd* (lute), but a freely-spoken courtier answered that everyone present was fully informed about the instrument, and no one more so than the khalif himself, at which sally 'Abd al-Malik was much amused. From the *Kitāb al-aghānī* we know that the khalif was sufficiently well acquainted with music to be able to ask for the *ḥudā'*, the *ghinā' al-rukbān*, and the *ghinā' al-mutqan*. The khalif's brother, Bishr ibn Marwān, was a staunch patron of music.

Al-Walīd I (705-15) reigned during a most eventful period. The banner of Islām was planted within the confines of China in the east, and on the shores of the Atlantic in the west. The Mediterranean was crossed, and the foundations of a western khalifate were laid in Spain. "In his reign," says Muir, "culture and the

[1] Muir, *Caliphate*, 314.
[2] Muir, *Caliphate*, 344. Al-Mas'ūdī, v, 310.
[3] *'Iqd al-farīd*, iii, 198.

arts began to flourish."[1] The cultivation of music, in spite of the high-handed measures of some of his governors, progressed by leaps and bounds. The chief musicians of Mecca and Al-Medīna,—Ibn Suraij and Ma'bad, were summoned to the court at Damascus, where they were received with even greater appreciation and honour than the poets. The khalif's favourite minstrel was Abū Kāmil al-Ghuzayyil, who, he declared, was indispensable to him.[2]

Sulaimān (715-17) was a man of pleasure. Music was for him not an art to be sought for itself alone, but as a mere concomitant with the joys of the feast or *ḥarīm*. The singing-girls alone had his attention.[3] When he was a prince, however, he had displayed a predilection for music, since he was keen enough to offer a prize for competition among the musicians of Mecca, and this during a pilgrimage! The first prize of 10,000 pieces of silver was carried off by Ibn Suraij, whilst a like amount was distributed among the other competitors.[4]

'Umar II (717-20) brought a change to the Khalifate. He was pious and to some extent a bigot. The result was that "poets, orators, and such-like soon found that his court was no place for them, while it was thronged by godly and devout divines."[5] Compared with his predecessors, it became a proverbial expression among the Arabs that whilst Al-Walīd I was for *art*, and Sulaimān was for *women*, 'Umar II was for *piety*.[6] Yet before he came to the throne he was not only fond of music, but was actually a composer. In the *Kitāb al-aghānī* he is claimed to have been the first khalif who composed songs, and the words and "modes" of these compositions are mentioned.[7] This was when 'Umar was governor of Al-Ḥijāz, and surrounded by a music-loving aristocracy. When he became khalif, however, *listening to music* was forbidden. It came to his notice on one occasion that a judge (*qāḍī*) of Al-Medīna had become a veritable slave to the accomplishments of one of his singing-girls.

[1] Muir, *Caliphate*, 361.
[2] *Aghānī*, vi, 144.
[3] Cf. *Aghānī*, iv, 60-2.
[4] *Aghānī*, i, 126.
[5] Muir, *Caliphate*, 369.
[6] *Fakhrī*, 173.
[7] *Aghānī*, viii, 149-50.

The khalif decided to dismiss him from office, but first sent for both the judge and his singing-girl. When they appeared before him, the latter was commanded to sing. The khalif was deeply moved by the charm of her voice and the sentiment of her song, and turning to the judge he said, "Thy crime is nothing. Return to thy post, and may Allāh guide thee."[1]

Yazīd II (720-24) brought back music and poetry to the court and public life, although he went to the very opposite extreme from his predecessor. Like his uncle, Yazīd I, he was a man "without religion" according to the orthodox annalists, and he cultivated music and the song on every hand. Ibn Suraij, Ma'bad, Mālik, Ibn 'Ā'isha, Al-Baidhaq al-Anṣārī, Ibn Abī Lahab and other musicians, were treated with generous bounty at his court. Here, too, we see the lavish favours bestowed on the singing-girls Sallāma al-Qass and Ḥabbāba, who played important rôles in political as well as musical affairs during his reign. Yazīd was utterly free from religious prejudices. The singer Ibn Abī Lahab, who had pleased the khalif with his singing one day was asked by whom he had been taught. The musician replied, "My father." Yazīd replied,—"If you had received no other heritage than this song, your father left you a considerable fortune." "But," urged the singer, "my father was an infidel and an enemy of the Prophet all his life!" "I know," said Yazīd, "yet he was such an excellent musician that I have a certain sympathy for him."[2] Some of this khalif's verses have been preserved.[3]

Hishām (724-43) had a prosperous reign and it was "one of the most exemplary of the Khalifate either before or after," says Muir.[4] Of his attitude towards music during his occupancy of the throne, we get no information in the *Kitāb al-aghānī*, although we know that he had musicians at court. Whilst he was a prince, he patronized the *doyen* of the musicians of Al-'Irāq, Ḥunain al-Ḥīrī,

[1] Al-Mas'ūdī, v, 428.
[2] Al-Mas'ūdī, v, 449.
[3] *Aghānī*, xiii, 161.
[4] Muir, *Caliphate*, 399. He abstained from wine (*nabīdh*).

during a pilgrimage even,[1] which would lead one to deduce that he was not quite in agreement with the conventional proscription.[2] Bar Hebræus[3] tells us that Hishām once admitted that he did not know the difference between a pandore (*tunbūr*) and a lute (*barbaṭ*), but this story probably belongs to the same class as those told of other khalifs. (See *ante* p. 61).

Al-Walīd II (743-44) cared little for political life, and it was from this time that the fortunes of the House of Umayya began to wane. Like Yazīd I, Al-Walīd I, and Yazīd II, this khalif was absorbed in pleasure and was an open-handed patron of the arts. Al-Mas'ūdī says "He loved music (*ghinā'*) and was the first to support musicians from abroad, showing publicly his pleasure in the wine-cup, the revels (*malāhī*) and the stringed instrument (*'azf*). . . . The cultivation of music spread not only among the leisured class, but with the people also, whilst the singing-girls became the rage."[4] At his court, musicians from all parts were welcomed with open arms, and among them: Ma'bad, 'Aṭarrad, Mālik, Ibn 'Ā'isha, Daḥmān (al-Ashqar ?), 'Umar al-Wādī, Ḥakam al-Wādī, Yūnus al-Kātib, Al-Hudhalī, Al-Abjar, Ash'ab ibn Jabīr, Abū Kāmil al-Ghuzayyil and Yaḥyā Qail. The khalif himself was a born *artiste*, and he excelled in both music and poetry, as we know from the *Kitāb al-aghānī*, where a chapter is devoted to his accomplishments in these arts. Besides being an excellent singer and a performer on the *'ūd* (lute) and the *ṭabl* (drum), he was a composer.[5] Unfortunately, he plunged into excesses, and this "alienated from him the regard of all the better classes."[6] This gave the 'Abbāsid faction, the enemy of the House of Umayya, the opportunity to further their propaganda against the "ungodly usurpers,"

[1] *Aghānī*, ii, 121.

[2] His reproof of Ibn 'Ā'isha for singing (*Aghānī*, xiii, 127) was only because it interfered with the progress of a caravan. Similarly his punishment of Yūnus al-Kātib was not on account of music, but because the words libelled a lady.

[3] Bar Hebræus, 207.

[4] Al-Mas'ūdī, vi, 4.

[5] *Aghānī*, viii, 161-2.

[6] Muir, *Caliphate*, 403.

as they termed the Umayyads. The reign of Al-Walīd II was short, but a great deal was done for music during those fleeting years. "The love of music," said Sayyid Amīr 'Alī, "grew almost into a craze, and enormous sums were spent on famous singers and musicians."[1]

Yazīd III (744) only reigned six months. He appears to have been equally favourable towards music, and he instructed his governor of Khurāsān, Naṣr ibn Sayyār, to furnish him with "every kind of musical instrument," as well as a number of singing-girls.[2] On the other hand, Al-Ghazālī hands down the saying attributed to this khalif, which bespeaks rigid orthodoxy on the question of "listening to music." Yazīd III is credited with these words: "Beware of singing for it maketh modesty to be lacking and increaseth lust and ruineth manly virtue; and verily it takes the place of wine and does what drunkenness does; and if ye cannot avoid having to do with it, keep it out of the way of women, for singing incites to fornication."[3]

Marwān II (744-50) was the last of the Umayyad khalifs in the East. The whole of his reign was taken up with internecine strife, which enabled the 'Abbāsids, whose seat was in Khurāsān, to raise the standard of revolt. On the 25th January, 750, the famous battle of the Zāb was fought. It sealed the fate of the Umayyads and culminated in the death of Marwān II. It was the end, too, of the purely Arabian period in the national music, which, in spite of Persian and Byzantine influences, seems to have held its own during the reign of the Umayyads. For a continuation of the old art we have to turn to the west, where a scion of the House of Umayya was to raise a sulṭānate and Khalifate in a land known as Al-Andalus (Spain).

§ II

The indifference of the Umayyads towards Islām augured well for musical art. The new khalifs represented

[1] Syed Ameer Ali, *Short History*.
[2] Muir, *Caliphate*, 406.
[3] Al-Ghazālī, *op. cit.*, 248-9.

the old Pagan ideas of the Arabs, and so far as they had any religion, says Muir, they were Unitarians, " and so might be called Muslims ; but in the matter of drinking wine and most other things, they set Islām at naught."[1] Among the " other things " was music, and indeed the Muslim purists did not forget to include music among the " sins " of the Umayyads. Al-Ḥasan al-Baṣrī (d. (728), a contemporary theologian, said concerning Mu'āwiya I, the least unorthodox of the Umayyads save 'Umar II, that he deserved damnation on four points, one of them being that he had left the Khalifate to Yazīd I, who was " a wine drinker, a player of the *ṭunbūr* (pandore) and a wearer of silken garments."[2] Yet we need give credit to but a tithe of the stories about the profligacy of the Umayyads, since the 'Abbāsid hatred of this dynasty accounts for many a canard.

With the exception of the reigns of Mu'āwiya I, 'Abd al-Malik and 'Umar II, the courts were thronged with musicians both male and female, and the greatest encouragement given to the art. The honours showered upon singers and instrumentalists and the largesses bestowed can only be equalled in the " Golden Age " of the 'Abbāsids. The Umayyads, however, had political as well as artistic reasons for these favours. It was the singer who, by setting the panegyrics and satires of the court poets to music, reached the ear of the populace.[3] As Lammens says, the singer and the poet were the journalists of their day.[4] A poet like Jarīr might affect to look down on the singer as he does in his *Naqā'id*, but it was readily acknowledged that a poem set to music had greater potency than when it was delivered by a mere reciter (*rāwī*).[5] Singers journeying from town to town and tribe to tribe passed on their songs which were taken up even by the singers in the caravans.[6] All this helped to consolidate the body politic as well as art.

[1] Muir, *Caliphate*, 431. Nicholson (*Lit. Hist. of the Arabs*) says: " They had little enough religion of any sort." For their contempt of the *Qur'ān* and the Holy places, see Jurjī Zaidān, 102.

[2] Al-Ṭabarī, ii, 146.

[3] *Aghānī*, ii, 153.

[4] Lammens, ii, 146.

[5] *Aghānī*, iii, 124.

[6] *Aghānī*, ii, 153.

Music and musicians had won back, to some extent, their places of esteem and honour in the social life of the Arabs which had once been theirs. Music was no longer an avocation for mere slaves, since we find freemen (*mawālī*) of good social standing and possession making music their profession. Yūnus al-Kātib, an official in the municipal adminstration of Al-Medīna, took up this vocation. We also see a musician named Burdān being appointed to a lucrative municipal post.[1] Even whilst it must be admitted that most of the professionals came from the freeman class, for the most part Persians by extraction, yet there were Arabs who did not think it beneath their dignity to be professional musicians, and among them Mālik, himself one of the aristocracy.

Yet musicians formed a class apart. This was not due to any official measure such as operated in Persia under the Sāsānids,[2] but was merely on account of the ban of Islām, and strengthened somewhat by craft consciousness. At first, looked upon as vagabonds, like the mediæval minstrels of Europe, musicians were naturally forced into a separate class, which assumed something of the nature of a brotherhood, just as in Europe they were compelled to form guilds. The leading musicians appear to have made rather comfortable livings. They were in constant demand at court, the houses of the nobility and the rich *bourgeoisie*, as well as at the innumerable festivities connected with Islām and social life generally.[3] Some of the *virtuosi* turned their residences into conservatories of music, where the rich *dilettanti* spent their leisure hours, and where they sent their singing-girls to be trained, for no house could be without its singing-girl.

The custom of audition at this period is of considerable interest. At the Umayyad court, whilst the khalif observed the Sāsānid custom[4] of having a thin curtain between the performers and himself during audition,

[1] *Aghānī*, vii, 168. [2] Al-Mas'ūdī, ii, 157.

[3] The "presents" bestowed on musicians are possibly exaggerated in some cases, but we must remember the Arab proverb, "Singing without silver is like a corpse without perfume." Burckhardt, *Arab. Prov.*, 464.

[4] Al-Mas'ūdī, ii, 158.

this does not appear to have always been the case, except when the ladies of the *ḥarīm* were with him. Even then, instances are given where the curtain was raised.[1] There were occasions indeed, when the musician performed face to face with his audience, and on one occasion actually occupied the same couch as the khalif.[2] Outside the court the musician was under no such restriction. Of course, the singing-girls, both at court and in private households, did not usually entertain guests without the customary curtain, although we read of some strange anomalies in this respect. The famous songstress, Jamīla, prepared a *fête* for 'Abdallāh ibn Ja'far and his *entourage*, in which the singing-girls who were studying at her house took a prominent part. The latter were gaily attired and performed without any curtain and in full view of the audience.[3] On the other hand, at her famous *fête* during the pilgrimage which the *Kitāb al-aghānī* makes so much of, we read that the singing-girls performed behind a curtain.[4] Again, in the house of 'Ā'isha bint Ṭalḥa, we find the songstress 'Azza al-Mailā' singing to the wives of the Quraish nobles, the whole of them being hidden from the men by a curtain.[5] Yet on another occasion we find Ibn Suraij and 'Azza al-Mailā' singing together at the house of Sukaina bint al-Ḥusain before the entire company quite openly.[6]

Perhaps the great musical advantage of the Umayyad period was gained on the theoretical side. According to Al-Mas'ūdī, it was not until the reign of Yazīd I (680-83) that music began to be seriously cultivated in Mecca and Al-Medīna.[7] This might very well be true of Mecca, but certainly not of Al-Medīna and elsewhere. Mecca, since the departure of the Umayyads for Syria, had fallen into strict orthodoxy, whilst Al-Medīna seems always to have maintained a more healthy secular outlook.[8] Mecca, at any rate, was later in its musical revival than

[1] *Aghānī*, iii, 99. [2] *Aghānī*, i, 117. [3] *Aghānī*, vii, 144.
[4] *Aghānī*, vii, 135. [5] *Aghānī*, x, 55.
[6] *Aghānī*, xv, 131-2. See *'Iqd al-farīd*, iii, 198, where instances are given of singing-girls performing openly before guests.
[7] Al-Mas'ūdī, v, 157. Jurjī Zaidān, 139, repeats this assertion.
[8] Cf. the opinion of Ibn al-Kirriya (Ibn Khallikān) *Biog. Dict.*, i, 239

Al-Medīna. During the "Orthodox Khalifate," most of the musicians belonged to Al-Medīna, which, of course, might have been due to the fact that it was the capital. Now, however, Mecca begins to produce musicians to rival Al-Medīna (and a rivalry did seriously exist), and it is Mecca that gives Arabian music its first schooled exponent in the person of Ibn Misjaḥ.

When last we saw the musicians of Al-Medīna, they were being captivated by the Persian melodies of the slaves. During the reign of Mu'āwiya I (661-80), Persian slaves were brought from Al-'Irāq to work on the buildings being erected at Mecca, and their singing immediately attracted attention just as it had already charmed the people of Al-Medīna. The first to take advantage of this exotic art was Ibn Misjaḥ, who is claimed to have been the "first who sang the Arabian song copied from the Persians," or again that he was the "first who transferred the Persian song (*ghinā'*) into the Arabian song."[1] More important perhaps were the other innovations of Ibn Misjaḥ.

It is highly probable that the Arabs of Al-Ḥīra and Ghassān possessed the Pythagorean scale, although those of Al-Ḥijāz still retained the old scale of the *ṭunbūr al-mīzānī*. When Al-Naḍr ibn al-Ḥārith introduced the *'ūd* (lute) from Al-Ḥīra about the close of the 6th century, some foretaste of the Pythagorean scale may have been introduced at the same time.[2] Yet there is no certainty on this question. All that we know is that the Arabs of Al-Ḥijāz had a system of music that was different from that of Byzantium and Persia. We get this information in the life of Ibn Misjaḥ already mentioned. This musician, we are told, was responsible for grafting sundry "foreign" musical ideas upon the native practice. Here is the whole passage from the *Kitāb al-aghānī*[3]:

"In Syria, he [Ibn Misjaḥ] learned the melodies (*alḥān*) of Byzantium and received instruction from the barbiton players (*barbaṭiyya*) and the theorists (*asṭūkhūsiyya*). He then turned to Persia, where he

[1] *Aghānī*, iii, 84-5. [2] See *ante* pp. 5, 19. [3] *Aghānī*, iii, 84.

learned much of their song (*ghinā'*), as well as the art of accompaniment. Returning to Al-Ḥijāz, he chose the most advantageous of the modes (*nagham*) of these countries, and rejected what was disagreeable, for instance, the intervals (*nabarāt*) and modes (*nagham*), which he found in the song (*ghinā'*) of the Persians and Byzantines, *which were alien to the Arabian song.* And he sang [henceforth] according to this method. and he was the first to demonstrate this [method] and after this the people followed him in this."[1]

Strange to say, his pupil, Ibn Muḥriz, is credited with a similar service to Arabian music. Like his master, he too travelled in Persia and Syria, where he learned the melodies (*alḥān*) and song (*ghinā'*) of the Persians and Byzantines. "Then," says the author of the *Kitāb al-aghānī*, "he laid aside from these what he did not consider good in the modes (*nagham*), and by a careful *mélange* he composed in this way songs (*aghānī*) which were set to the poetry of the Arabs, *the like of which had not been heard* before."[2]

What was actually borrowed from Persia and Byzantium we cannot be sure of. We certainly know that benefit was derived from the Persian contact on the instrumental side. The word *dastān* is Persian for "fret," and this was borrowed by the Arabs for their finger-places on the finger-board of the *'ūd* (lute) and *ṭunbūr* (pandore). Further, there are reasons for believing that the Arabs altered their *accordatura* of the *'ūd* to the Persian method. The old Arabian *accordatura* appears to have been C-D-G-a, but with the new Persian method it was tuned A-D-G-c. This probably accounts for the Persian names *zīr* and *bamm* being given to the first and fourth strings whilst the second and third, which had not been touched, retained their Arabic names of *mathnā* and *mathlath.*[3]

[1] See my *Facts for the Arabian Musical Influence*, p. 57, and Appendix 23.

[2] See the *Burhān-i qāṭi'*, sub "sī laḥn." *Mafātīḥ al-'ulūm*, 238. See also my article "The Old Persian Musical Modes" in the *J.R.A.S.* January, 1926.

[3] Cf. Land, *Remarks*, 161-2, and my *Facts for the Arabian Musical Influence*, Appendix, 24.

What was gained from Byzantine theory or practice is equally uncertain. The general principles of the Byzantine theorists (*asṭūkhūsiyya*)[1] could scarcely have been borrowed, or at least not much, since one of the Al-Kindī treatises informs us that the system of the *asṭūkhūsiyya* of Byzantium was different from that of the Arabs.[2] Probably the Pythagorean system was more rigidly fixed owing to this Byzantine influence, and perhaps the two "Courses" (sing. *majrā*) were also of the same origin, although they may, indeed, have already been known, and may have belonged to ancient Semitic teachings.[3]

Yet whilst a considerable alien influence was at work in Arabian music, we must not forget however that this was a period of strong national feelings, when the old Pagan ideals were gloried in.[4] As Land points out, "*the Persian and Byzantine importations did not supersede the national music, but were engrafted upon an Arabic root with a character of its own.*"[5]

The rhythmic and melodic modes now appear in a more definite form than we saw them during the "Orthodox Khalifate." Six rhythmic modes (*īqā'āt*) are mentioned at this period—the *thaqīl awwal, thaqīl thānī, khafīf thaqīl, hazaj, ramal* and *ramal ṭunbūrī*. Two of these were invented during the Umayyad period, since the *ramal* was introduced by Ibn Muḥriz.[6]

The melodic modes (*aṣābi'*) were classified according to their "course" (*majrā*), as either in the *binṣir* (third finger, i.e., with the *Major Third*) or *wusṭā* (middle finger, i.e., with the *Minor Third*).

The "courses" had their species named after their

[1] See Professor D.S.Margoliouth's remarks in *J.R.A.S.*, July, 1925. My opinion as there expressed was based on the assumption of Kosegarten (*Lib. Cant.*, 34), but the appearance of the word in Al-Kindī as quoted below, leads me to prefer the meaning of "theorists" for *asṭūkhūsiyya* (√στοιχεῖα).

[2] Al-Kindī, *Berlin MS.*, 5530, fol. 30. See my article "Some Musical MSS. Identified," in *J.R.A.S.*, January, 1926.

[3] The *majrā al-binṣir* is called "masculine," and the *majra al-wusṭa* "feminine." The idea is Chaldæan and Pythagorean.

[4] *'Iqd al-farīd*, ii, 258. *Aghānī*, xix, 153, xx, 169.

[5] Land, *Remarks*, 156.

[6] *Aghānī*, i, 152.

tonics (*mabādī*), such as *muṭlaq* (= open string), *sabbāba* (= first finger), *wusṭā* (= second finger), *binṣir* (= third finger). The "species" or "modes" (*aṣābi'*) bore such names as *muṭlaq fī majrā al-binṣir* (=" open string in the 'course' of the third finger") or *Sabbāba fī majrā al-wusṭā* (=" first finger in the 'course' of the second finger"). There were eight of these "modes."

Although the *Kitāb al-aghānī* contains innumerable verses that had been set to music during the Umayyad period, not a solitary note has come down to us. All that we know is the metre (*'arūḍ*) of the verse, together with the melodic mode (*aṣba'*), and the rhythmic mode (*īqā'*), which the great musicians sang in. Whether the *virtuosi* knew of a notation or tablature at this period, we cannot say, although something of the sort was practised under the 'Abbāsids. Possibly, the idea of a notation was contrary to the interests of the musicians, who looked upon their compositions, so far as theory and practice is concerned, as something secret.[1] There were schools and cliques that passed on the tricks and special accomplishments from master to pupil.[2] All the evidence at this period seems to show that music was learned "by rote" and auricularly.

All music was melodic or homophonic (in the Greek sense of the term). Whether a musician had his song accompanied by one or fifty instruments, nothing save the melody was performed, for as the author of the *Kitāb al-aghānī* says, everyone "played as one."[3] One departure, however, was allowed from this, and that was the admission of the *zā'ida* or "gloss." This was a science of decorating or festooning the melodic outline by graceful figurations such as we know of in Western music as the *appoggiatura*, shake, trill and other graces, and including perhaps another note struck simultaneously, as with the Greeks.[4] Harmony, in our sense of

[1] Cf. C. S. Myers, *Anthropological Essays Presented to E. B. Tylor*, p. 240. Some musicians believed, like their Pagan forebears, that some of the music that they composed was actually given them by the *jinn* (*genii*).

[2] *'Iqd al-farīd*, iii, 187.

[3] *Aghānī*, vii, 135.

[4] Reinach, *La musique grecque* (1926), 69-70.

the word, was unknown.[1] Its place was taken by rhythm (*īqā'*), which one writer on Arabian music has termed "rhythmic harmony."[2]

Ibn Suraij tells us what was expected of a good musician in these days:

> "The best musician is he who enriches the melodies [by means of the 'gloss'?] and who quickens souls[3]; who gives proportion to the measures (*awzān*) and emphasizes the pronunciation; who knows what is correct and establishes the grammatical inflection (*i'rāb*); who gives full duration to the long notes (*nagham al-ṭiwāl*) and makes definite the cutting off of the short notes (*nagham al-qiṣār*); who 'hits the mark' in the various genres of rhythm (*īqā'*) and grasps the places of the intervals (*nabarāt*), and completes what resembles them in the beats (*nuqarāt*) of the accompaniment (*ḍarb*)."[4]

On the instrumental side, we see a few changes. It has already been noted that there was a change in the *accordatura* of the lute. This may have been due especially to Ibn Suraij, and not necessarily Ibn Misjaḥ. In 684, 'Abdallāh ibn al-Zubair brought Persian workers to help in the construction of the Ka'ba. From these slaves Ibn Suraij borrowed the Persian lute (*'ūd fārisī*)[5]; and he is said to have been "the first in Mecca to play Arabian music on it."[6] This lute continued to be in favour until the first half-century of the 'Abbāsids, when a lute called the *'ūd al-shabbūṭ* was invented by Zalzal. Sometimes, the Persian name for the lute, which was *barbaṭ*, is mentioned by the chroniclers, but the term was scarcely in common use as we know from a story of Yazīd II (720-24), who was hardly uninformed

[1] By "harmony" I mean the modern art of *chords*. "Harmony," in the Greek sense of *ἁρμονία*, *i.e.*, an ordered succession of intervals, the Arabs certainly recognized.

[2] See my *Music and Musical Instruments of the Arab*, p. 45. It reminds one of the "*armonia rithmica*" mentioned in Trevisa's translation of *Bartholomaeus de proprietatibus rerum*.

[3] Or "prolongs the breath."

[4] *Aghānī*, i, 125.

[5] Persian "lutes" are mentioned as though there were several kinds.

[6] *Aghānī*, i, 98.

in musical matters. The *barbaṭ* had been mentioned to him one day, and he pleaded that he was unacquainted with such an instrument.[1] In Al-'Irāq, where the *ṭunbūr* (pandore) was favoured, the *'ūd* (lute) appears to have been strung and perhaps tuned the same as the former.[2] At least we read of a two-stringed lute in the *'Iqd al-farīd* in the time of Bishr ibn Marwān (d. 694), and its strings were termed the *zīr* and *bamm.*[3] The *ṭunbur* was now in more general use in Al-Ḥijāz and Syria.[4] Those who still had a taste for the old Pagan songs of the "Days of Idolatry," indulged in the tones of the *ṭunbūr al-mizānī*, with its curious scale. The *jank* or *ṣanj* (harp) also had its votaries.[5]

Wood-wind instruments came into more accepted use by the *virtuosi*, as we frequently read of the *mizmār* sustaining the melody of the song whilst the *'ūd* was used for the accompaniment.[6] Both the *ṭabl* (drum) and *duff* (square tambourine) were also used for the accompaniment by marking the rhythm.[7] Martial music consisted of drums and kettledrums.[8] With untutored musicians, we find the *qaḍīb* or wand being used to accentuate the metrical or rhythmical beats.[9]

One of the great musical events of the Umayyad period was the pilgrimage of the famous songstress, Jamīla, to Mecca, and the consequent *fêtes*. All the principal musicians, male and female, of Al-Medīna, took part in this affair, as well as the poets Al-Aḥwaṣ, Ibn Abī 'Atīq, Abū Miḥjan Nuṣaib, and a crowd of *dilettanti*, together with some fifty singing-girls (*qaināt*). The magnificence of the litters and the *cortège* in general was much commented on. When it arrived at Mecca, the leading musician and the poets 'Umar ibn Abī Rabī'a, Al-'Arjī, Ḥārith ibn Khālid al-Makhzūmī, received it in admirable style. On the return to Al-Medīna, a

1 *'Iqd al-farīd*, iii, 201.
2 Cf. Land, *Remarks*, 157, 161, and my *Facts*, etc., Appendix 24.
3 *'Iqd al-farīd*, iii, 181.
4 Bar Hebræus, 207. Al-Ṭabarī, ii, 146.
5 Al-Farazdaq, 684.
6 *Aghanī*, ii, 121.
7 *Aghānī*, ix, 162.
8 Syed Ameer Ali, *Short History*, 65.
9 *Aghānī*, i, 97.

series of musical *fêtes* were held for three days, the like of which had not been experienced in Al-Ḥijāz before. During the first two days, performances were given either singly or by two or three together, by Jamīla, Ibn Misjaḥ, Ibn Muḥriz, Ibn Suraij, Al-Gharīd, Ma'bad, Mālik, Ibn 'Ā'isha, Nāfi' ibn Ṭunbūra, Nāfi' al-Khair, Al-Dalāl Nāfidh, Fand, Nauma al-Ḍuḥā, Bard al-Fu'ād, Budaiḥ al-Malīḥ, Hibat Allāh, Raḥmat Allāh and Al-Hudhalī. On the third day, Jamīla assembled fifty of the singing-girls, with their lutes, behind a curtain, whilst she herself, lute in hand, sang to their accompaniment. This same orchestra played for the performances of other famous songstresses, such as Sallāma al-Zarqā', 'Azza al-Mailā' (?), Sallāma al-Qass, Ḥabbāba, Khulaida, Rabīḥa, Al-Fariha (or Al-Far'a), Bulbula, Ladhdhat al-'Aish and Sa'īda (or Sa'da).

Although the accounts of this pilgrimage and the *fêtes* are based on the chronicle of a contemporary musician, Yūnus al-Kātib, a considerable amount of legend has crept in.[1] The pilgrimage probably took place during the reign of Al-Walīd I (705-15).[2]

It was during the Umayyad *régime* that the first musical *littérateur* of the Arabs, Yūnus al-Kātib, began to collect biographical and historical materials concerning the native music, although Ibn al-Kalbī (d. 819) had already accomplished much in this direction. His *Kitāb al-nagham* (Book of Melodies) and *Kitāb al-qiyān* (Book of Singing-Girls) laid the foundation for the later musical literature, including the famous *Kitāb al-aghānī* of Abū'l-Faraj al-Iṣfahānī (d. 967).

The old Pagan notions of the elemental powers of music still obtained. Islām had banished idolatry, but superstition held its own, and the genii (*jinn*), charms, phylacteries, and even magic, had their place. What else could be expected, seeing that Ja'far al-Ṣādiq (d. 765)

[1] See *Encyclopædia of Islām*, i, 1012. *J.A.*, Nov.-Dec., 1873, p. 451.

[2] The dates of 'Azza al-Mailā', Sallāma al-Qass, Ḥabbāba, and the various poets are some guide to this. At any rate, it could scarcely have occurred during the reigns of Sulaimān (715-17) or 'Umar II (717-20). Both Ṭuwais (d. 710) and Ibrāhīm al-Mauṣilī (b. 742) are mentioned in the pilgrimage, but it is extremely doubtful if the first-named was present, and the latter certainly was not.

the sixth *imām*, taught the theory of magical numbers, which was closely connected with music. On the whole, perhaps, magic and charms were discountenanced, except where they had a religious import. Poetry and song, however, were known as "lawful magic," a phrase which reveals the Pagan past. The wonderful effect of music could not help but clothe it with a magical or mystical significance. There is a chapter in the *'Iqd al-farīd* concerning those who fainted or died through listening to music.[1] Music, as a means of exciting religious devotion was even recognized in these days, although it was reserved for the later *ṣūfī* to develop it. When the Arabs came in contact with the writings of the ancient Greeks during the 'Abbāsid period, the doctrine of the "influence" (*ta'thīr*=ἦθος) of music confirmed the older dogmas.[2]

Summing up the musical situation during the Umayyad days, one might emphasize three distinct features: (1) The revival of the Pagan Arab predilection for music due to the indifference of the Umayyads to Islām; (2) the impress of Syria, which came with the removal of the capital to Damascus, when a North-Greco Semitic culture helped to mould a new musical theory; (3) the influence of Persia, which made itself felt on the instrumental side. Yet, as I have already pointed out, these external promptings must not be overstated. Ibn Khaldūn says for instance that musicians from Persia and Byzantium, passing into Al-Ḥijāz, playing on the *'ūd* (lute), *ṭunbūr* (pandore), *mi'zaf* (? barbiton), and *mizmār* (reed-pipe), led to the Arabs adopting Persian and Byzantine melodies for their poetry.[3] That is only a partial truth. That the Arabs adapted Persian and Byzantine melodies is generally admitted,[4] but they possessed the *'ūd, ṭunbūr, mi'zaf* and *mizmār* in the "Days of Idolatry." Further, there is not one Byzantine musician mentioned by the annalists during the first

[1] *'Iqd al-farīd*, iii, 199.
[2] For a discussion of this question see my lecture, *The Influence of Music: From Arabic Sources* (1926).
[3] Ibn Khaldūn, ii, 360.
[4] See *ante* pp. 46, 48, 70.

century of the *Hijra*, and all the musicians, save perhaps Nashīṭ al-Fārisī, even the so-called Persian musicians (i.e., of Persian extraction), were either born or educated in Arabia. Indeed, only four musicians of importance came from beyond the confines of Al-Hijāz, and they were Nashīṭ al-Fārisī (the Persian), Abū Kāmil al-Ghuzayyil of Damascus, Ibn Ṭunbūra of Al-Yaman, and Ḥunain al-Ḥīrī from Al-'Irāq.

The conservatory of music was Al-Ḥijāz, a circumstance which scandalized the provinces. Al-'Irāq, once the very seminal ground of Semitic musical culture, lagged behind, having fallen into the hands of the purists of Islām, who proscribed music, although one of its greatest theologians, Al-Ḥasan al-Baṣrī (d. 728), said, "Music (*ghinā'*) is a good help in obedience to Allāh, and man learns through it the ties of friendship."[1]

§ III

The lives of the *virtuosi* of the Umayyad period are replete with most interesting details of the social as well as the artistic life. Much of the material has been handed down on the authority of a contemporary musician, Yūnus al-Kātib, and for that reason it may be considered reliable so far as music is concerned.

Ibn Misjaḥ,[2] or in full, Abū 'Uthmān Sa'īd ibn Misjaḥ (d. *ca.* 715), was the first and greatest musician of the Umayyad era. He was born at Mecca, and was a freeman of the Banū Jumḥ. During the reign of Mu'āwiya I (661-80) his master heard him singing Arabic verses to Persian melodies, and it led to his emancipation. Ibn Misjaḥ then took it into his head to go abroad so as to ascertain what else there was to be learned from foreigners. This took him to Syria and Persia, as we have already mentioned, and on his return to Al-Ḥijāz we see that new methods were superimposed on Arabian music. His fame spread with amazing rapidity and during the reign of 'Abd al-Malik (684-705) his popularity roused the

[1] *'Iqd al-farīd*, iii, 179.

[2] This is the vocalization in the *Fihrist*, p. 141, and it is followed by Guidi. Kosegarten however (*Lib. Cant.*, 9) has Musajjij, whilst Caussin de Perceval writes Musajjiḥ. (*J.A.*, Nov.-Dec., 1873, p. 414.)

indignation of the stricter Muslims, who laid a charge against him before the governor of Mecca, saying that he was seducing the " Faithful " by means of his profane art.[1] The khalif, apprised of this, commanded that Ibn Misjaḥ be sent to Damascus. On his arrival at the capital he fell in with the cousins of the khalif, who, being fond of music, took him to their palace, which adjoined that of the " Commander of the Faithful." Owing to the proximity, the khalif heard Ibn Misjaḥ singing, and immediately commanded that he be summoned to his presence. Before the khalif we read of the musician singing the *ḥudā'*, the *ghinā' al-rukbān* (a form of the *naṣb*), and the *ghinā' al-mutqan* (the artistic song). He was not only pardoned by the khalif, but awarded a handsome present. Ibn Misjaḥ returned to Mecca, where he lived until the reign of Al-Walīd I (705–15). We do not know the date of his death, but it appears to have taken place during the latter reign.[2] Ibn Misjaḥ has been designated " the first in the art of music," and by general consent is included among the " four great singers." Among his pupils were: Ibn Muḥriz, Ibn Suraij and Yūnus al-Kātib, all of whom are famed in Arabian musical annals.[3]

Ibn Muḥriz,[4] or Abū'l-Khaṭṭāb Muslim (or Salm) ibn Muḥriz (d. *ca.* 715), belonged to Mecca, where his father, a Persian freeman, was one of the guardians of the Ka'ba. Ibn Muḥriz himself is said to have been a freeman of the Banū Makhzūm, and besides having been taught music by Ibn Misjaḥ, he had learned the art of accompaniment from 'Azza al-Mailā'. Unfortunately, he was afflicted with leprosy, and for that reason he made no appearance at court or public engagements, but led a wandering life, spending only three months of the year

[1] In the *Rauḍat al-Ṣafā'*, ii (1) 57, we read that it was the Devil's jealousy of the Prophet David's beautiful voice that led him to invent musical instruments, " and thereby decoyed men from the straight path, precipitating them into the valley of perdition."

[2] *J. A.*, Nov.-Dec., 1873, p. 421.

[3] *Aghānī*, iii, 84-88.

[4] In both editions of the *Kitāb al-aghānī* and elsewhere, he is called Ibn Muḥriz. On the other hand, Al-Buḥturī (*Dīwān*, i, 134) calls him Ibn Muḥarrar.

at Mecca, the remaining time being taken up at Al-Medīna and other towns. He is counted with his master, Ibn Misjaḥ, as one of the contributors to the improvement of the native art.[1] He certainly had a considerable reputation, and was said to be " the best of men in music (*ghinā'*)," whilst popular voice dubbed him " The harpist or cymbalist (*ṣannāj*) of the Arabs."[2] His songs were in great demand, and although he kept aloof from the public on account of his infirmity, these songs were introduced by a singing-girl. Two musical innovations stand to his credit—the rhythmic mode called *ramal*, and the practice of singing the couplet (*zauj*). The beauty of his melody was its simplicity, and the annalists say, " It seems as though his singing was created from the very heart of man, since every man could sing it."[3] Among the " four great singers " we find the name of Ibn Muḥriz.[4]

Ibn Suraij, or Abū Yaḥyā 'Ubaidallāh[5] ibn Suraij (*ca.* 634-726)[6] was the son of a Turkish slave born at Mecca. He was a freeman of the Banū Naufal ibn 'Abd al-Muṭṭalib or the Banū'l-Ḥārith ibn 'Abd al-Muṭṭalib. He had been taught music by Ibn Misjaḥ, and had received instruction from Ṭuwais at Al-Medīna, where he also attended the concerts of 'Azza al-Mailā'.[7] Returning to Mecca, he took upon him the calling of a *nā'iḥ* (singer of elegies), and we find him at the court of 'Uthmān. At this time he only sang the improvisation (*murtajal*) to the accompaniment of the *qaḍīb* or wand. Up to his fortieth year he was practically little known, but in 683 he attracted notice by his elegy (*nauḥ*) on the slain of Al-Medīna during that rebellious year. Im-

[1] See *ante* p. 70.
[2] That is, " the *ṣanj* player of the Arabs." Here, the instrument is undoubtedly meant, not like the title given to the Pagan poet Al-A'shā, who was called, " The *ṣannāja* (fem.) of the Arabs," meaning probably " The rhythmist (in poetry) of the Arabs." See Lane, *Lexicon*, s.v., but cf. Nicholson, *Literary History of the Arabs*, 123. De Perceval, *Essai sur l'hist. des Arabes*, ii, 396. *Aghānī* (Sāsī Ed.), i, 146.
[3] *Aghānī*, i, 150-2.
[4] See p. 80.
[5] Cf. Kosegarten, *Lib. Cant.*, 12. *J.A.*, Nov.-Dec., 1873, p. 457.
[6] He could scarcely have lived until the reign of Al-Hādī (785-6) as suggested in one place. (*Aghānī*, vi, 67.)
[7] *Aghānī*, ii, 174. iii, 84. xvi, 14. *'Iqd al-farīd*, iii, 187.

mediately he sprang into fame and Sukaina bint al-Ḥusain became his patroness.

We have already seen that about 684 Ibn Suraij took up the *'ūd al-fārisī* or "Persian lute." This circumstance, together with the fact that a pupil of his named Al-Gharīḍ, had already outshone him as a *nā'iḥ*, led him to relinquish this profession and become a practical musician (*mughannī*). In this sphere he was equally successful, and he won the prize offered by Sulaimān (afterwards khalif) at a tournament of song at Mecca. He was later invited to the court of Al-Walīd I (705-15), at Damascus, where he was lodged in a splendid pavilion and loaded with honours. On his return to Mecca however, he found that the new governor, Nāfi' ibn 'Alqama, had forbidden music and wine in the city; yet so great was the prestige of Ibn Suraij that the ordinance was relaxed in his favour. Hishām ibn Mirya said, "After the Prophet David, Allāh created no musician comparable with Ibn Suraij." He was considered the supreme exponent of the *ramal* rhythmic mode, whilst his famous "Seven Songs" rivalled those of Ma'bad. Yūnus al-Kātib names him as one of the "four great singers."[1]

Al-Gharīḍ was the nickname (meaning "The good singer")[2] of Abū Yazīd[3] (or Abū Marwān) 'Abd al-Malik. He belonged to a Barbary family of slaves, and was a freeman of the famous sisters known as the 'Abalāt in Mecca. He afterwards passed into the household of Sukaina bint al-Ḥusain, who had him trained as a *nā'iḥ* by Ibn Suraij. He then persevered with the song (*ghinā'*) proper, and soon became a serious rival to his teacher. We next find him at the court of Al-Walīd I (705-15) at Damascus, where he was accompanying his singing with the *qaḍīb*, *duff*, and *'ūd*. When Nāfi' ibn 'Alqama, the governor of Mecca, issued his decree against

[1] *Aghānī*, i, 97-129. Yūnus al-Kātib gives the "four great singers" as Ibn Suraij, Ibn Muḥriz, Al-Gharīḍ and Ma'bad. Isḥāq al-Mauṣilī says that they were Ibn Suraij, Ibn Muḥriz, Ma'bad and Mālik. 'Ubaid ibn Ḥunain al-Ḥīrī mentions Ibn Suraij, Al-Gharīḍ, Ma'bad and Ḥunain al-Ḥīrī.

[2] Cf. Kosegarten, *Lib. Cant.*, 14. *J. A.*, Nov.-Dec., 1873, 460.

[3] Kosegarten has Abū Zaid.

wine and music, Al-Gharīḍ was compelled to seek refuge in Al-Yaman, where he is said to have died in the reign of Sulaimān (715-17). In another account, however, he is mentioned at the court of Yazīd II (720-24))[1] According to the *'Iqd al-farīd*, Al-Gharīḍ died at a festive gathering in the bosom of his family. He had just finished singing to them when " the *jinn* (genii) twisted his neck and he died."[2] He, too, has been claimed among the " four great singers."[3]

Ma'bad,[4] or Abū 'Abbād Ma'bad ibn Wahb (d. 743), was a mulatto, his father being a negro. He belonged to Al-Medīna and was a freeman of 'Abd al-Raḥmān ibn Qaṭan. In his youth he was an accountant, but having taken music lessons from Sā'ib Khāthir, Nashīṭ al-Fārisī and Jamīla, he became a professional musician. After a sort of musical pilgrimage, he returned to his native city, and at a tournament of song organized by Ibn Ṣafwān, a noble of the Quraish, he carried off first prize. He then sang at the courts of Al-Walīd I (705-15), Yazīd II (720-24) and Al-Walīd II (743-44). Ma'bad was treated very handsomely by Yazīd II, and one day this khalif said that he had noticed in Ma'bad's compositions a certain strength (*matāna*) and solidity which did not exist in those of Ibn Suraij, whose works appeared to him to be more pliable (*inḥinā'*)[5] and tender (*layyin*). To this Ma'bad replied, " Ibn Suraij cultivates a light (*khafīf*) style, whilst I adopt a grandiose (*kāmil tāmm*) mode. He moves towards the East, and I towards the West."[6] Upon the death of Ibn Suraij, Ma'bad came to be recognized as the leading singer, and when Al-Walīd II was called to the throne in 743, he was invited to the court at Damascus. Here he was received with much consideration and was rewarded with a gift of 12,000 pieces of gold! The next time that he was commanded to court, he was ill, and although he was lodged in the

[1] *Aghānī*, vii, 11-12.
[2] *'Iqd al-farīd*, iii, 187.
[3] See *ante*, p. 80.
[4] Burton, *Arabian Nights* (Isobel Burton's Edit.), iii, 252, writes *Ma'abid*.
[5] Cf. *J.A.*, Nov.-Dec., 1873, p. 488.
[6] *Aghānī*, i, 116.

palace itself, and treated with the utmost attention, paralysis intervened and Ma'bad died. At his funeral, the khalif and his brother, Al-Ghamr, dressed in simple tunics, accompanied the bier to the palace boundaries, whilst the renowned songstress, Sallāma al-Qass, one of Ma'bad's pupils, chanted one of the old singer's elegies.

Isḥāq al-Mauṣilī said, " Ma'bad was a consummate singer and his compositions reveal a talent superior to all his rivals." A poet of Al-Medīna also wrote:

> " Ṭuwais, and after him Ibn Suraij, excelled [in music],
> But no musician outstripped Ma'bad."

Poets like Al-Buḥturī (d. 897) and Abū Tammām (d. 846) have shown the place of Ma'bad in Arabian music.[1] Among his famous songs were seven known as the " Fortresses " (*ḥuṣūn Ma'bad*) or " Cities " (*mudun Ma'bad*), whilst five others were celebrated as the *Ma'badāt*.[2] Among his pupils were: Ibn 'Ā'isha, Mālik, Sallāma al-Qass, Ḥabbāba, Yūnus al-Kātib and Siyyāṭ.[3]

Ibn 'Ā'isha, or Abū Ja'far Muḥammad ibn 'Ā'isha (d. *ca.* 743) belonged to Al-Medīna, and was the son of 'Ā'isha (his father's name being unknown), a female hairdresser in the service of Al-Kathīr ibn al-Ṣalt al-Kindī. In music, Ma'bad and Jamīla were his teachers, and he possessed a voice of extraordinary quality. We read of his musical abilities as early as 'Abd al-Malik (685-705).[4] At the courts of Yazīd II (720-24) and Al-Walīd II (743-44) he created a deep impression. Indeed, the former was so completely ravished by the music of Ibn 'Ā'isha that on one occasion he gave vent to such exclamations in his ecstasy, that they were considered impious.[5] At Al-Walīd's court, he was wine-bibbing with

[1] Al-Buḥturī, *Dīwān* (Const. Ed.), ii, 160, 193, 218. Abū Tammām, *Dīwān* (Bairūṭ Ed.), 103.
[2] *Aghānī*, viii, 91. Ibn Khallikān, *Biog. Dict.*, ii, 374.
[3] *Aghānī*, i, 19-29. *'Iqd al-farīd*, iii, 187. See also my article on Ma'bad in the *Encyclopædia of Islām*.
[4] *Aghānī*, xviii, 127.
[5] Al-Mas'ūdī, vi, 9-10.

the khalif's brother, Al-Ghamr, on a balcony, when they quarrelled. A struggle ensued, and the musician either fell or was thrown from the balcony and was killed. This is said to have been about 743.[1] Ibn al-Kalbī says of Ibn 'Ā'isha, "He was the best of mankind in singing," whilst his brilliant style gave rise to the saying, "Like the beginning of a song of Ibn 'Ā'isha." During his recitals he would preface the performance with an explanatory lecture on the poetry of the song, the music to which it was set, and the composer of it.[2]

Yūnus al-Kātib, or Yūnus ibn Sulaimān (d. *ca.* 765), was a freeman of 'Amr ibn al-Zubair. He was the son of a lawyer of Persian origin, and had been educated at Al-Medīna, where he became an official in the municipal service, hence his surname al-Kātib ("the secretary"). At first, music was merely a pastime, but after studying under Ibn Muḥriz, Ibn Suraij, Al-Gharīḍ and Muḥammad ibn 'Abbād al-Kātib,[3] he became a good all-round musician, even so proficient as to arouse the jealousy of Ibn 'Ā'isha. During the reign of Hishām (724-43) he was patronized by the khalif's nephew, who afterwards became Al-Walīd II.[4] Unfortunately he got into trouble with the "authorities" by reason of having set to music some verses about a young lady of noble birth named Zainab, which had become popularly known as the *Zayānib*. The lady's family were incensed at the liberty taken in this way and Yūnus al-Kātib and the poet had to flee the country. On the accession of Al-Walīd II (743), Yūnus returned and was invited to the Damascus court where he remained until the death of this pleasure-loving monarch in 744. After this date we have no trace of Yūnus, but he possibly lived until the middle of the reign of Al-Manṣūr (754-75).

The chief merit of Yūnus al-Kātib was on the literary side. He was a highly esteemed author and quite a

[1] Cf. *Aghānī*, v, 17, 54. viii, 86.

[2] *Aghānī*, ii, 62-79. *'Iqd al-farīd*, iii, 187. In the index to De Meynard's edition of Al-Mas'ūdī's *Prairies d'or*, the singer Ibn 'Ā'isha is confused with the traditionist and others of the same name.

[3] *Aghānī*, vi, 15.

[4] An account of this friendship is given in the 684th Night of the *Arabian Nights.*

good poet.[1] His books on music, already adverted to, are mentioned in the *Fihrist* (*ca.* 988). They are a *Kitāb al-nagham* (Book of Melodies) and a *Kitāb al-qiyān* (Book of Singing-Girls).[2] The first-named, says the author of the *Kitāb al-aghānī*, was " the first collection of song (*ghinā'*)," that is to say, it was the first attempt made to collect the songs of the Arabs, together with information about their melodies, modes, authors and composers. Among the pupils of Yūnus were Siyyāṭ and Ibrāhīm al-Mauṣilī.[3]

Mālik al-Ṭā'ī, or Abū Walīd Mālik ibn Abī'l-Samḥ (d. *ca.* 754) was an Arab of noble birth, his father being a member of the Banū Thu'l, a branch of the Banū Ṭai', whilst his mother came of the Banū Makhzūm and was therefore a Quraishite. He was born in the mountain home of Ṭai', but was left an orphan, when he was adopted by 'Abdallāh ibn Ja'far of Al-Medīna. In his house, Mālik received a good education, but in the year 684, Mālik heard the celebrated singer, Ma'bad at the house of Ḥamza ibn 'Abdallāh ibn al-Zubair, and the event changed his whole career. He asked leave to take singing lessons from Ma'bad, and before long he astonished Al-Medīna by his musical abilities. The court and nobility favoured him, and in company with Ma'bad and Ibn 'Ā'isha he appeared before Yazīd II (720-24) and Al-Walīd II (743-44).[4] On the death of his protector, 'Abdallāh ibn Ja'far (*ca.* 700),[5] he attached himself to Sulaimān ibn 'Alī the Hāshimite. On the accession of the 'Abbāsids to power (750), Sulaimān was appointed governor of the Lower Tigris, and Mālik accompanied him to his seat at Al-Baṣra. After a short stay at this city, Mālik returned to Al-Medīna, where he died upwards of eighty years of age about the year 754. As a singer, Mālik was ranked very high, and according to one version was one of the " four great singers." Apparently he was not an original composer, and he did not even play

[1] Brockelmann, *Gesch. der Arab. Lit.*, i, 49.
[2] *Fihrist*, i, 143.
[3] *Aghānī*, vi, 7.
[4] Cf. *J.A.*, Nov.-Dec., 1873, 499.
[5] Cf. *Encyclopædia of Islām*, i, 23.

the *'ūd* (lute), which was a considerable drawback. At first he only sang the "improvisation" (*murtajal*), and we are told that Ma'bad had to rectify his songs for him.[1]

'Aṭarrad, Abū Hārūn (d. *ca.* 786) was a freeman of the Anṣār and a pupil of Ma'bad. He was held in high esteem at Al-Medīna by reason of his legal erudition as well as on account of his music. He was "pre-eminently a good singer and possessed a fine voice." We read of him in connection with the best families in Al-Medīna, including Sulaimān ibn 'Alī. When Al-Walīd II (743-44) was khalif, he was called to court at Damascus, where his music so affected the khalif that he tore his robes in twain in his excitement. 'Aṭarrad was rewarded with a thousand pieces of gold, the khalif saying, "When you return to Al-Medīna you may be inclined to say, 'I have sung before the Commander of the Faithful and so entranced him that he tore his garments,' but, by Allāh, if a word escapes your lips of what you have seen, you will lose your head for it."[2] 'Aṭarrad lived as late as the reign of Al-Mahdī (755-85), and perhaps even into the time of Hārūn (786-809).[3]

Among the famous songstresses of the Umayyad era there are four outstanding names: Jamīla, Sallāma al-Qass, Ḥabbāba and Sallāma al-Zarqā'.

Jamīla (d. *ca.* 720) was a freewoman of the Banū Sulaim, or rather the Banū Bahz, a branch of the former. Whilst she was with this latter family, Sā'ib Khāthir was their neighbour, and Jamīla was clever enough to memorize the notes (*naghamāt*) of his songs which she heard him singing, and one day she surprised her mistress by singing not only the songs of Sā'ib Khāthir, but also a composition of her own.[4] Al-Medīna soon rang with the praises of the new singer, and she was in great demand as a teacher, with the result that a crowd of slaves were to

[1] *Aghānī*, iv, 168-75. *'Iqd al-farīd, iii*, 187. See my life of Mālik al-Ṭā'ī in the *Encyclopædia of Islām*.

[2] A similar story is told of Ma'bad. A khalif said to him: "If you desire to continue to receive the favour of kings, guard their secrets."

[3] *Aghānī*, iii, 96-9.

[4] *Aghānī*, vii, 188.

be found at her house being prepared as "singing-girls" (*qaināt*). Having gained her freedom, she married, and established herself in a splendid residence, which eventually became the centre of attraction for the musicians and *dilettanti* of Al-Medīna and Mecca. Many musicians of later fame, such as Ibn Misjaḥ, Ibn Muḥriz, Ibn Suraij, Al-Gharīḍ, Ma'bad, Ibn 'Ā'isha, and Mālik, as well as the poets 'Umar ibn Abī Rabī'a, Al-Aḥwaṣ and Al-'Arjī, were frequent auditors at her concerts, some indeed being her pupils. One of the most imposing events of her career was her famous pilgrimage.

Although the dates of the *Kitāb al-aghānī* are rather confusing we can be fairly certain that Jamīla flourished during the first half of the Umayyad period. In one place (*Aghānī*, vii, 148) she is mentioned as having sung before 'Umar I (634-44), and in another as singing the verses of Al-Aḥwaṣ before Yazīd II (720-4). Clearly, the first date is too early, and apparently she did not live much later than Al-Walīd I (d. 715). Jamīla held a high place in the estimation of her contemporaries, especially as a teacher. Ma'bad said, "In the art of music (*ghinā'*) Jamīla is the tree and we are the branches."[1]

Sallāma al-Qass was a singing-girl of a Quraishite noble of the Banū Zuhra named Suhail. She was a handsome mulatto who was brought up, if not born, at Al-Medīna. She counted among her teachers, Jamīla, Ma'bad, Ibn 'Ā'isha and Mālik. At the death of Suhail she passed into the possession of his son, Muṣ'ab, who sold her to Yazīd II, whilst he was a prince, for 3,000 pieces of gold. Yazīd was considerably influenced by Sallāma, but when he became khalif, he transferred his affections to another singing-girl, Ḥabbāba. Sallāma al-Qass continued at court, however, under successive khalifs.[2]

Ḥabbāba, the second favourite of Yazīd II, was procured by him when he was a prince for 4,000 pieces of gold from a certain Ibn Rummāna or Ibn Mīna of the Banū Lāshik. The affair greatly displeased his

[1] *Aghānī*, vii, 124-48.
[2] *Aghānī*, iii, 115-117. Al-Mas'ūdī, v, 446, etc.

brother, the Khalif Sulaimān, and Yazīd was compelled to send her back. When the latter became khalif (720), Ḥabbāba became his constant companion until her death in 724. Yazīd was prostrated with grief, and for a long time clung to the lifeless body. He never lifted his head again, and was dead within a week. Ḥabbāba had been taught by 'Azza al-Mailā', Jamīla, Ibn Muḥriz, Ibn Suraij, Ma'bad and Mālik.[1]

Sallāma al-Zarqā' was a pupil of Jamīla and took part in her celebrated *fêtes*. She went to the court of Yazīd I (680-83) and was presented to the poet Al-Aḥwaṣ, who had fallen in love with her. She was a celebrated beauty as well as an accomplished singer, and she passed into the hands of several masters. We read of her finally at the court of Yazīd II (720-24).[2] Her sister Rayyā' also won some fame.[3]

There are also some less famed musicians who deserve passing mention.

Muḥammad ibn 'Abbād al-Kātib, a freeman of the Banū Makhzūm, was one of the good singers of Al-Ḥijāz. He is specially mentioned on account of his interview with Mālik ibn Anas (d. 795), one of the great legists of Islām. He was one of the teachers of Yūnus al-Kātib. He died at Baghdād in the reign of Al-Mahdī (775-85).[4]

'Amr ibn 'Uthmān ibn Abī'l-Kannāt, a contemporary of Ibn 'Ā'isha, was credited with a phenomenal voice. There is a story how a procession of pilgrims was held up by its charm.[5]

Ibn Ṭunbūra was a musician who came from Al-Yaman, and is classed among the most skilful executants in the *hazaj* rhythmic mode.[6] He may be identified with Nāfi' ibn Ṭunbūra, who flourished during the "Orthodox Khalifate."[7]

Al-Burdān was a pupil of Ma'bad, and was contemporary even with 'Azza al-Mailā', Jamīla and Ibn Muḥriz. It

[1] *Aghānī*, xiii, 154-65. Al-Mas'ūdī, v, 447, etc.
[2] *Aghānī*, viii, 89-90. If the account in the *Aghānī* (xxi, 5) of her being at the court of Yazīd II (cf. Guidi, 381, who says Yazīd III) is correct, she must have been about fifty years of age.
[3] *Aghānī*, viii, 7, 9. [4] *Aghānī*. vi, 15-16. [5] *Aghānī*, xviii, 126-8.
[6] *'Iqd al-farīd*, iii, 187. [7] *Aghānī*, vii, 135, 163.

was through him that the classical musical traditions of the Umayyad school were passed on to the *virtuosi* of the 'Abbāsid court. In his old age he gave up the musical profession and became an inspector of markets in Al-Medīna.[1]

Yaḥyā Qail[2] was a freeman of the famous 'Abalāt family. He gave music lessons to Khalif Al-Walīd II (743-4), even during a pilgrimage to Mecca, which scandalized the devout.[3]

'Umar al-Wādī, whose real name was 'Umar ibn Dā'ūd ibn Zādhān, was a freeman of 'Amr ibn 'Uthmān ibn 'Affān. He is said to have been a *muhandis*, i.e., a geometrician, and must therefore have been one of the first to be acquainted with this science among the Arabs.[4] As a musician he was a great favourite with Al-Walīd II (743-4), who called him, "The joy of my life." He was actually singing to this artistic khalif when the latter was assassinated. At his native place, Wādī al-Qurā, he is said to have been the first of the singers (? of artistic music), and is claimed to have been the teacher of Ḥunain al-Ḥīrī. His date, however, rather precludes these attributions, and perhaps it is his father who is meant.[5]

Abū'l-'Alā' Ash'ab ibn Jubair was another favourite of Al-Walīd II, and he once sang before this khalif dressed in pantaloons made from the skin of an ass, much to his master's delight. He possessed not only an excellent voice, but a fund of buffoonery.[6]

Daḥmān (al-Ashqar ?)[7] 'Abd al-Raḥmān ibn 'Amr was a well-known singer who had a contest with Ḥakam al-Wādī. He is mentioned as late as Faḍl ibn Yaḥyā the Barmakide in the eighth century.[8]

Abū 'Abd al-Raḥmān Sa'īd ibn Mas'ūd, commonly called al-Hudhalī, was a sculptor by profession, but a

[1] *Aghānī*, vii, 168-9.
[2] Guidi writes Qīl, whilst Huart (*Arab. Lit.*, 58) has Fīl. Kosegarten (*Lib. Cant.*, p. 18) calls him Qail.
[3] *Aghānī*, iii, 11-12. viii, 162.
[4] Unless *muhandis* here means "an architect, or engineer."
[5] *Aghānī*, vi, 141-44.
[6] *Aghānī*, xviii, 83-105.
[7] Cf. Kosegarten, *Lib. Cant.*, 21. Guidi, s.v.
[8] *Aghānī*, iv, 141-46.

skilful singer as well. He found a considerable audience among the gentry of the Quraish, and he married a daughter of Ibn Suraij, who taught him her father's songs.[1]

Al-Baidhaq al-Anṣārī sang before Yazīd II (720-24).[2] Abū Kāmil al-Ghuzayyil was at the court of Al-Walīd II (743-4) and of this minstrel the khalif once said, "When he is away I am like one bereft."[3] Another singer was Ibn Mush'ab of Al-Ṭā'if in Al-Ḥijāz.[4] Bard al-Fu'ād, Hibat Allāh and Raḥmat Allāh took part in the Jamīla pilgrimage.[5] Other musicians of passing fame were: Abū Ṭālib 'Ubaidallāh (or Muḥammad) ibn al-Qāsim, better known as Al-Abjar,[6] and 'Abdallāh ibn Muslim ibn Jundab.[7]

Among the less famed female musicians were: Ṭanbī, at the court of Sulaimān,[8] and Umm 'Auf, who belonged to the circle of Yazīd II.[9] Shuḥda (or Shahda) was a singing-girl of Al-Walīd I (705-15), and her daughter 'Ātika became famous during the 'Abbāsid *régime*.[10] Khulaida, Bulbula, Ladhdhat al-'Aish and Al-Fariha were among those who assisted at the Jamīla *fêtes*.[11]

[1] *Aghānī*, iv, 152.
[2] *Aghānī*, xiii, 163.
[3] *Aghānī*, vi, 144-6. He is called Abū Kāmil al-'Azīz in the various copies of the *'Iqd al-farīd* that I have consulted.
[4] *Aghānī*, iv, 82-3.
[5] *Aghānī*, vii, 135, 139.
[6] *Aghānī*, iii, 115-17.
[7] *Aghānī*, v, 145.
[8] *Aghānī*, ix, 20.
[9] *Aghānī*, xiii, 164.
[10] *Aghānī*, vi, 57-8.
[11] *Aghānī*, vii, 124, 135.

CHAPTER V

THE 'ABBĀSIDS

(" The Golden Age," 750-847)

" The art of music continued to make progress with the Arabs, and under the 'Abbāsids it was carried to perfection."

Ibn Khaldūn, *Al-Muqaddima.*

WHEN the House of 'Abbās rose on the ruins of the Umayyad dynasty, a new era dawned for the Arabs, and the foundations of the great intellectual life of subsequent centuries were laid. The more liberal intercourse with Byzantium, and the encouragement given to the people of Persia and Khurāsān, were the main causes of this. Although Persia and contiguous lands had been thoroughly subdued, and almost every trace of their national life effaced under Arab domination and Islāmic penetration, yet there still remained the mind of the Aryan, which became a weighty factor in the artistic, philosophic and scientific ideas of Islāmic civilization. Under the Umayyads, the Arabs, as we have seen, formed a sort of military and administrative aristocracy. The time had now arrived, however, when the Arabs, sated with conquest, power and dominion, began to " settle down." They scorned even the best administrative positions, preferring to admit their erstwhile slaves (*mawālī*), Persians for the most part, to a number of them. Side by side with this political decline, there was a retrogression in the purely Arabian arts and literature. Poetry especially was affected, and the number of Persian and other foreign poets who sprang up after the 'Abbāsids came into power is considerable.

The arts became similarly influenced. Persian costume and decoration were encouraged at court, whilst Persian scholars and philosophers were welcomed. Indeed there are many proofs of a considerable domination of the Aryan over the Semitic spirit, for a time at least, in this direction.[1] In music, however, this influence did not reveal itself until a much later period. This was probably owing to the fact that musicians formed quite a special and distinct class of society, which, by reason of its insularity, was very narrow and conservative. In this particular, it will be noticed that nearly all the musicians of the "Golden Age" were Arabs either by race or birth, and came mostly from Al-Ḥijāz, the home of the Arabian art.[2]

The 'Abbāsid period that comes within our purview at present, falls into three cycles of culture epochs, which, for the sake of historical convenience, may be divided into "The Golden Age" (750-847), "The Decline" (847-945), and "The Fall" (945-1258). Herein, as in the previous chapters, the individual khalifs will be used to illustrate the determining political factors in the culture conditions. Everywhere they form excellent milestones, as it were, for this purpose, since all culture seems to depend on the body politic.

§ I

Abū'l-'Abbās, surnamed Al-Saffāḥ (750-54), was the first 'Abbāsid khalif. In choosing the capital, the new dynasty would have nothing to do with Syria, which had been the home of the Umayyads. It was perilously near the Byzantine frontier, and it was too far away from Persia and Khurāsān, whose people had given the 'Abbāsids the throne.[3] Al-Kūfa in Al-'Irāq was therefore made the capital, and the khalif built his first palace, the Hāshimiyya, at Al-Anbār, where there began those brilliant courts which soon became the by-word of the Mediæval world. Abū'l-'Abbās was a despot and a tyrant, but a

[1] Muir, *Caliphate*, 465. Huart, *Arab. Lit.*, 64. Von Kremer, *Streifzüge*, 32.

[2] Lichtenthal, *Dizionario e bibliografia della musica*, calls it, "The Golden Age of Persian music with the Arabs." As a matter of fact, Persian influence was extremely slight at this period in music. It was during "The Decline" that Persian music really came into favour.

[3] Le Strange, *Baghdād during the 'Abbāsid Caliphate*, 4.

patron of the arts withal. His interest in Persia and Khurāsān, where music and Islām did not come into conflict, had made him partial to the art, and in this respect he carried on the best traditions of the old Sāsānid kings of Persia, of whose patronage of music the khalif was no feeble imitator. No clever musician ever left the presence of Abū'l-'Abbās, says Al-Mas'ūdī, without a gift of money.[1]

Al-Manṣūr (754-75), his brother, is said to have been the greatest ruler among the 'Abbāsids. During his reign the Persian family of Barmak were given high administrative positions. Khālid al-Barmakī, his son Yaḥyā al-Barmakī, and his grandsons Ja'far and Faḍl al-Barmakī, all played significant parts in the cultivation of the arts, and music especially, during the "Golden Age." In the year 762, Al-Manṣūr founded the city of Baghdād, which became not only the capital of the Empire and the centre of the Eastern world, but the very home of art, literature and science, and indeed of all intellectual activity, the glories of which became quite fabulous. The tales which were spread abroad concerning this wonderful city of Al-Manṣūr, with its two gorgeous palaces—the Bāb al-Dhahab and the Khuld, soon attracted intellectuals from all parts, as well as a crowd of poets and musicians who were soon to shed lustre on the Khalifate. Al-Manṣūr, we are told, was "completely insensible to the charms of music."[2] Ḥakam al-Wādī was the leading musician of the day, and although his talents were the talk of Baghdād, yet Al-Manṣūr could see nothing clever in his performance except, as he once said, that Ḥakam was certainly "clever" to be able to extort money from his patrons.[3] Yet Al-Manṣūr did not impose his personal dislike or indifference in this matter upon others, since we find the nobility of Baghdād, such as the khalif's cousins, the two sons of Sulaimān ibn 'Alī, his own son Al-Mahdī, and his nephew Muḥam-

[1] Al-Mas'ūdī, vi, 121-2.

[2] Bar Hebræus says that Al-Manṣūr pretended that he did not know what a *ṭunbūr* (pandore) was. We have seen the story told of so many of the khalifs, that it looks suspicious.

[3] *Aghānī*, vi, 67.

mad ibn Abī'l-'Abbās, all eager to patronize music and musicians.

Al-Mahdī (775-85) was particularly fond of music, and his court in the new Qaṣr al-Mahdī palace was crowded with musicians, and among them: Ḥakam al-Wādī, Siyyāṭ, Ibrāhīm al-Mauṣilī and Yazīd Ḥaurā'. At the same time, he would not allow his two sons Al-Hādī and Hārūn to meddle with music, and two eminent musicians were punished for entering the princes' palace contrary to his orders.[1] There is a good story told of Al-Mahdī and the court musician, named Siyyāṭ, that is worthy of a place here. Siyyāṭ had two instrumental accompanists—one named Ḥibbāl, who played the *mizmār* (reed-pipe), and the other named 'Uqqāb, a performer on the *'ūd* (lute). The names of these individuals in Arabic, if pronounced in a slightly different way, stand for " whips," " ropes " and " punishment." One day Al-Mahdī, during a court reception (*majlis*), was heard to address some words to his chief eunuch, and all that the courtiers could hear were the above words of sinister import, which led them to conclude that one or more of their number had fallen into disfavour and were about to pay the penalty. Imagine their relief when Siyyāṭ, and his two accompanists, Ḥibbāl and 'Uqqāb, appeared on the scene.[2] Muir says of the period of Al-Mahdī, " Music, literature, and philosophy, refined the age."[3] Al-Mahdī himself was fond of singing, and Ibn Khallikān says that " no man had a finer voice than he."[4]

Mūsā al-Hādī (785-6) only reigned a short time. The two musicians who had been punished by his father for entering his palace when he was a prince, were sent for on his accession, and they were installed as court musicians. They were Ibrāhīm al-Mauṣilī and Ibn Jāmi'. These, with the older Ḥakam al-Wādī, were the special favourites. This khalif had a son, 'Abdallāh, who was an accomplished singer and performer on the *'ūd* (lute).[5]

[1] *Aghānī*, v, 4.
[2] *Aghānī*, vi, 7.
[3] Muir, *Caliphate*, 467.
[4] Ibn Khallikān, *Biog. Dict.*, iii, 464.
[5] *Aghānī*, ix, 99.

Hārūn al-Rashīd (786-809) is the khalif whose name has become a household word not merely in the East, but in the West. The magnificence of his palaces at Baghdād, Al-Anbār and Al-Raqqa, has been abundantly commented on. His court "was the centre to which, from all parts, flocked the wise and the learned, and at which rhetoric, poetry, history and law, as well as science, medicine, *music*, and the arts, met with a genial and princely reception—all of which bore ample fruit in the succeeding reigns."[1] The enchanting pages of *The Thousand and One Nights* have revealed Hārūn quite in harmony with this picture. The galaxy of musical talent which clustered at his court must have had millions disbursed in their favour, and among those who benefited were: Ḥakam al-Wādī, Ibrāhīm al-Mauṣilī, Ibn Jāmi', Yaḥyā al-Makkī, Zalzal, Yazīd Ḥaurā', Fulaiḥ ibn Abī'l-'Aurā,' 'Abdallāh ibn Daḥmān, Al-Zubair ibn Daḥmān, Isḥāq al-Mauṣilī, Mukhāriq, 'Allūyah, Muḥammad ibn al-Ḥārith, 'Ibthar (?), 'Amr al-Ghazzāl, Abū Ṣadaqa, Barṣaumā, and Muḥammad al-Raff. The favourite son of Hārūn, who was named Abū 'Īsā, was also a good musician, and we find him at the court, with his brother Aḥmad, taking part in the musical festivities.[2]

Al-Amīn (809-13) and Al-Ma'mūn, became joint rulers of the Empire, the one controlling the West from Baghdād, and the other the East from Merv. They both took the title of khalif, and this arrangement lasted until 813, when war was declared between them. It resolved itself finally into a struggle between the Arab and Persian factions, culminating in the defeat of the former, and the death of Al-Amīn. This khalif was a man of pleasure, who spent his whole time, we are told, with musicians and singing-girls. The latter were gathered for their beauty "from all parts of the Empire." His festivities "were of the most sumptuous kind," and we read on one occasion that a hundred singing-girls sang before him.[3] Whatever his faults were he was a patron of the arts. Isḥāq al-Mauṣilī, Mukhāriq and 'Allūyah were among the

[1] Muir, *Caliphate*, 486. [2] *Aghānī*, v, 63. ix, 143.
[3] Muir, *Caliphate*, 488-9.

famous musicians who received his bounty.[1] He gave protection to his uncle, Prince Ibrāhīm ibn al-Mahdī, who was one of the most accomplished musicians of the day. The talents of his kinsman had a particular charm for him,[2] and in the khalif's last days, when the army of Al-Ma'mūn was investing Baghdād, Al-Amīn found solace in the songs of Ibrāhīm. Al-Mas'ūdī has drawn a pathetic picture of this khalif, just before the end, sitting by the banks of the Tigris, listening to the voice of his favourite singing-girl, Ḍu'afā.[3] His son 'Abdallāh was quite a talented musician.[4]

Al-Ma'mūn (813-33) assumed full control of the Khalifate on the overthrow of Al-Amīn, although he remained at Merv until 819. During the interval, both Syria and Al-'Irāq rose in rebellion, and in Baghdād, Prince Ibrāhīm ibn al-Mahdī was actually proclaimed khalif. This step greatly shocked the stricter Muslims because Ibrāhīm openly professed himself a musician. Di'bil the poet, suiting the occasion, wrote some bitter verses against Ibrāhīm, saying, " If Ibrāhīm is fit to reign, then the Empire has devolved by right to Mukhāriq, Zalzal, and Ibn al-Māriqī [the court musicians]."[5] He further asked what good could be expected from a khalif " who made the *barbaṭ* (lute) his *Qur'ān*."[6] Ibrāhīm's attempt to seize the Khalifate failed, and he threw himself on the mercy of Al-Ma'mūn, who spared his life. But from the day of his triumphal entry into Baghdād in 819 until 823, Al-Ma'mūn would not listen to a note of music, nor permit a musician to be near him, so exasperated was he with the perfidy of his musical kinsman, Ibrāhīm.[7] The first to break the silence, we are told, was Muḥammad ibn al-Ḥārith, who was admitted to the khalif's presence.[8] On the other hand, the *'Iqd al-farīd* says that the silence

[1] A concert is described in the *Aghānī*, xvi, 138.
[2] *Aghānī*, ix, 56, 62, 63. xxi, 242.
[3] Al-Mas'ūdī, vi, 426-30.
[4] *Aghānī*, ix, 102-3.
[5] Ibn Khallikān, *Biog. Dict.*, i, 18. See also the lines by Bashshār ibn Burd preserved by Abū'l-'Alā al-Ma'arrī, *Risālat al-ghufrān*, 97.
[6] *Aghānī*, xviii, 30.
[7] *Aghānī*, ix, 52, 67.
[8] *Aghānī*, ix, 52, 60, 61.

only lasted twenty months, and that the first musician who was listened to was another musical kinsman, Abū 'Īsā, the talented son of Hārūn.[1] At any rate, as soon as the proscription was raised, the famous Ma'mūnī palace rang with the sound of voices and instruments. Here appeared Isḥāq al-Mauṣilī, Mukhāriq, 'Allūyah, Muḥammad ibn al-Ḥārith, 'Amr ibn Bāna, Aḥmad ibn Ṣadaqa and 'Aqīd.

Of great importance to musical culture and learning in general was Al-Ma'mūn's patronage of the Greek sciences. Inclined to Rationalism, he made the *Mu'tazalī* doctrine the state religion, which gave more freedom to independent thought. At Baghdād he instituted a college called the *Bait al-ḥikma* or " House of Wisdom," where he installed Yaḥyā ibn Abī Manṣūr, the Banū Mūsā and other learned men, who devoted their lives to the translation of the Greek sciences and their study, including the study of music, which had already started under earlier khalifs.

Al-Mu'taṣim (833-42) was equally favourable to the arts and sciences, and especially encouraged the translators from the Greek and Syriac. He held out the hand of friendship to the famous Arab philosopher and music theorist, Al-Kindī, whose writings became the text-books for several centuries. Al-Mu'taṣim built a new palace in the Mukharrim quarter of Baghdād, which became his residence until 836, when he removed to Sāmarrā, where he built another costly palace. Here, as brilliant a scene was enacted as anything Hārūn of *The Thousand and One Nights* had staged. The palace sheltered all the musical *virtuosi* of the day, and their *doyen*, Isḥāq al-Mauṣilī, was the khalif's "boon companion." The khalif's uncle, the musical Prince Ibrāhīm ibn al-Mahdī, also found favour at his court.[2] Among other musicians of his munificence were: Aḥmad ibn Yaḥyā al-Makkī, Zurzūr al-Kabīr,[3] and Muḥammad ibn 'Amr al-Rūmī.[4]

Al-Wāthiq (842-47) was the first of the 'Abbāsid

[1] *'Iqd al-farīd*, iii, 188. Cf. *Aghānī*, v, 106.
[2] *Aghānī*, viii, 58.
[3] *Aghānī*, xii, 92.
[4] *Aghānī*, vi, 190.

khalifs who was actually a real musician. Ḥammad ibn Isḥāq al-Mauṣilī testifies that he was the most learned of the khalifs in this art, and that he was an excellent singer and a skilled performer on the *'ūd* (lute).[1] His songs are mentioned in the *Aghānī*. So much did the art find support and flattery at his court that one might think that it had been turned into a conservatory of music with Isḥāq al-Mauṣilī as Principal, instead of it being the *majlis* of the " Commander of the Faithful." Even the khalif's son Hārūn was a gifted musician and a brilliant instrumentalist. Among the older musicians at the court were: Isḥāq al-Mauṣilī, Mukhāriq, 'Allūyah, Muḥammad ibn al-Ḥārith, 'Amr ibn Bāna, whilst among the new-comers were 'Abdallāh ibn al-'Abbās al-Rabī'ī, Ibn Fīlā' al-Ṭunbūrī, Ibrāhīm ibn al-Ḥasan ibn Sahl and Al-Ḥasan al-Masdūd. Al-Wāthiq carried forward the spirit of Rationalism inaugurated by Al-Ma'mūn, and gave the fullest encouragement to art and letters. His death in 847 brought to a close the first period of the 'Abbāsid *régime*, generally known as " The Golden Age " of Islām, by the side of which the civilization of contemporary Europe might be considered mere barbarism.

In Al-Andalus (Spain), at the Western extremity of the Empire, another Khalifate had sprung into being.[2] This land, as Stanley Lane-Poole has said, was to become " the marvel of the Middle Ages." Al-Andalus, " when all Europe was plunged in barbaric ignorance and strife, alone held the torch of learning and civilization bright and shining before the Western world."[3]

As early as 710 the Muslim armies, after conquering the northern coast of Africa, crossed the Mediterranean and invaded Spain. By 713, the whole of Spain practically, up to the Pyrenees, and even further, had fallen to the invaders. Under the Umayyads, governors were appointed to this land, a system which continued under the early 'Abbāsids. In the year 755, however, a refugee landed in Al-Andalus who was to change the fortunes

[1] *Aghānī*, viii, 172.
[2] The rulers of Al-Andalus however, did not call themselves khalifs until the time of 'Abd al-Raḥmān III (912).
[3] S. Lane-Poole, *Moors in Spain*, 43.

of the country. This was 'Abd al-Raḥmān, the sole survivor of the House of Umayya who had managed to escape the swords of the 'Abbāsids. Thousands flocked to his banner, and in the following year he made his triumphal entry into Cordova, the capital, and was proclaimed sulṭān. Henceforth, this land has a history apart from the Khalifate of the East.

'Abd al-Raḥmān I (756-88) laid the foundations for the future greatness of Al-Andalus. The Arab tribal factions, the Berbers, the *muwalladūn* (Spaniards turned Muslims), whose internecine strife had for a quarter of a century been a menace to the body politic, were now checked. In spite of the fact that his reign was almost entirely taken up by politics, art and letters flourished. We read of his favourite singing-girl 'Afzā, who sang to the *'ūd*.[1]

Hishām I (788-96) was, unlike his predecessor, extremely pious. This did not prevent him from surrounding himself with men of science, poets and sages. What his attitude was towards music we are not told by the annalists. From the fact that the court was dominated by the theologians of the Mālikī school, it is possible that music may have been proscribed.

Al-Ḥakam I (796-822) refused to be governed by the theologians, and they, in turn, fomented rebellion. The new sulṭān was a true son of the House of Umayya. "He was gay and sociable, and enjoyed life as it came to him, without the slightest leaning to asceticism. Such a character was wholly objectionable to the bigoted doctors of theology."[2] Al-Ḥakam was a free-handed patron of letters, art and science, and it was during his reign that music began to assume a high importance in Al-Andalus. Among the court musicians were: Al-'Abbās ibn al-Nasā'ī, Al-Manṣūr (a Jew), 'Alūn and Zarqūn.

'Abd al-Raḥmān II (822-52) did not inherit the strength of mind of his predecessor, and the theologians soon regained power. Yet they did not interfere with the artistic and intellectual tastes of the court, always the index of the general culture, which reached a very high

[1] *Aghānī*, xx, 149. Al Maqqarī, *Analectes*, ii, 97-8.
[2] S. Lane-Poole, *Moors in Spain*, 74.

pinnacle during his reign.[1] Music and musicians received greater attention than ever, a fact borne out by the life of Ziryāb, the chief court musician. He was the " boon companion " of the sulṭān, who shared his meals with the musician. The great musical feature of the period was the school of Ziryāb, and the importation of singers from Al-Medīna for the propagation of the old Arabian musical ideals. The school lasted until the extinction of the Western Khalifate. On the death of 'Abd al-Raḥmān II in 852, Al-Andalus was split up into a number of petty kingdoms, although a sulṭān still ruled at Cordova

§ II

The 'Abbāsid Empire during the early years of the " Golden Age " extended westward through Egypt, Tripoli, Tunisia, Algeria, Morocco, into Spain and France, and eventually into Italy.[2] Northward, it included Syria, a portion of Asia Minor, Kurdistān, Armenia and Georgia. Eastward, it stretched through 'Irāq 'Ajamī, Ṭabaristān, Khurāsān, Khwārism, Bukhārā to the borders of Tartary, and through Persia, Afghanistān to Sind. Baghdād was the capital of this vast Empire, and Al-'Irāq was the emporium of the East. Baghdād was a city of great populousness and magnificence. The wealth of the khalifs, nobility and merchants was almost fabulous.[3] Al-Mahdī spent six million pieces of gold on a single pilgrimage! Hārūn, richer still, was able to give away two and a half million at one time, whilst at his death the treasury showed nine hundred million sterling. The magnificence of the palaces, mosques, colleges, and official residences, the luxurious appointments and furnishings of the interiors, the gorgeous retinues and equipages, the sumptuous *fêtes*, banquets,

[1] Casiri, *Bibl. Arab.-Hisp. Escur.*, ii, 34.

[2] Some of these divisions were not, of course, known in these days, and so far as Spain and Italy is concerned the 'Abbāsids only held a very slight control on the former.

[3] However much we may feel inclined to doubt the veracity of the annalists in these matters, it has to be confessed that the figures quoted, from the highest to the lowest, are invariably proportionate.

and other gatherings, together with the splendour of social life, not only in the capital, but in all the great cities from Cordova to Samarqand, surpasses anything of its kind in history.

Yet one may ask, "What has all this to do with music?" A great deal. Everywhere we see culture progress dependent upon economic and political forces, and side by side with this material luxury and political grandeur we find intellectual weal and æsthetic splendour. It has been called "The Augustine Age of Arabian literature," for not only *belles lettres*, but science (including the science and theory of music) and philosophy were patronized with zeal. Colleges were opened, libraries founded, observatories, hospitals and laboratories built, and "all this brilliance of literary and scientific attainment is contemporary with Charlemagne, in other words when the whole of Christian Europe was submerged in a barbarism very insufficiently tempered by the educational reform which he initiated."[1]

The art of music naturally fared well under such propitious conditions. The courts were crowded with professional musicians and singing-girls, who were treated with unheard-of favours and generosity, the memory of which is proverbial with the Arabs to-day. Much of this was due to Persian example, since the 'Abbāsids desired to emulate the glories of the Sāsānids of old.[2] Ibrāhīm al-Mauṣilī received 150,000 pieces of gold in one gift from Khalif Al-Hādī. Mukhāriq took a present from Hārūn of 100,000 pieces. Ḥakam al-Wādī had nearly 600,000 pieces of silver bestowed on him in two gifts from Hārūn and Ibrāhīm ibn al-Mahdī. These people were certainly the *virtuosi*, but even the ordinary professional musician made a small fortune by his art in these days.

It has already been shown that the favours showered on musicians were resented by the theologians (*'ulamā*), who objected to music on religious grounds. Now, however, even the poets are aroused to jealousy. It was

[1] Owen, J., *Skeptics of the Italian Renaissance*, 65.
[2] Al-Mas'ūdī, ii, 158.

the poet Abū Nuwās (d. *ca.* 810) who wrote the line, "The mien of a singer (*mughannī*) and the elegance of a freethinker (*zindīq*)." Even the singing-girls were the object of envy, since the poetess Faḍl once said, "They never ask less than a gold-mine, and treat a poor man as if he were a dog."

Yet although we see these musicians enjoying wealth and patronage, and some of them like Ibrāhīm al-Mauṣilī, his son Isḥāq al-Mauṣilī, Mukhāriq, and others, were even the "boon companions" of the khalifs,[1] yet their avocation placed them in an anomalous position. The "letter" of the law proscribed them because they were the practitioners of an art which, even if it were not actually "sinful" (*ḥaram*), was "religiously unpraiseworthy" (*makrūh*), as Burton says.[2] However much the Arabs delighted in a musician's company, it was apparently some spiritual consolation and satisfaction that they recognized him as a "sinner." Indeed, musicians had no standing at law, at any rate in regard to their calling.[3] Even their professional life was not so serene as might be imagined, for often their duties were most arduous and exacting.[4] Many, too, tasted both the whip and the dungeon at the hands of the khalifs and nobility.[5] Still, on the whole, their lot was certainly better than that of Haydn and Mozart at European courts nine centuries later.

[1] The *virtuosi*, like the "boon companions," were expected to be able to do justice to the wine-cup, and not infrequently we find them under the influence of wine. Al-Amīn however, although fond of the wine-cup himself, did not extend its bounty to his musicians. *Aghānī*, vi, 72.

[2] Burton, *Arabian Nights* (Isobel Burton's edit.), vi, 59.

[3] A musician named Ja'far al-Ṭabbāl brought an action against Prince Ibrāhīm ibn al-Mahdī for payment of lessons given to a singing-girl. Before the judge, he offered to prove that he had fulfilled his contract, by getting the girl to sing. The judge would have none of it, and walked out of court crying: "The curse of Allāh on all you musicians." Judgment therefore went by default against the musician. *Aghānī*, xiv, 5. Musicians, like modern "bookmakers," were tolerated in their avocation, but dared not go to law on account of it. Even to-day, in Islāmic lands, a singer cannot sue for wages. *Al-Hidāya*, iv, 212.

[4] *Aghānī*, xvi, 138. If the musicians of the Umayyads were the journalists of the day, they were more so under the 'Abbāsids. Knowing that music went hand-in-hand with the wine-cup, and that "men in wine speak the truth," the 'Abbāsids even used their musicians as spies. *Aghānī*, v, 113.

[5] *Aghānī*, iii, 162, v, 7

Besides the *virtuosi* there were two other classes of musicians, the instrumentalist (*ālātī*) and the singing-girl (*qaina*). These were either slaves or freemen who were attached to the *virtuosi* as accompanists, but their position as freemen was an inferior one. The second class were slaves who, when they were betrothed or became mothers, were given their freedom.[1] At the courts some ten or twelve of the *virtuosi* were always to be found, whilst thirty, fifty or even a hundred or more singing-girls were part of the establishment.

As in the Umayyad days, the singing-girls were usually taught by the *virtuosi*, more frequently at their schools of music. In the "Golden Age," the famous Ibrāhīm al-Mauṣilī, the leading musician of the time, had his music school for the training of singing-girls. High prices were asked for these female musicians, for they were invariably highly accomplished, not only in music, but in other departments of culture.[2]

It still continued to be the custom at court for the *virtuosi* to be hidden from the khalif by a curtain, although according to Lane it would appear that what really took place was that there was a dais or stage for the musicians, which was screened off.[3] The accounts of the author of the *Kitāb al-aghānī* do not admit of this interpretation generally. Ibn Jāmi' describes the music saloon of the court in the following story:

"I was led into a large and splendid saloon, at the end of which there hung a gorgeous silk curtain. In the middle of the room were several seats facing the

[1] *Aghānī*, xix, 136.

[2] In the *Alf laila wa laila*, ii, 493, we read of a singing-girl versed in syntax, poetry, jurisprudence, exegesis, philosophy, *musical science*, arithmetic, geodesy, geometry, fables of the ancients, the *Qur'ān*, *ḥadīth*, medicine, logic, rhetoric, composition, and the art of playing the *'ūd* (*lute*). See also i, 280; iv, 163. *'Iqd al-farīd*, ii, 198. Ibrāhīm al-Mauṣilī selling a singing-girl to Ja'far al-Barmakī, asked rather a high price. The latter said: "What is her particular merit that she is priced so high?" The musician replied: "Though she had no other merit than of singing this melody which is mine, she is worth the price and more." It is highly probable that the singing-girl of Egypt to-day hands down in her name,—*'ālima* ("learned"),—the old status of her class. Cf. Lane, *Modern Egyptians*, 355, who says that the word might perhaps be derived from the Hebrew word *'almāh* ("a girl").

[3] See Lane's "Notes" to the *Arabian Nights*, i, 203.

curtain, and four of these seats had been already taken by four musicians, three females and one male, with lutes (*'īdān*) in their hands. I was placed next to the man, and the command was given for the concert to commence. After these four had sung, I turned to my companion and asked him to accompany me with his instrument, saying, 'Sharpen (*shadd*) the string of your lute thus, to raise the pitch (*ṭabaqa*), and go down to this fret (*dastān*) thus when playing.' I then sang a melody of my own composition, and when finished, five or six eunuchs came from behind the curtain and demanded the name of the melody. I replied, 'It is my own.' After they had returned with the message, Sallām al-Abrash [the chief eunuch] came from behind the curtain and said, 'You lie! It is by Ibn Jāmi'.' . . . Again we all sang in the same order, and again I sang one of my own compositions, and again I was asked the composer, and once more I said, 'It is my own,' and once more did the chief eunuch say, 'You lie! It is by Ibn Jāmi'.' Then I said, 'Yes, and I am he.' As soon as I had uttered these words. the curtain opened, and Faḍl ibn Rabī' cried, 'The Commander of the Faithful,' and Hārūn appeared upon the arm of Ja'far al-Barmakī, and, approaching me said, 'Ah, it is you, Ibn Jāmi'.' . . . Hārūn then reclined upon a divan and commanded me to sing some new melody. I then sang my song of the negress."[1]

In this account we see the khalif behind the curtain listening to music, and then practically *tête à tête* with the performer. A similar sort of thing occurs over and over again in the pages of the *Kitāb al-aghānī*. In the *'Iqd al-farīd* we read that when Isḥāq al-Mauṣilī and Khalif Al-Mahdī became reconciled, the musician used to say, "I reclined with the khalif [on a divan] and he patted me with his hand as a familiar friend would do."[2] Of course, the singing-girls continued to be screened off.[3]

[1] *Aghānī*, vi, 78-80. Abridged.
[2] *'Iqd al-farīd*, iii, 188.
[3] Abū'l-'Alā al-Ma'arri gives as an argument against girls going to school that they sit without a curtain, when "even the singing-girls sit behind one." *Luzūmiyyāt*, p. 62.

During the period covered by the "Golden Age," Arabian music made greater progress than during any other period. This was due primarily to two causes, which can be viewed quite apart from industrial prosperity or political poise. These causes were the influence of *Shī'a*[1] and *Mu'tazilī*[2] ideas upon Islāmic thought, and the dominant note of Greek scientific culture in secular life. The former brought a more tolerant attitude towards music in so far as Islām was concerned. Strange to say, however, the theologians had considerable power at court. Whilst the Umayyads kept the theologian to his private and domestic sphere, the 'Abbāsids brought him into the court and made him take part in public policy. Favouring the theologian in this way was evidently considered a better policy than keeping him at a distance. The personal contact seems to have enabled the khalifs to get their own way to a considerable extent, and certainly it obtained so far as the *malāhī* were concerned, including music. Hārūn said to Ibrāhīm ibn Sa'd al-Zuhrī the theologian one day, "I hear that Mālik ibn Anas makes singing a crime." The court theologian replied, "Has Mālik the right to loose and bind? . . . If I heard Mālik condemning it, and I had the power, I would improve his education."[3] Hārūn was amused at the reply. Indeed, what other reply could Al-Zuhrī have made, seeing that everyone knew, many to their cost, that it was Hārūn alone who could "loose and bind." Of course, the orthodox still murmured, and we have the poet Bashshar ibn Burd, himself a Rationalist, voicing their opinion in a satire, saying how incongruous it was to find a "Successor of the Prophet in the midst of wine-bottle and lute."[4] The pasquinade brought him to his death.

Proficiency in the theoretical side of musical art had

[1] The Shi'ites were the sect (*shī'a*) or followers of 'Alī. They were always more tolerant and open-minded on the question of music than the Sunnites or orthodox Muslims. The Persians are Shi'ites.

[2] The Mu'tazilites ("Seceders") were the Rationalists of the day.

[3] *'Iqd al-farīd*, iii, 180.

[4] *Aghānī*, ii, 71. De Meynard translates the passage as "lutes and oboes," but the text has *ziqq wa'l-'ūd*. Cf. the line quoted by Abū'l-'Alā al-Ma'arrī, where it runs,—"*nāy* (flute) and the *'ūd* (lute)."

long been established, but this did not prevent further progress. In general culture we see the influence of both Byzantium and Persia, the latter perhaps the most marked. Persian influence, especially that from Khurāsān, made itself felt on the accession of Al-Ma'mūn (813), for the reason that the latter event pushed back the Arabian ascendancy which Al-Amīn represented.[1] Its effect on music, however, was considerably less than in other spheres, and perhaps quite unimportant. Byzantium contributed very little to musical culture. What the Arabs got from Byzantium were the ancient treatises on Greek theory of music, which were practically unknown to the Byzantines save by name. Indeed, it was not until the Syrian and Arab translators turned these treasures into Arabic that the East revived its interest in them. From these sources the Arabs certainly borrowed, but the loaning did not assume much import until the Golden Age had passed.[2]

On the whole, theoretical progress during the period under survey was practically indigenous. Isḥāq al-Mauṣilī came forward as the chief musician of his day, to lay down and fix definitely the theory which appears to have fallen into neglect since the time of Yūnus al-Kātib in the days of the Umayyads. It was Isḥāq, says the author of the *Kitāb al-aghānī*, who first established methodically the genres (*ajnās*) of the melodic modes (*aṣābi'*) and the different kinds (*ṭarā'iq*) of rhythmic modes (*īqā'āt*), which, in the works of Yūnus al-Kātib, had been insufficiently indicated. Al-Khalīl ibn Aḥmad, one of the most famous scholars of the time, contributed the first really scientific treatises it would seem on musical theory in his *Kitāb al-nagham* (Book of Notes) and *Kitāb al-īqā'* (Book of Rhythm).[3] More important still were the treatises of the celebrated Al-Kindī, no less than seven of these standing to his credit.[4] From the latter we get a close insight into the theory and practice of the *virtuosi* of the age, together with the

[1] Jurjī Zaidān, 185-6.
[2] *Aghānī*, v, 53. See my *Facts*, etc., pp. 55-6.
[3] *Fihrist*, 43.
[4] *Fihrist*, 257.

theories derived from the Ancient Greeks. Collectors of songs such as Yaḥyā al-Makkī, Aḥmad ibn Yaḥyā al-Makkī, Fulaiḥ ibn Abī'l-'Aurā', and Isḥāq al-Mauṣilī, issued several works, whilst the last named compiled a dozen or so biographies of famous musicians.[1] It is here that we see how considerably the Arabian traditions were preserved in the music of the period.[2]

The rhythmic modes (*īqā'āt*) appear to have been little different from what we saw in Umayyad times. They are fully described in the *Risāla fī ijzā' khabariyya al-mūsīqī* by Al-Kindī, now preserved at Berlin.[3] The only apparent difference is the substitution of a *khafīf al-khafīf* instead of a *ramal ṭunbūrī*. The Persians adopted the rhythmic modes of the Arabs, although it was not until the time of Hārūn (786-809) that they took the *ramal* mode, which was introduced by a musician named Salmak.[4]

In the melodic modes (*aṣābi'*) the old principles still obtained. Isḥāq al-Mauṣilī had composed a song which attracted the attention of Prince Ibrāhim ibn al-Mahdī, who wrote to the composer asking him to let him have it. Isḥāq replied by letter giving him particulars of the verse, together with "its rhythm (*īqā'*) and its division (*basīṭ*), its course (*majrā*) and its melodic mode (*aṣba'*), its proportionate dividing (*tajzi'a*) and its parts (*aqsām*), the succession of its notes and the places of the rests (*maqāṭi'*), the particulars of its compound modes (*adwār*) and its measures (*awzān*)."[5]

The passage above gives us a fair example of the technical nomenclature of the period. *Īqā'*, *aṣba'*, and *majrā*, we are already acquainted with. The *busūṭ* (sing. *basīṭ* or *basāṭ*) appear to have been the divisions of the rhythmic modes (*īqā'āt*). The word for the proportionate dividing of the melody or rhythm has its root in *jaza'a*, which opens an interesting speculation for the origin of the modern word *jazz*.[6] The *maqāṭi'* (rests)

[1] *Fihrist*, 141-3. *Aghānī*, i, 183. vi, 17, 18. xv, 159.
[2] Isḥāq al-Mauṣilī sang the old melodies. *Aghānī*, xviii, 175.
[3] *Berlin MS.*, No. 5503, fol. 31, v.
[4] *Aghānī*, i, 151. [5] *Aghānī*, ix, 54, 56.
[6] See my *Facts*, etc., p. 14.

are detailed in the rhythmic modes given by Al-Kindī. The *adwār* (sing. *daur*)[1] were made up of the first tetrachord of one melodic mode (*aṣba'*) and the second tetrachord of another. Transposition scales called *ṭabaqāt* (sing. *ṭabaqa*) were practised. These were, of necessity, innumerable, and Isḥāq al-Mauṣilī says that it took him ten years to learn them. These *ṭabaqāt* were like changes of key signature.

There is another very interesting passage which reveals the fact that the Arabs employed *genres* similar to the Ancient Greeks. The tetrachord was the theoretical landmark of the Arabs, and it was contained with the stretch of the hand on the *'ūd* (lute).[2] The Greeks called their variations of the tetrachord—*genres* (=γένη), of which there were three, the *diatonic*, *chromatic*, and *enharmonic*. In the 10th century these were known to the Arabs as the *qawī*, *khunthawī*, and *rāsim* respectively.[3] That the Arabs of the period concerned with used these *genres* is quite likely, as the following passage appears to show[4]:

> "I read in one of the books that Muḥammad ibn al-Ḥasan (and I think that he is Ibn Muṣ'ab) mentions Isḥāq al-Mauṣilī. He says, 'His art was correct in principles (*uṣūl*), and his notes wonderful of arrangement (*tartīb*), and his division (*qism*) just of measures (*awzān*). And he used to perform in all the divisions (*busūṭ*) of the rhythms (*īqā'āt*), and whichever division (*basāṭ*) he wished to sing a song in, he used the *aqwā* (= *qawī*) song which was the division (*basāṭ*) of the ablest of the older people (*qudamā'*). . . . Sometimes he would seek the very threshold of the ancients (*awā'il*) and would follow their manner in their methods. Then he would build upon the *rāsim*, and work it out

[1] Both editions of the *Kitāb al-aghānī* have *awāra*. De Meynard (*J.A.*, Mars-Av., 1869, p. 325) rightly suggests that this should be *adwār*. Strange to say Kosegarten (*Lib. Cant.*, 183), in quoting this passage, actually omits this word.

[2] This point is worth noting in connection with Wead's theories in his *Contributions to the History of Musical Scales*, 433.

[3] *Mafātīḥ al-'ulūm*, 243-4.

[4] *Aghānī*, v, 53.

according to their example. He would then make it *qawī*, and so his work became strong and firm, uniting in it two states—the strong in nature (and it is easy of method), and the *khunthā* (= *khunthawī*), in which are many notes (*nagham*) and their arrangement (*tartīb*) between the high (*ṣiyyāḥ*) and the low (*isjāḥ*). This art is more akin in the *ṭabaqāt* (scales) to that of the ancients (*awā'il*) than to the less remote people.[1]"

Discussions on the theory of music, even before the khalifs, both by the *virtuosi* and the scientific musicians, were not uncommon, and they certainly reveal the temper of the period.[2] That a phonetic notation was known during the Golden Age is highly probable. Perhaps the letter of Isḥāq to Prince Ibrāhīm mentioned above contained a notation. We certainly read that khalif Al-Ma'mūn (in 819) "waited twenty months without hearing a *letter* (*ḥarf*) of music (*ghinā'*)."[3] Al-Kindī (d. *ca.* 874) uses a notation in his *Risāla fī khubr ta'līf al-alḥān*, which is the earliest definite use of it among the Arabs.[4]

Considerable changes had taken place on the instrumental side, and during the second half of the 8th century, one of the court musicians, Zalzal, introduced a new type of *'ūd* (lute), which was soon generally adopted in the place of the *'ūd al-fārisī* or Persian lute that had been in common use. This "perfect lute" was called the *'ūd al-shabbūṭ*, which Land thinks to have been the instrument in which the neck and fingerboard gradually broadened out to the body.[5] It was still mounted with four strings,[6] although in Al-Andalus, a musician named Ziryāb had added a fifth.[7] This Ziryāb, whilst he was at the court of Hārūn (786-809), introduced some novel

[1] By the "ancients" we may presume that the Greeks are meant, whilst the "older people" probably refers to his immediate predecessors. By "less remote people" we may infer that the Byzantines are intended.

[2] *Aghānī*, v, 22, 23, 53, 60-1. ix, 74.

[3] *'Iqd al-farīd*, iii, 188. Perhaps *ḥarf* stands for "particle."

[4] *British Museum MS.*, Or. 2361, fol. 167, v.

[5] Land, *Remarks on the Earliest Development of Arabic Music*, p. 161-2.

[6] Al-Kindī, *Berlin MS.*, 5530, fol. 30. *Aghānī*, v, 53.

[7] Al-Maqqarī, *Moh. Dyn.*, ii, 116.

improvements to the lute. Whilst his instrument was "equal in size and made of the same wood" as the lute in general use, it was heavier by nearly one-third. His silk strings were made differently from those of his confrères,[1] whilst his second, third and fourth strings were made from the entrails of a young lion, which he claimed to be "far superior to those of any other animal in point of strength, depth of tone, and clearness of sound." Besides this he asserted that they would bear much longer wear and were not so liable to change of temperature.[2]

We read of large bands of singing-girls playing lutes in these days, for these were the special instruments of accompaniment. Only occasionally do we read of the *mi'zafa* (? psaltery) or the *ṭunbūr* (pandore) being used. More general for the accompaniment, after the lute, were the wood-wind instruments (*mazāmīr*) of the flute type, the *ṭabl* (drum) and the *duff* (square tambourine). Open-air music consisted of the *ṭabl* (drum) and *surnāy* (reed-pipe),[3] and the court military band of Al-Amīn was thus constituted,[4] which shows that the old ideas of the Pagan Arabs concerning martial music still obtained.

Some writers have imagined that these bands were directed by a conductor with *bâton* in hand.[5] This conjecture appears to have been due to a misinterpretation of a passage in the *'Iqd al-farīd*, which runs, "*Ibrāhīm* [al-Mauṣilī] was the first to beat the rhythm (*īqā'*) with a *qaḍīb* (wand)."[6] This "beating" has already been described, and was much older than Ibrāhīm al-Mauṣilī.[7]

The doctrine of the *ēthos* (*ta'thīr*) was now definitely linked up with music. This old Semitic idea had been strengthened by the doctrines of the Ṣābi'a of Ḥarrān and the theories of the ancient Greeks and Byzantines.

[1] Cf. the text.
[2] Al-Maqqarī, *Analectes*, ii, 88. *Moh. Dyn.*, ii, 116-21, 410.
[3] The text has *surnāb*.
[4] *Aghānī*, xvi, 139.
[5] Syed Ameer Ali, *Short Hist.*, 451. Perron, *Femmes Arabes*. F. Salvador-Daniel, 98. Fétis, *Hist. Gen.*, ii, 121. The latter attributes the *'Iqd* account to Isḥāq al-Mauṣilī.
[6] *'Iqd al-farīd*, iii, 188.
[7] Cf. *Aghānī*, i, 97, and see *ante* pp. 16, 47, 74.

Almost everything terrestrial was "influenced" by something celestial. The seven notes of the scale corresponded to the planets. The twelve signs of the zodiac were associated with the four pegs, four frets, and four strings of the *'ūd*. The four strings were affiliated with the primeval elements, the winds, the seasons, the humours, the mental faculties, colours, perfumes, the quarters of the zodiac, moon, and the world. Al-Kindī deals with this question at considerable length.[1] In Al-Andalus also, the doctrine was in full swing.[2]

The Music School of Ibrāhīm al-Mauṣilī at Baghdād has been mentioned. Unfortunately we get little or no information about the didactic methods which obtained there. In Al-Andalus, however, we get some details of the Music School founded by Ziryāb. Before the advent of Ziryāb, the professors of music had no other method of teaching their pupils to sing than mere practical example.[3] Ziryāb changed all this. He divided the curriculum of his pupils into three parts—first, the rhythm, metre, and words of a song were taught to the accompaniment of a musical instrument. Then, the melody in its simple state was mastered. Finally, the "gloss" (*zā'ida*) was introduced.

The following account is given of the method adopted by Ziryāb with beginners. "Whenever a youth came to him for the purpose of taking lessons in vocal music, he made him sit down on the round cushion called *miswara*, and bade him exert the full power of his voice. If his voice was weak, he was made to tie his turban round his waist, a practice which is well known to increase the voice. . . . If the youth stammered, or could not well open his mouth, or if he had the habit of clenching his teeth whenever he spoke, he bade him put inside his mouth a small piece of wood three inches (three fingers) in width, which he was to keep there day and night until his jaws were well expanded. This being done, he made him cry out at the top of his voice, *yā ḥajjām* or

[1] Al-Kindī, *Berlin MS.*, 5530, fol. 30.

[2] Al-Maqqarī, *Moh. Dyn.*, ii, 118. See my *Influence of Music: From Arabic Sources.*

[3] See Ribera, *La enseñanza de los musulmanes espanoles.*

ah! telling him to protract the sound as much as possible: if he found that he uttered those words in a clear, powerful, and sonorous voice,[1] he admitted him into the number of his pupils, and spared no trouble or fatigue to make him an accomplished singer; if the contrary, he took no further pains with him."[2]

Notwithstanding the inordinate elevation of musical art and *belles lettres* during the "Golden Age," the great classical standards fell into desuetude. The old *qaṣīda* which "breathed of the desert," was a thing of the past. The *littérateurs* were Persians for the most part, and, as citizens of gay and festive communities, they saw little interest in the stern ideals of Arab life which formed the background of Arabic poetry. Hence a new school arose in which we find "the maddest gaiety and the shamefullest frivolity; strains of lofty meditation mingled with a world-weary pessimism; delicate sentiment, unforced pathos, and glowing rhetoric; but seldom the manly self-reliance, the wild, invigorating freedom and inimitable freshness of *badawī* song."[3]

Music, dependent on the song, which was far more in favour than instrumental performance, became similarly affected. As far back as the days of Ma'bad and Ibn Suraij, there had been a growing preference for a lighter (*khafīf*) rhythmic mode in place of the more serious one (*kāmil tāmm*).[4] The craze for the former grew and the *hazaj* and *mākhūrī* rhythmic modes were the most frequent in demand. Ḥakam al-Wādī, being upbraided by his son for pandering to the taste of the public in this way with the *hazaj* rhythm, answered him thus, "My son: For thirty years have I sung in the *thaqīl* rhythmic modes and hardly gained a living, yet in the three years of singing in the *hazaj* I have earned more money than thou hast seen in thy life." It was the old story, the musician had to get his living, and art must necessarily go by the board. Even a great *artiste* like Isḥāq al-Mauṣilī had

[1] Literally, "Without any roughness, nor straightness, nor narrowness of production."
[2] Al-Maqqarī, *Moh. Dyn.*, ii, 121. *Analectes*, ii, 88-9.
[3] Nicholson, *Lit. Hist. of the Arabs*, 291.
[4] *Aghānī*, i, 116.

to bow to the demand for the *hazaj* rhythm,[1] whilst his father made his name with the *mākhūrī*.[2]

§ III

The *virtuosi* of the "Golden Age" won undying fame. How real this has been we know from the pages of the *'Iqd al-farīd*, the *Kitāb al-aghānī*, the *Fihrist*, the *Nihāyat al-arab*, and the *Thousand and One Nights*. Take away those alluring musical interludes, those escapades of the *virtuosi* and the singing girls that we read of in the last-named work, and there would be a relish wanting.

The first great musician of the 'Abbāsid era was Ḥakam al-Wādī, or Abū Yaḥyā Ḥakam ibn Maimūn al-Wādī. He was a freeman of Al-Walīd I (705-15), and was born at Wādī al-Qurā, his father, of Persian origin, having been a hairdresser who amassed a small fortune. On his father's death, Ḥakam became a successful trader in oil, but taking a liking for music he went to his compatriot, 'Umar al-Wādī, for lessons, and in due course his teacher presented him at the court of Al-Walīd II (743-44), where his performance brought him a reward of one thousand pieces of gold. He remained at court until the death of this khalif. After this he languished in obscurity until the time of Al-Manṣūr (754-75) when he set out for Baghdād. Here, he was immediately patronized by the khalif's cousin, Muḥammad ibn Abī'l-'Abbās. Fame came rather late to him, for he was then over fifty years of age. Yet he was recognized as the leading musician in the capital. Having made a fortune he retired to his native town, but he soon returned to Baghdād, and was present at the courts of Al-Mahdī (775-85), Al-Hādī (785-86), and Hārūn (786-809). At the court of Al-Hādī he managed to defeat Ibrāhīm al-Mauṣilī and Ibn Jāmi' in a tournament of song, carrying off the first prize of 300,000 pieces of silver. Later, Ḥakam went to the court of Prince Ibrāhīm ibn al-Mahdī, then governor of Damascus, where he composed no less than 200

[1] *Aghānī*, v, 83, 89, 115.
[2] *Aghānī*, vi, 66.

melodies for this prince, for which he received 299,000 pieces of silver.[1] Retiring finally to Wādī al-Qurā, he died about the middle of Hārūn's reign, at the age of about 81.[2] Ḥakam is classed among the great singers of the Arabs,[3] and was an acknowledged expert in the *hazaj* rhythm.[4]

Siyyāṭ (d. 785) was the popular cognomen of Abū Wahb 'Abdallāh ibn Wahb, a freeman of the Banū Khuzā'a. He was born at Mecca about 739, and, although his career was short, it was a distinguished one. He had two excellent teachers who were well versed in the best musical traditions of the Orthodox and Umayyad periods. These were Yūnus al-Kātib, the author of the first *Kitāb al-aghānī*, and Burdān, an old musician who had heard 'Azza al-Mailā', Ibn Muḥriz, Ibn Suraij, Jamīla and Ma'bad.[5] Siyyāṭ became one of the foremost lutenists and singers of his day, as well as being a composer of repute.[6] During the reign of Al-Mahdī (775-85) he established himself in Baghdād, and soon won success at court. He died in the prime of life in 785. His two greatest pupils were Ibrāhīm al-Mauṣilī and Ibn Jāmi'. One day the former was asked by his son, Isḥāq al-Mauṣilī, who was the composer of a certain song, when Ibrāhīm replied, "The composer was a man who, had he lived, would not have taken a second place to me or to any other musician who is at present favoured by the khalif. This melody is by Siyyāṭ."[7]

Yaḥyā al-Makkī, or Abū 'Uthmān ibn Marzūq al-Makkī, was a freeman of the House of Umayya and belonged to Mecca as his name tells us. He was an estimable *artiste* and was justly considered the *doyen* of the musicians of Al-Ḥijāz in his day. It was he who taught Ibn Jāmi', Ibrāhīm al-Mauṣilī, and Fulaiḥ ibn Abī'l-'Aurā' the classical traditions of the Ḥijāzian music.[8] He was present at court from the time of Al-Mahdī (775-85) to Al-Ma'mūn (813-33). Al-Amīn (809-13) thought so

[1] This broken amount was "policy" on the part of the prince. To have given as much as the khalif would probably have been considered *lèse majesté*.

[2] *Aghānī*, vi, 64-8.
[3] *Aghānī*, v, 9.
[4] *Aghānī*, v, 36. vi, 13, 66.
[5] *Aghānī*, vii, 141.
[6] *Aghānī*, v, 9.
[7] *Aghānī*, vi, 7-10.
[8] *Aghānī*, vi, 17.

highly of his abilities that he paid him 10,000 pieces of silver for one music lesson given to his brother, Prince Ibrāhīm ibn al-Mahdī. As a singer, he was praised by no less a person than Ibrāhīm al-Mauṣilī. His fame, however, rests more upon his literary work, since his *Kitāb fī'l-aghānī* (Book of Songs), comprising the best examples of the ancient song (*ghinā' al-qadīm*) became the standard collection until his son Aḥmad issued a revised edition which comprised some 3,000 songs. Although Yaḥyā is classed among the foremost who composed works of this kind, Al-Iṣfahānī, the author of the great *Kitāb al-aghānī*, points out that his classification of the " modes " displays " confusion." He does not appear to have been a careful chronicler, and it is possibly due to him, although perhaps more so to 'Amr ibn Bāna, that so many errors have been perpetuated. There is a story told of Isḥāq al-Mauṣilī who, knowing how unreliable Yaḥyā was as an historian, set a trap for him. One day before Hārūn, Ishāq invented the name of an individual and then asked Yaḥyā for information concerning him. Yaḥyā began expatiating on this man's genealogy When Isḥāq explained that the individual had no existence, Yaḥyā's reputation as a genealogist was at an end so far as Hārūn was concerned.[1]

Abū Ja'far Aḥmad ibn Yaḥyā al-Makkī (d. 864), son of the above, was " one of the most praiseworthy of the narrators (*ruwāt*) of music (*ghinā'*), and the most learned in its science." Not content with revising the work of his father[2] he issued a collection known as the *Kitāb mujarrad fī'l-aghānī* (Book of Choice Songs), which became one of the text-books for later investigators. It was compiled for Muḥammad ibn 'Abdallāh ibn Ṭāhir, a brother of the musical theorist, and it comprised some 14,000 songs. As a practical musician he was praised by Isḥāq al-Mauṣilī, which was the means of his receiving a gift of 20,000 pieces of silver from Khalif Al-Mu'taṣim (833-42). He first appeared at the court of Al-Ma'mūn (813-33),[3] and finally at that of Al-Mutawakkal (847-61).[4]

[1] *Aghānī*, vi, 16-24.
[2] *Aghānī*, v, 104.
[3] *Aghānī*, vi, 17-18.
[4] *Aghānī*, xiii, 22.

He is sometimes called Ẓunain al-Makkī[1] and in the *'Iqd al-farīd* there is an account of Ẓunain and two other musicians named Al-Ḥasan al-Masdūd and Dubais at the house of Abū 'Īsā ibn al-Mutawakkal, and here they are called "the cleverest men in singing." Aḥmad ibn Yaḥyā al-Makkī died in 864.[2]

Ibn Jāmi', whose full name was Abū'l-Qāsim Ismā'īl ibn Jāmi', was born at Mecca. He was an Arab of noble blood, since both his father and mother belonged to the house of Saḥm, one of the principal branches of the Quraish. He was originally destined for a profession suitable to one of such a station, and he received an excellent education, especially in law, and he knew the Qur'ān by heart. Whilst he was a youth, he lost his father, and his mother having married the musician Siyyāṭ[3] the career of a singer soon attracted the young and impressionable Ibn Jāmi'. Although his step-father was his first teacher, he also received lessons from Yaḥyā al-Makkī. When Siyyāṭ left Mecca for Baghdād and became a favourite at Al-Mahdī's court, Ibn Jāmi' and another of Siyyāṭ's pupils named Ibrāhīm al-Mauṣilī were countenanced by the khalif's sons, Hārūn and Al-Hādī. The khalif, however, fearing lest this liking for music by his heirs might offend the people, forbade these two young musicians the princes' apartments. The instruction was ignored, and Ibn Jāmi' and Ibrāhīm al-Mauṣilī were arrested. The latter was sentenced to 300 strokes of the lash, whilst Ibn Jāmi', protesting his noble birth, was banished. "You," cried the khalif, "one of the Quraish, and following the profession of music! What a disgrace. Out of my sight. Leave Baghdād instantly."[4] Ibn Jāmi' fled to Mecca, but when the khalif died (785) and Al-Hādī came to the throne, Ibn Jāmi' was sent for and was presented with 30,000 pieces of gold. With this fortune, Ibn Jāmi' thought he

[1] The *'Iqd al-farīd* has "Zunain." See Guidi, s.v. and also *sub* "Ṭunain."

[2] *Aghānī*, xv, 65-8. *'Iqd al-farīd*, iii, 191.

[3] See *ante* p. 113.

[4] "Sovereigns are of the Quraish" runs the tradition. *'Iqd al-farīd*, ii, 40.

would retire to Mecca, but through reckless living he fell on evil days, and was compelled to take to music once more, making an appearance at the court of Hārūn (786-809). Here he found his old fellow pupil, Ibrāhīm al-Mauṣilī, who was the chief court minstrel, and a bitter jealousy arose between them. Even the other court minstrels took part in this, and two rival parties actually existed at court in consequence. There can be little doubt that Ibn Jāmiʿ was a finished performer, although inferior perhaps to his rival. Ibn ʿAbd Rabbihi says that "Ibrāhīm al-Mauṣilī was the greatest of the musicians in versatility, but Ibn Jāmiʿ had the sweetest note."[1] Barṣaumā, a favoured court minstrel, was asked by Hārūn for his opinion of Ibn Jāmiʿ, when he replied, "Why not ask my opinion about honey?"[2]

Ibrāhīm al-Mauṣilī or Al-Mauṣilī (d. 804) were the usual names given to Ibrāhīm ibn Māhān (or Maimūn)[3] al-Mauṣilī, who was born at Al-Kūfa in 742. He came of a noble Persian family, but was brought up by an illustrious Arab of the Banū Tamīm. Running away from his protector, he settled at Al-Mauṣil, which gave him his surname, and it was here that he took his first music lessons. Later he went to Al-Raiy in Northern Persia, where he acquired a comprehensive knowledge of both Persian and Arabian music (*ghinā'*). Here he met a representative of Khalif Al-Manṣūr, who enabled him to go to Al-Baṣra to further prosecute his musical studies.[4] Finally he directed his steps to Baghdād, where he studied under Siyyāṭ. We have already seen how he suffered on account of the sons of Al-Mahdī, and when the latter died, his successor, Al-Hādī (785-86), repaid Ibrāhīm for his punishment on his account by a gift of 150,000 pieces of gold. With Hārūn (786-809) he was elevated to the foremost position among the court musicians, and became the "boon companion" of the khalif, hence his nickname—Al-Nadīm.[5]

[1] *ʿIqd al-farīd*, iii, 179. [2] *Ibid. Aghānī*, vi, 12, 69-92.
[3] Māhān was his father's Iranian name, but the Arabs changed it to Maimūn.
[4] Ahlwardt, *Abū Nuwās*.
[5] See how he is respected in the *Alf laila wa laila*, iv, 232.

The rival camps of Ibrāhīm al-Mauṣilī and Ibn Jāmi' caused a great stir at court. Among the supporters of the former were: Isḥāq his son, Zalzal his brother-in-law, and Muḥammad al-Raff, whilst the latter had Mukhāriq and 'Aqīd among his adherents. An audition was being held by Ibrāhīm one day in which some thirty singing-girls were playing their lutes, and Ibn Jāmi' complained that one of them was playing out of tune. Ibrāhīm immediately named the culprit and actually mentioned the string that was out of tune. The court was amazed, much to the chagrin of Ibn Jāmi'.

Ibrāhīm became extremely rich, for not only did he receive a court pension of 10,000 pieces of silver a month, but the liberalities of the khalif and nobility in his favour almost pass credence. He also derived a large income from his lands, and his Music School alone brought him a total profit of twenty-four million pieces of silver. His mansion was the talk of Baghdād, and one person says, "A more spacious and nobler dwelling I had never seen."[1]

As a singer and instrumentalist, Ibrāhīm was without a peer.[2] As a composer he also stood unrivalled, and no less than 900 compositions stood to his credit.[3] Ibn Khallikān credits him with the introduction of "several new modes."[4] Other writers say that he was the first to make a name with the *mākhūrī* rhythmic mode.[5] When the great musician was on his deathbed, Khalif Hārūn was ever present, and at his funeral the prayers were recited by Al-Ma'mūn himself. Besides his son Isḥāq, he had several eminent pupils, and among them: Zalzal, Mukhāriq, 'Allūyah, Abū Ṣadaqa, Sulaim ibn Sallām and Muḥammad ibn al-Ḥārith. The name of Ibrāhīm al-Mauṣilī has been made famous in the West as well as in the East by the *Thousand and One Nights.*[6]

[1] *Iqd al-farīd*, iii, 188.
[2] 'Ibn Khallikān, *Biog. Dict.*, i, 21. Cf. '*Iqd al-farīd*, iii, 188.
[3] *Aghānī*, v, 17. xviii, 176.
[4] Ibn Khallikān, *Biog. Dict.*, i, 21.
[5] *Aghānī*, vi, 66. Al-Mas'ūdī, viii, 98.
[6] *Alf laila wa laila*, iii, 388. This is his adventure with the Devil, told also in the *Aghānī*, v, 36, and by Al-Ghuzūlī, i, 241. His escapade with the singing-girls (*Aghānī*, v, 41; Al-Ghuzūlī, i, 243; Ibn Badrūn, 272), is told in the *Alf laila wa laila*, ii, 437, of his son Isḥāq.

Yazīd Ḥaurā' Abū Khālid was a musician of Al-Medīna, and a freeman of the Banū Laith ibn Bakr. Settling in Baghdād, he made a reputation at the court of Al-Mahdī (775-85). His voice was of an extraordinary quality and Ibrāhīm al-Mauṣilī employed him at his Music School, but it is said that Yazīd was unable to impart to his pupils the secret of his charming vocalization. He excelled also as a composer, and both Ibrāhīm al-Mauṣilī and Ibn Jāmi' sang his compositions. Hārūn (786-809) was devoted to Yazīd, and on the deathbed of the latter the khalif never failed to send his chief eunuch to enquire each day after his favourite. He was a personal friend of the poets Abū'l-'Atāhiya and Abū Mālik al-A'raj, and it was the latter who wrote the elegaic verses on his death. As an all-round musician, he is ranked with Ibrāhīm al-Mauṣilī and Ibn Jāmi'.[1]

Zalzal, or Manṣūr Zalzal al-Ḍārib (d. 791),[2] was a very important musician of the early 'Abbāsid period. The author of the *'Iqd* says of him, "Zalzal was the most pleasant of the stringed instrumentalists, and there was not his equal either before or after."[3] Isḥāq al-Mauṣilī testified at the court of Al-Wāthiq, that Zalzal had no equal as a lutenist.[4] He was the special accompanist of Ibrāhīm al-Mauṣilī, whose brother-in-law he was, and apparently his *forte* was as an accompanist, hence his surname (al-Ḍārib), since he did not sing much.[5] He is better known in musical history as a reformer of the scale, for it was he who introduced the famous neutral third (22:27) on the lute. He was also the inventor of a "perfect lute" called the *'ūd al-shabbūṭ*, which superseded the Persian lute hitherto in use. Unfortunately, he incurred the displeasure of Hārūn and was flung into prison, where he languished for years. On his release

[1] *Aghānī*, iii, 73-75.
[2] Carra de Vaux, *Traité des rapports*, 56, and Caussin de Perceval, *J.A.*, Novembre-Decembre, 1873, p. 548, write Zolzol. The above however, is the pronunciation indicated in the *Mafātīḥ al-'ulūm*, 239. Guidi writes Zilzil. See also Ibn Khallikān, *Biog. Dict.*, i, 21. Land, *Recherches*, 61, Von Hammer, *Lit. der Arab.*, iii, 764.
[3] *'Iqd al-farīd*, iii, 190.
[4] *Aghānī*, v, 57-8.
[5] Cf. *'Iqd al-farīd*, iii, 190.

his beard was quite white, and his health was ruined. He died in 791.[1] During his lifetime Zalzal had a well dug at Baghdād, and at his death he left this to the people of Baghdād with sufficient funds to keep it in repair. For centuries it was known as the *Birkat al-Zalzal.*[2]

Fulaiḥ ibn Abī'l-'Aurā' was a native of Mecca and a freeman of the Banū Makhzūm. He was a pupil of Yaḥyā al-Makkī, and was considered one of the chief singers at the court of Al-Mahdī (775-85), being the only musician (so it is said) who appeared before that khalif without the customary curtain. He was one of the three musicians commissioned by Hārūn (786-809) to make a collection of songs for him, his collaborators being Ibrāhīm al-Mauṣilī and Ibn Jāmi'. The collection was called "*The Hundred Songs.*"[3] Isḥāq al-Mauṣilī praises him as a singer.[4] Among his pupils were the songstresses Badhl and Danānīr.[5]

Prince Ibrāhīm ibn al-Mahdī, Abū Isḥāq (779-839) was the younger brother of Hārūn, but by another mother, whose name was Shikla. Born at Baghdād, he received a very careful education, and his profound knowledge of the poets, the sciences, jurisprudence, dialectic, and traditions, is commented on by the annalists. His abilities as a musician, however, outshone all these other accomplishments. Losing his father, Al-Mahdī, when six years of age, and being confided to his mother's care, Ibrāhīm was nurtured in the *ḥarīm*, where music played so large a part. His mother, who came from Al-Dailam, was a musician, and so was Maknūna the mother of his step-sister 'Ulayya. So we find these two spoilt children being initiated very early into the practice of music. Hārūn himself evinced extreme interest in the musical education of his brother and sister, and although it was not considered "good form" for a Muslim of any social standing to indulge in the profane art of music, yet Hārūn encouraged them to perform before him, and was

[1] *Aghānī*, v, 22-24.
[2] Le Strange, *op. cit.*, 62.
[3] *Aghānī*, iv, 98-101.
[4] *Aghānī*, v, 9.
[5] *Aghānī*, xv, 144. xvii, 77.

even delighted to see them competing with the court musicians.[1]

When Al-Amīn became khalif (809) he sent for his musical nephew Ibrāhīm ibn al-Mahdī, so that his court might have the benefit of his talents. After the accession of Al-Ma'mūn, Ibrāhīm allowed himself to be proclaimed khalif during the Baghdād rebellion of 817. The glory was but short-lived, and the would-be khalif sought safety in flight, but, apprehended,[2] he begged for his life at the feet of Al-Ma'mūn. It was granted him, and henceforth the prince was only known as a professional musician.[3] For a time, however, musicians were banned at court, as we have seen.[4]

Ibrāhīm ibn al-Mahdī eventually became the leader of the Persian Romantic music movement, and through it there began an historic struggle between this school and that of Isḥāq al-Mauṣilī, who stood for the old Arabian traditional school. Ibrāhīm continued as favourite at court until the time of Al-Mu'taṣim. Two of his sons, Yūsuf and Hibat Allāh, published biographical notices of their illustrious father, the former going out of his way to calumniate Isḥāq al-Mauṣilī, his father's rival, an act justly condemned by the author of the great *Kitāb al-aghānī*. The other son, however, was a fount of information for the latter author. Among the most notable pupils of Ibrāhīm were Muḥammad ibn al-Ḥārith and 'Amr ibn Bāna.

Ibrāhīm ibn al-Mahdī had a magnificent voice of tremendous power,[5] with a compass of three octaves.[6] " No other singer in the world was capable of this feat," says Al-Iṣfahānī. As a theorist and instrumental performer he was of outstanding ability. The *Kitāb al-aghānī* says, " Ibrāhīm was one of the most proficient of

[1] Both Ibrāhīm al-Mauṣilī and Ibn Jāmi' acknowledged the cleverness of the young prince. *Aghānī*, ix, 51.

[2] The *Aghānī* and the *Arabian Nights* (Burton, 274th night), both say that Prince Ibrāhīm was denounced to the authorities by Ibrāhīm al-Mauṣilī. This cannot be correct, since the latter had been dead for many years.

[3] *Aghānī*, ix, 60-1.

[4] *Aghānī*, ix, 60-1.

[5] *Aghānī*, ix, 51, 72. Even Isḥāq al-Mauṣilī conceded his talents. *Aghānī*, v, 119.

[6] *Aghānī*, ix, 51.

mankind in the art of the notes (*nagham*), in the knowledge of the rhythms (*īqā'āt*), and in performing on stringed instruments." He even essayed to play the *mizmār* (reed-pipe) and the *ṭabl* (drum).[1]

Mukhāriq (d. *ca.* 845) or Abū'l-Mahannā' Mukhāriq ibn Yaḥyā,[2] was born at Al-Medīna (or Al-Kūfa), and was a slave of 'Atika bint Shudha, a famous songstress. From her, Mukhāriq received his first lessons in music, and was purchased for Faḍl al-Barmakī, who, in turn, passed him on to Hārūn. Ibrāhīm al-Mauṣilī took him as a pupil and Hārūn gave him his freedom. Soon after this he won high favour at court, was rewarded with 100,000 pieces of gold, and honoured with a seat by the side of the khalif himself.[3] Al-Amīn (809-13) had Mukhāriq at his court. One day this capricious monarch was riding in his *manège* to the music of his military band of pipes (*surnāyāt*) and drums (*ṭubūl*), and he commanded Mukhāriq to sing along with these instrumentalists. This was kept up continuously during the night, the khalif being absolutely indifferent to the fatigue of this demand.[4] Under Al-Ma'mūn (813-33), Al-Mu'tasim (833-42), and Al-Wāthiq (842-47), he remained a conspicuous favourite at court, and he appears to have died in 845. He was a close friend of the poet Abū'l-'Atāhiya, who, on his deathbed, sent for Mukhāriq, that he might hear the great singer intone those verses of his which had been set to Mukhāriq's music, beginning, "When my life closes, the sorrow of women will be short."[5] Ibn Taghrībirdī says in his *Nujūm al-zāhira* that whilst Ibrāhīm al-Mauṣilī and his son Isḥāq sang well to the accompaniment of the *'ūd*, in pure vocal work Mukhāriq outshone them both.

Muḥammad ibn al-Ḥārith ibn Buskhunr (or Buskhunnar)[6] Abū Ja'far was of foreign extraction, since his

[1] *Aghānī*, xiv, 54.
[2] Cf. Ibn Khallikān, *Biog. Dict.*, i, 18. Kosegarten, *Lib. Cant.*, 30. Von Hammer, *Lit. der Arab.*, iii, 784.
[3] *Aghānī*, viii, 20. [4] *Aghānī*, xvi, 139. See *ante*, p. 109.
[5] *Aghānī*, xxi, 220-56.
[6] Both the Būlāq and Sāsī editions of the *Aghānī* have Bashkhīr or Shakhīr, but the *Taṣḥīḥ kitāb al-aghānī* has Buskhunnar and the *Nihāyat al-arab* has Buskhunr.

family came from Al-Raiy. His father, who had been a judge (*qāḍī*), was fond of music and was noted for his singing-girls.[1] At first, Muḥammad contented himself with the "improvisation," but he became the pupil of Ibrāhīm al-Mauṣilī and we find him playing on the *mi'zafa* (? psaltery) and later on the *'ūd* (lute), which he learned from Ibrāhīm ibn al-Mahdī. When al-Ma'mūn pardoned the latter for his treachery in 817-19, he made him virtually a prisoner within the palace under the charge of the *wazīr* Muḥammad ibn Mazdād. The latter appointed Muḥammad ibn al-Ḥārith to see that the prince did not break his parole. It was this musician who was able to persuade the khalif to remove this irksome surveillance.[2] One day, however, Muḥammad sang some verses in praise of the Umayyads which so enraged the khalif that the latter ordered the imprudent musician to be beheaded, and it was with the utmost difficulty that the *wazīr* was able to stay the hand of the khalif. Muḥammad ibn al-Ḥārith appears to have lived to a ripe old age, since we find him at the court of Al-Wāthiq (842-47).[3]

Abū Ṣadaqa, or Miskīn ibn Ṣadaqa, was a minstrel of Al-Medīna. Called to the court of Hārūn (786-809), he won a considerable reputation as a story-teller as well as a musician. His talents are said to have been discovered by Ibrāhīm al-Mauṣilī. Historians say that he was particularly clever in the extemporization (*iqtirāḥ*) and in the rhythmic modes (*īqā'āt*), which, like the earlier musicians, he marked with a *qaḍīb* (wand). At a concert given before Hārūn, when most of the *virtuosi* were present, the khalif commanded that a certain song should be performed by each of them in turn. None of the renditions pleased the "Commander of the Faithful" until the *sattār* or "Guardian of the Curtain," commanded Abū Ṣadaqa to sing. At the conclusion, the khalif showered the most extravagant encomiums on this minstrel, and, drawing aside the curtain, listened to a story from the lips of Abū Ṣadaqa concerning the origin of this particular song. His son, Ṣadaqa ibn Abī Ṣadaqa, and

[1] *Aghānī*, xx, 83.
[2] *Aghānī*, x, 161-4. xx, 82.
[3] *Aghānī*, ix, 61.

his grandson, Aḥmad ibn Ṣadaqa ibn Abī Ṣadaqa, both became celebrated minstrels.[1]

'Allūyah (or 'Allawaya)[2] al-A'sr Abū'l-Ḥasan 'Alī ibn 'Abdallāh ibn Saif was a freeman of the House of Umayya. He belonged to Al-Medīna, and was a grandson of a musician named Saif, who lived in the days of Al-Walīd ibn 'Uthmān ibn 'Affān. He was taught music by Ibrāhīm al-Mauṣilī and became a skilful performer. His first court appearance was with Hārūn (786-809), who, on one occasion, punished him.[3] With Al-Amīn (809-13) he was shown some partiality, although once again punishment fell upon him. Al-Ma'mūn (813-33) also extended his patronage to 'Allūyah, and it was through the latter that Isḥāq al-Mauṣilī was re-instated in the khalif's good graces after a long estrangement.[4] When the Romantic movement, headed by Prince Ibrāhīm ibn al-Mahdī, took definite form, 'Allūyah joined this party, and he and Isḥāq al-Mauṣilī became enemies.[5] Yet after the prince's death these two great *virtuosi* patched up their differences. In the *'Iqd al-farīd*, 'Allūyah is blamed for the introduction of Persian notes into Arabian music,[6] and it was this which eventually contributed to the loss of much of the classical music of Arabia.[7] 'Allūyah died in the reign of Al-Mutawakkil (847-61).[8]

Al-Zubair ibn Daḥmān was a musician of Mecca and a freeman of the Banū Laith ibn Bakr. His father was a well-known musician of the Umayyads. Although successful in commercial life, he became enamoured with music, and in the reign of Hārūn (786-809) he was called to court. Here he took part in the rivalry between the factions of Prince Ibrāhīm and Isḥāq al-Mauṣilī, both he and his brother 'Abdallāh,[9] also a court musician, joining the former party. Iṣḥāq, however, paid a warm tribute to his ability, and Hārūn bestowed his favours. On one occasion it was a musical setting of Al-Zubair to a pre-

[1] *Aghānī*, xxi, 153-64. Al-Mas'ūdī, 342-47.
[2] See *Nihāyat al-arab*, v, Fihrist. [3] *Aghānī*, v, 45.
[4] *Aghānī*, v, 106. *'Iqd al-farīd*, iii, 188.
[5] *Aghānī*, v, 60, 64, 91.
[6] *'Iqd al-farīd*, iii, 188.
[7] *Aghānī*, i, 2. [8] *Aghānī*, x, 120-32. [9] *Aghānī*, xx, 144-5.

scribed piece of verse that carried off the prize of 20,000 pieces of silver, with twenty competitors.[1] Among his pupils was the songstress Qalam al-Ṣālaḥiyya.[2]

Isḥāq al-Mauṣilī (767-850) or in full Abū Muḥammad Isḥāq ibn Ibrāhīm al-Mauṣilī, became the chief court musician on the death of his father. Born at Al-Raiy in 767, he came to Baghdād with his father. He received a fine education, and we are told that he began his daily studies with the traditions under the guidance of Hushaim ibn Bushair. The next hour took him to Al-Kisā'ī and Al-Farrā' for the study of the *Qur'ān*. His uncle Zalzal then initiated him into the craft of the lutenist, and the science of the rhythmic modes (*īqā'āt*). He then passed into the hands of 'Atika bint Shudha, the famous songstress, who taught him her art. Finally, he closed his day's studies with Al-Aṣma'ī and Abū 'Ubaida ibn al-Muthannā, from whom he learned history and *belles lettres*.

His attainments were such that, as soon as he was old enough, he was admitted to the circle of the court minstrels by Hārūn (786-809) and the Barmakids, all of whom lavished untold wealth and unprecedented favours upon him. Each succeeding khalif seemed anxious to outdo his predecessor in paying honour to this savant musician. Much of his reputation was also due to his gifts outside of music, for his talents as a poet, *littérateur*, philologist, and jurisconsult, won deserved appreciation. Al-Ma'mūn (813-33) was so impressed that he said, "Were Isḥāq not so publicly known as a musician, I would have appointed him a judge (*qāḍī*), for he is more deserving of it than any of the judges that we now have, and he surpasses them all in virtuous conduct, piety and honesty." Al-Ma'mūn permitted Isḥāq to take his stand with *littérateurs* and savants at the court receptions (*majālis*), and not with the musicians who held a lower rank. Later, he granted him the privilege of wearing the black 'Abbāsid robes, which were reserved for legists, and he even allowed him to assist

[1] *Aghānī*, xvii, 73-8.
[2] *Aghānī*, xii, 115.

at the Friday prayer from the tribune of the khalif. Al-Wāthiq (842-47) said, "Isḥāq never yet sang to me but what I felt that my possessions were increased." When Isḥāq died in 850,[1] from the results of the Ramaḍān fast, Al-Mutawakkil (847) paid this tribute, "With the death of Isḥāq my Empire is deprived of an ornament and a glory."

As an all-round musician, Isḥāq was the greatest that Islām had produced. Although his voice was probably not so good in quality as some of his contemporaries, yet his absolute artistry gave him a decided superiority. As an instrumentalist he certainly was supreme. As a theorist, whilst he may not have been a scientific thinker like Al-Kindī, yet he was able to reduce the conflicting theories of the practice of the art to a definite system. This we are told was accomplished "without his having known a solitary book of the Ancients (*awā'il*)," meaning the Greeks. As a *littérateur* his library was one of the largest in Baghdād, and it was especially rich in Arabic lexicography.[2]

The *Fihrist* places nearly forty works to his pen, and in this monumental work, written at the close of the tenth century, Isḥāq is described as "a recorder of poetry and antiquities . . . a poet, clever in the art of music (*ghinā'*), and versatile in the sciences." Among his books on music and musicians were: *Book of Songs sung by Isḥāq*, *Book of Stories of 'Azza al-Mailā'*, *Book of the Songs of Ma'bad*, *Book of Stories of Ḥunain al-Ḥīrī*,[3] *Book of Stories of Ṭuwais*, *Book of Stories of Ibn Misjaḥ*, *Book of Stories of Al-Dalāl*, *Book of Stories of Ibn 'Ā'isha*, *Book of Stories of Al-Abjar*, *Book of the Selected Songs of Al-Wāthiq*, *Book of Dancing* (*Kitāb al-raqaṣ wa'l-zafan*), *Book of Notes and Rhythm* (*Kitāb al-nagham wa'l-īqā'*), *Book of the Singing-Girls of Al-Ḥijāz*, *Book of the Singing-Girls*, *Book of Stories of Ma'bad and Ibn Suraij and their Songs*, *Book of Stories of Al-Gharīḍ*, and the *Grand Book of Songs*. This last-named

[1] Abū'l Fidā' says 828.
[2] He allowed a pension to Ibn al-'Arabī, the lexicographer.
[3] The text has Al-Khīrī.

book, which became very popular, was not entirely from the pen of Isḥāq, but was a compilation by a bookseller named Sindī ibn 'Alī. Only the licence (*rukhṣa*) was by Isḥāq, the remaining material being selected from his other works by this editor. Biographies of Isḥāq al-Mauṣilī were written by his son Ḥammād, and by 'Alī ibn Yaḥyā ibn Abī Manṣūr, and others.[1]

Al-Khalīl ibn Aḥmad (718-791), one of the famous scholars of the Al-Baṣra school of Arabic philology, was perhaps the only great musical theorist of his day. He is universally known as the compiler of the first Arabic lexicon, the *Kitāb al-'ain*, and the systematizer of the rules of prosody. His investigations into the science of music were made public in two works—a *Kitāb al-nagham* (Book of Notes) and a *Kitāb al-īqā'* (Book of Rhythm).[2] Ḥamza ibn al-Ḥasan al-Iṣfahānī (tenth cent.) says of him, "Islām never produced a more active spirit than Al-Khalīl for the discovery of the sciences which were unknown, even in their first principles, to be learned by the Arabs."[3]

Ḥunain ibn Isḥāq al-'Ibādī, Abū Zaid (809-73), was a Christian belonging to the 'Ibād of Al-Ḥīra. In this city, where his father was an apothecary, Ḥunain received his earliest education. He then proceeded to Baghdād and became a pupil of the famous physician Yaḥyā ibn Māsawaihi. His education was completed in Asia Minor, where he learned Greek. Returning to Baghdād he entered the *Bait al-ḥikma* (College of Science) in the service of the Banū Mūsā. Later he became personal physician to Al-Mutawakkil (d. 861). Ḥunain became famous for his translations of Greek works into Syriac and Arabic.[4] It is highly probable that some of the Greek treatises on music that were known in Arabic, were his translations. We certainly know that the Arab theorists learned much of the physical and physiological aspects of the theory of

[1] *Aghānī*, v, 52-131. *Fihrist*, 141-3. *'Iqd al-farīd*, iii, 188. *Nihāyat al-arab*, v, 1-9.
[2] *Fihrist*, 43.
[3] Ibn Khallikān, *Biog. Dict.*, i, 494.
[4] *Fihrist*, 294. Ibn al-Qiftī. Ibn Abī Uṣaibi'a, i, 184. Ibn Khallikān, *Biog. Dict.*, i, 478.

sound from Ḥunain's translations of Aristotle's *De anima* (*Kitāb fī'l-nafs*), *Historia animalium* (*Kitāb al-ḥayawān*), and Galen's *De voce* (*Kitāb al-ṣaut*), although the first two had already been dealt with by Yūḥannā ibn Baṭrīq (d. 815).[1] The Staatsbibliothek at Munich possesses an Arabic MS. by Ḥunain, which contains material on music gathered from the Greeks.[2] It was also translated into Hebrew.[3]

Al-Kindī, whose full name was Abū Yūsuf Ya'qūb ibn Isḥāq al-Kindī (d. *ca.* 874), was an Arab of noble descent. He was born at Al-Baṣra about 790, and rose to favour in the days of Al-Ma'mūn (813-33) and Al-Mu'taṣim (833-42). Under the orthodox reaction in the reign of Al-Mutawakkil (847-61) his identification with the Mu'tazilites led to the confiscation of his library. Al-Kindī has been called "The Philosopher of the Arabs" by his own countrymen, since he seems to have been the first to have devoted special attention to natural phenomena from a rationalist standpoint.[4] He was a voluminous writer, and among his books on music are: a *Kitāb risālat al-kubrī fī ta'līf* (Grand Treatise on Composition), *Kitāb risāla fī tartīb al-nagham*(Treatise on the Arrangement of the Notes), *Kitāb risāla fī'l-īqā'* (Treatise on Rhythm), *Kitāb risāla fī'l-madkhal ilā ṣinā'at al-mūsīqī* (Introduction to the Art of Music), *Kitāb risāla fī khubr ṣinā'at al-ta'līf* (Information concerning the Art of Composition), *Kitāb risāla fī akhbār 'an ṣinā'at al-mūsīqī* (Stories about the Art of Music), *Mukhtaṣar al-mūsīqī fī ta'līf al-nagham wa ṣan'at al-'ūd* (Compendium of Music in the Composition of Melodies and the Art of the Lute.)[5]

Three if not four of these works have come down to us, although the titles are slightly different. In the British Museum we have a *Risāla fī khubr ta'līf al-alḥān*,[6] and the Berlin Staatsbibliothek has a *Risāla fī ijzā'*

[1] Wenrich, *De auct. Graec.*, 129, 253.
[2] No. 651 (Aumer) fols. 25, v.-39.
[3] See A. Löwenthal, *Hunain ibn Ischāqs Sinnsprüche der Philosophen ...*
[4] Steiner, *Die Mu'taziliten*, 15.
[5] *Fihrist*, 255-7. Ibn al-Qiftī, 370. Ibn Abī Uṣaibi'a, i, 210.
[6] *Brit. Mus.*, Or. 2361.

khabariyya al-mūsīqī,[1] and a *Risāla fī'l-luḥūn.*[2] Another work in this library may also be by Al-Kindī.[3] In the British Museum MS. there is another work mentioned by name—a *Kitāb al-'azm fī ta'līf al-luḥūn.*[4] Al-Kindī's treatises had a fairly considerable influence on later writers for two centuries at least.[5]

The Banū Mūsā, whose names were Muḥammad (d. 873), Aḥmad, and Al-Ḥasan, were the sons of Mūsā ibn Shākir, one of the first algebraists. They were among the most celebrated scholars of their day, and were at the *Bait al-ḥikma* (a college founded at Baghdād by Al-Ma'mūn) contemporary with Yaḥyā ibn Abī Manṣūr (d. *ca.* 831). In the *Fihrist* we read that their favourite sciences were geometry, mechanics, music, and astronomy." Ibn Khallikān also assures us that music and mechanics were among their accomplishments. Yet, not a solitary work on music is mentioned under their name in the *Fihrist,* nor by Ibn al-Qifṭī, unless the *Kitāb al-urghanun* (Book on the Organ), mentioned in another part of the *Fihrist* in connection with them, is to be placed to their credit.[6] Casiri mentions a *Liber de musica* on their account, but the treatise corresponds in the text with a *Kitāb al-qarasṭūn* which has no concern with music.[7] One musical work by the Banū Mūsā has fortunately survived. It is a treatise on automatic musical instruments, including the hydraulic organ. The MS. is preserved at the Greek Orthodox College at Bairūt known as "The Three Moons." The work is entitled *Al-ālat illatī tuzammir binafsihā* (The Instrument which Plays by Itself), the text of which has been published in the *Mashriq.*[8]

Ziryāb was the nickname of Abū'l-Ḥasan 'Alī ibn

[1] *Berlin MS.,* Ahlwardt, 5503. [2] *Berlin MS.,* Ahlwardt, 5531.
[3] *Berlin MS.,* Ahlwardt, 5530.
[4] *Brit. Mus. MS.,* Or. 2361, fol. 165, v.
[5] *Brit. Mus. MS.,* Or. 2361, fol. 229, v. [6] *Fihrist,* 285.
[7] See Dozy, *Suppl. Dict. Arabes,* sub "Qarasṭun." Suter, *Math. Verz. im Fihrist,* 20. Steinschneider, *Die Arab. Ueber.*
[8] *Fihrist,* 271. Ibn Khallikān, *Biog. Dict.,* iii, 315. Ibn al-Qifṭī, 441. Casiri, i, 418. *Al-Mashriq,* xvi, 444. See the present author's work entitled *The Organ of the Ancients from Eastern Sources,* F. Hauser's *Über das Kitāb al-ḥijal . . . der Benū Mūsā,* and *Centenario della nascitā di M. Amari,* ii, 169.

Nāfi'. It was given him "on account of his dark complexion and his eloquence of speech."[1] He was the most famous musician among the Western Arabs of Al-Andalus. We first read of him at Baghdād, as a freeman of Al-Mahdī (775-85) and a pupil of Isḥāq al-Mauṣilī, although he did not make his first appearance at court until the time of Hārūn (786-809), where his remarkable personality, quite apart from his musical talents, so struck the khalif that he was predicted as the coming master. At his first audition before Hārūn, he refused to play on the lute of his teacher, Isḥāq al-Mauṣilī, and insisted on using his own, which he said was of different structure.[2] Ziryāb soon captured Hārūn's fancy, and this aroused the jealousy of Isḥāq, who immediately gave Ziryāb to understand that he would not tolerate a rival at court, and insisted on his leaving Baghdād. It would have been folly to have defied so eminent a man as Isḥāq, and so the young minstrel emigrated to the West (North Africa), where he soon rose to fame. Whilst in the service of Ziyādat Allāh I (816-37), the Aghlabid sulṭān of Qairawān, near Tunis, he sang a song of 'Antara one day. It was the one beginning, "If my mother were as black as a crow," and the sulṭān was so furious at this verse that he had Ziryāb whipped and banished. The musician then crossed the Mediterranean and entered Al-Andalus, where the sulṭān, 'Abd al-Raḥmān II (822-52), took him into his service. So says the author of the *'Iqd al-farīd*.[3]

Al-Maqqarī says that it was in the year 821 that Ziryāb landed at Algeciras, and offered his talents to sulṭān Al-Ḥakam I (796-822), who immediately sent one of his court musicians, a Jew, Al-Manṣūr, to invite him to Cordova. Just then the sulṭān died, but his successor, 'Abd al-Raḥmān II, equally anxious to obtain Ziryāb's services, confirmed the previous invitation. Great respect was paid to Ziryāb during his journey to Cordova, and the sulṭān himself actually rode out of the city to meet

[1] Ziryāb is the name for a dark bird that has a sweet note. In Persian it stands for a solution of gold for gilding.

[2] See *ante*, p. 108.

[3] *'Iqd al-farīd*, iii, 189.

him.[1] For several months he was fêted at the palace, and finally he was lodged in a splendid mansion with a pension and emoluments amounting to 40,000 pieces of gold annually.

Ziryāb soon eclipsed all other musicians in Al-Andalus. Al-Maqqarī says, " Ziryāb was deeply versed in every branch of art connected with music, and was, moreover, gifted with such a prodigious memory that he knew by heart upwards of one thousand songs, with their appropriate airs : a greater number than that recorded [?] by Ptolemy, who established rules on the science of music, and wrote upon it." Ziryāb, like many of the other musicians, believed that the *jinn* (*genii*) taught him his songs in the middle of the night. When thus inspired, he would call his two favourite singing-girls, Ghazzālan and Hīnda, and bid them commit to memory the music which had come to him by these means.

Like Isḥāq al-Mauṣilī, the great Ziryāb " had a deep acquaintance with the various branches of polite literature. He was likewise learned in astronomy and in geography."[2] Indeed, his accomplishments were such that Al-Maqqarī says, " There never was, either before or after him, a man of his profession who was more generally beloved and admired." He introduced *plectra* of eagles' talons instead of those of wood, and added a fifth string to the lute.[3] His greatest fame was made through his Music School at Cordova, which became the conservatory of Andalusian music,[4] and its pupils were looked upon as one of the glories of the country.[5] The date of Ziryāb's death is not recorded, but it is doubtful whether he lived later than the reign of Muḥammad (852-86). His sons and daughters became well-known musicians.

Al-Andalus had a few other well-known musicians who deserve mention.

[1] Ibn Khaldūn, *Prolegomena*, ii, 361.

[2] This was requisite for those who taught the influence of the " Music of the Spheres " and its cosmical potency. See my *Influence of Music : From Arabic Sources*.

[3] Al-Maqqarī, *Moh. Dyn.*, ii, 116-21.

[4] *Ibid.*, ii, 117. Von Hammer, *op. cit.*, iv, 727.

[5] Ibn Khaldūn, ii, 361.

'Alūn and Zarqūn were "the first of the musicians who entered Al-Andalus [from the East] in the days of Al-Ḥakam I (796-822), and they were maintained by him [at his court]." They became the most eminent of the *virtuosi* until Ziryāb came and wrested the laurels from them.[1]

'Abbās ibn al-Nasā'ī was the chief musician at the court of Al-Ḥakam I, and he is mentioned as the singer of the songs of this sulṭān.

Al-Manṣūr was a Jewish musician who stood high in favour at the court of Al-Ḥakam I. It was he who was sent to conduct Ziryāb to Cordova.[2]

Among the minor musicians in the Baghdād khalifate at this period were the following:

Muḥammad ibn Ḥamza Abū Ja'far was a freeman of Al-Manṣūr (754-75). He was a pupil of Ibrāhīm al-Mauṣilī and was counted "among the foremost of the singers, players, and story-tellers of the day." He was at the court of Hārūn (786-809).[3]

Ismā'īl ibn al-Harbidh was a freeman of the Banū Zubair ibn al-'Awwām or the Banū Kināna, and he sang at the courts from the time of Al-Walīd II (743-4) to Hārūn.[4]

Sulaim ibn Sallām Abū 'Abdallāh belonged to Al-Kūfa, and was an intimate friend of Abū Muslim and Ibrāhīm al-Mauṣilī. He possessed "an excellent voice."[5]

Barṣaumā al-Zāmir was a pupil of Ibrāhīm al-Mauṣilī and a talented performer on the *zamr* or *mizmār* (reed-pipe). He seems to have been trusted as a critic of contemporary musicians by Hārūn.[6]

Zunām was also a famous performer on the *mizmār*, and he is mentioned in the 18th *maqāma* of Al-Ḥarīrī, as a well-known musician. He was also the inventor of a reed-pipe called the *nāy zunāmī* or *nāy zulāmī*, as the Western Arabs misnamed it. He was at the courts of Hārūn, Al-Mu'taṣim and Al-Wāthiq.[7]

[1] *Ibid.* [2] Al-Maqqari, *Analectes*, ii, 85.
[3] *Aghānī*, v, 45. xvi, 226.
[4] *Aghānī*, vi, 150. [5] *Aghānī*, vi, 12-15.
[6] *Aghānī*, v, 34. vi, 12. *'Iqd al-farīd*, iii, 188. He is called Jūssūn by Von Hammer, *Lit. der Arab.*, iii, 766, and Fétis, ii, 14.
[7] Steingass, *Assemblies of Ḥarīrī*, i, 137. Chenery, *Assemblies of Al-Ḥarīrī*, 209. Cf. *Ency. of Islām*, ii, 136.

Muḥammad ibn 'Amr al-Raff (or al-Ziqq) was a freeman of the Banū Tamīm and came from Al-Kūfa. He was a fine performer on the *'ūd*, and a man of handsome appearance. He was a partisan of Ibrāhīm al-Mauṣilī against the rival clique of Ibn Jāmi'.[1]

'Amr al-Ghazzāl,[2] Al-Ḥusain ibn Muḥriz,[3] Muḥammad ibn Dā'ūd ibn Ismā'īl,[4] and 'Abd al-Raḥīm ibn Faḍl al-Daffāf,[5] were at Hārūn's court, whilst Ma'bad al-Yaqṭīnī,[6] Ja'far al-Ṭabbāl,[7] and Abū Zakkār[8] were the favoured minstrels of the Barmakids.

The singing-girls and songstresses of the "Golden Age" were even more famous than those of the Umayyad days, as we know from the pages of *The Thousand and One Nights*, although, strange to say, most of the names handed down in this entertaining work have no place in the *Kitāb al-aghānī*, *Nihāyat al-arab*, and kindred works.

Baṣbaṣ ("Caress") was a half-caste singing-girl of Yaḥyā ibn Nafīs, who was famed for his concerts at Al-Medīna. Here 'Abdallāh ibn Muṣ'ab heard Baṣbaṣ sing, which led him to compose verses specially for her. It was these verses that so charmed Khalif Al-Manṣūr (754-75) that he learned them by heart. Ibn Khurdādhbih avers that Al-Mahdī (775-85) bought Baṣbaṣ from Yaḥyā whilst he was a prince for 17,000 pieces of gold. Whilst she was at Al-Medīna she was the idol of the Quraish, and her beauty was praised by the poets.[9]

'Uraib (d. 841) was a songstress who had a most extraordinary career, which deserves recording as it gives an insight into the social life of the period. Handsome, accomplished as poetess, writer and musician, 'Uraib won a tremendous reputation. She "surpassed all the songstresses of Al-Ḥijāz and was particularly skilful in the art and science of the notes (*nagham*), and stringed

[1] *Aghānī*, xiii, 19-22. See Guidi, 601.
[2] *Aghānī*, xi, 34. xx, 64. [3] *Aghānī*, vi, 12. xiii, 9.
[4] *Aghānī*, iii, 57. xxi, 226.
[5] *Aghānī*, iii, 80-81. See Guidi, 435.
[6] *Aghānī*, xii, 168-70. *Nihāyat al-arab*, v, 13.
[7] *Aghānī*, xiv, 54.
[8] *Aghānī*, vi, 212. Al-Mas'ūdī, vi, 359. Ibn Khallikān, i, 317.
[9] *Aghānī*, xiii, 114-18. *Nihāyat al-arab*, v, 70.

instruments (*awtār*)." She is ranked with 'Azza al-Mailā' and Jamīla of old. Isḥāq al-Mauṣilī said that he knew of no better performer on the *'ūd* (lute), nor a more gracious or artistic woman. She is credited with knowing 21,000 melodies by heart. Her first owner was 'Abdallāh ibn Ismā'īl, Captain of the Galleys under Hārūn, but she fled with a lover to Baghdād. Here she sang in the public gardens, but was discovered and compelled to return to her master. She was then acquired by Al-Amīn (809-13), and at his death she reverted to her old proprietor, but again fled with a lover, who married her. Al-Ma'mūn (813-33) then possessed her, and at his court she held a high place as a musician. Under Al-Mu'taṣim (833) she was still captivating all hearts and minds by her beauty and accomplishments. She died in 841. Al-Mu'tamid (870-92) ordered a collection of her songs to be made.[1]

'Ubaida, surnamed al-Ṭunbūriyya, was "one of the best of the songstresses and the foremost of them in art and literature." Isḥāq al-Mauṣilī said, "In the art of *ṭunbūr* playing, anyone who seeks to go beyond 'Ubaida makes mere noise." Jaḥẓa al-Barmakī, the historian of the ṭunbūrists, remarked that 'Ubaida was "an excellent musician and a remarkable *virtuoso*." She received her first lessons from a certain Al-Zubaidī al-Ṭunbūrī, who used to stay at her father's house. On her parents' death she became a public singer, visiting all and sundry for a few coins. She was then acquired by a certain 'Alī ibn al-Faraj al-Zajḥī, by whom she had a daughter. Divorced, she entered the household of a cadet of the family of Ḥamza ibn Mālik, himself a good singer and a performer on the *mi'zafa* (? psaltery). Her cleverness as an instrumentalist was generally acknowledged. At a concert given in the presence of the most celebrated ṭunbūrist of his day, Masdūd, the latter refused to play in front of "a mistress of the musical art" like 'Ubaida. Jaḥẓa al-Barmakī possessed her *ṭunbūr*, and underneath the neck was written, "In love one can endure almost

[1] *Aghānī*, xviii, 175-91. *Nihāyat al-arab*, v, 92, where the name is vocalized as *'Arīb*.

anything except faithlessness." The instrument had been given her by Ja'far ibn al-Ma'mūn. 'Ubaida seems only to have been true to her art.[1]

Shāriyya was a native of Al-Baṣra, her father belonging to the Banū Sāma ibn Lu'ai, and her mother to the Banū Zuhra a branch of the Quraish. In spite of her origin, she was put up for the highest bidder by her mother, and was purchased by Ibrāhīm ibn al-Mahdī. He had her taught by the best singing-girls in his household, including the famous Raiq (" Bloom of Youth "), and he then made a present of her to his daughter, Maimūna. The prince afterwards freed her, and made her his wife. Al-Mu'taṣim (833-42) was annoyed at this, but Ibrāhīm argued that she was one of the Quraish. On the death of Ibrāhīm she entered the *ḥarīm* of Al-Mu'taṣim and remained at court under several khalifs. Muḥammad ibn al-Ḥārith, asked his opinion of the respective merits of Prince Ibrāhīm and Shāriyya as musicians, awarded the palm to the latter. One of her best pupils was Farīda.[2]

Badhl (" Gift ") was a songstress of Al-Medīna who flourished at the courts from Al-Amīn (809-13) to Al-Mu'taṣim (833-42). She belonged at first to Ja'far ibn al-Hādī, but Al-Amīn, having heard her sing, begged his cousin to sell her to him. Ja'far replied, " Men of rank do not sell their slaves." Finally, however, Al-Amīn obtained her. She was a most accomplished *artiste*, Fulaiḥ ibn Abī'l-'Aurā' having been one of her teachers. She had a prodigious memory and boasted of a repertory of 30,000 songs. So perfect was her knowledge of the songs that even Isḥāq al-Mauṣilī stood abashed. Abū Ḥashīsha, the musical biographer, says that in the time of Al-Ma'mūn (813-33) she composed a *Kitāb al-aghānī* (Book of Songs) of some 12,000 specimens for 'Alī ibn Hishām. This resulted in a reward of 10,000 pieces of silver. She left a large fortune.[3] Among her pupils were Danānīr and Mutayyim al-Hāshimiyya [4]

[1] *Aghānī*, xix, 134-7. *Nihāyat al-arab*, v, iii. Written '*Abīda* by Guidi, 355, but cf. 500.
[2] *Aghānī*, xiv, 109-14. *Nihāyat al-arab*, v, 80.
[3] *Aghānī*, xv, 144-7. *Nihāyat al-arab*, v, 85.
[4] *Aghānī*, vii, 31-8. xvi, 136.

Danānīr (" Wealth "), surnamed al-Barmakiyya, was a slave of a man of Al-Medīna, who sold her to Yaḥyā ibn Khālid al-Barmakī, who set her free. She was well-educated and was a gifted poetess. Among her music teachers were Ibrāhīm al-Mauṣilī, Isḥāq al-Mauṣilī, Ibn Jāmi', Fulaiḥ, and Badhl. She sang before Hārūn (786-809) and was the authoress of a *Kitāb mujarrad al-aghānī* (Book of Choice Songs).[1] She refused to marry the court musician 'Aqīl, on the ground that she could not ally herself with a second-rate performer.[2]

'Ātika bint Shuhda[3] was the daughter of Shuhda, the famous songstress at the court of Al-Walīd II (743-44). Like her mother, she was an excellent singer, and Yaḥyā ibn 'Alī, the musical theorist, said that she was one of the best of people in singing. At the court of Hārūn (786-809) she was a great favourite, and among her pupils were Isḥāq al-Mauṣilī and Mukhāriq.[4]

Mutayyim (" Enslaving ") al-Hāshimiyya[5] was a free-woman of Al-Baṣra, where she lived all her life. Taught by Ibrāhīm al-Mauṣilī and his son Isḥāq, and Badhl, she became a well-known singer and poetess. She was acquired by 'Alī ibn Hishām and became the mother of his children. Both Al-Ma'mūn (813-33) and Al-Mu'taṣim (833-42) had heard her sing.[6]

Qalam al-Ṣāliḥiyya was a singing-girl of Ṣāliḥ ibn 'Abd al-Wahhāb. She was counted " a clever singer and performer," and was bought from this man by Al-Wāthiq (842-7) for 10,000 pieces of gold.[7]

Dhāt al-Khāl (" Mistress of the Beauty Spot ") was originally purchased by Hārūn (786-809) for 70,000 pieces of silver, but was afterwards given to his favourite slave, Ḥammawaihi, in marriage. On her husband's death she re-entered the *ḥarīm* of Hārūn, and she was one of the three favourites that the poets sang about, the other two being Siḥr (" Charm ") and Ḍiyā' (" Splendour ").[8]

[1] *Aghānī*, xvi, 136-9. *Nihāyat al-arab*, v, 90.
[2] Von Hammer and Fétis have *'Aqīd.*
[3] Kosegarten writes Shahda. *Lib. Cant.*, 22. [4] *Aghānī*, vi, 57-8.
[5] Kosegarten writes Hishāmiyya. *Lib. Cant.*, 29.
[6] *Aghānī*, vii, 31-8. *Nihāyat al-arab*, v, 62.
[7] *Aghānī*, xii, 115-17. *Nihāyat al-arab*, v, 68.
[8] *Aghānī*, xv, 79, 80. *Nihāyat al-arab*, v, 88.

'Inān was another singing-girl who captivated Hārūn. She was formerly in the service of a certain Al-Naṭifī. One day when the khalif had heard one of her verses recited by a court minstrel, he approached her owner with a view to purchase. The price was 30,000 pieces of gold. Al-Aṣma'ī said that Hārūn was never infatuated with anyone more than with 'Inān.[1]

Other singing-girls of passing note were: Ḥasana,[2] Raiq,[3] Daman,[4] Wahba,[5] Dufāq,[6] Samḥa,[7] and Qumriyya.[8]

In Al-Andalus there were some famous songstresses. Afzā was the favourite singing-girl of 'Abd al-Raḥmān I (756-88). She was purchased in the Orient, and was considered "the most excellent of people in music (*ghinā*)."[9]

Faḍl was originally in the service of a daughter of Hārūn at Baghdād, but later went to Al-Medīna, and from there she journeyed with a companion 'Alam, to Al-Andalus, and became famous at the court of 'Abd al-Raḥmān II (822-52). We are told that she excelled in music (*ghinā*).[10]

Qalam was a Biscayan songstress who was obtained by 'Abd al-Raḥmān II. She is spoken of as a scholar, an excellent scribe, a historian of poetry, a reciter of stories, well versed in the various forms of polite literature, and "devoted to music (*al-samā'*)."[11]

Muṣābiḥ was a singing-girl of Abū Ḥafṣ 'Umar ibn Qalhīl of Al-Andalus. In music she is said to have reached "the highest point of excellence and skill, together with sweetness of voice." Ibn 'Abd Rabbihi has a poem in her honour. She had Ziryāb as a teacher.[12]

Mut'a was another of Ziryāb's pupils, and when she grew up she so captivated the sulṭān, 'Abd al-Raḥmān II (822), that Ziryāb presented her to him.[13]

[1] *Aghānī*, x, 101. xx, 76. *'Iqd al-farīd*, iii, 199. *Nihāyat al-arab*, v, 75.
[2] *Aghānī*, xii, 108.
[3] *Aghānī*, iii, 184. Rīq in Kosegarten, *Lib. Cant.*, 29.
[4] *Aghānī*, v, 58-9.
[5] *Aghānī*, xiii, 126.
[6] *Aghānī*, xi, 98-100. *Nihāyat al-arab*, v. 67. In the latter as in Kosegarten and Von Hammer, she is called Duqāq.
[7] *Aghānī*, iii, 115.
[8] *Aghānī*, vi, 17.
[9] Al-Maqqarī, *Analectes*, ii, 97-8. *Aghānī*, xx, 148, 149.
[10] Al-Maqqarī, *Analectes*, ii, 96.
[11] *Ibid*, i, 225.
[12] Al-Maqqarī, *Analectes*, ii, 90.
[13] *Ibid.*

CHAPTER VI

THE 'ABBĀSIDS

(The Decline, 847–945)

"I like the man who cultivates poetry for self-instruction, not for lucre, and the man who practises music for pleasure, not for gain."
Ibn Muqla (10th cent.).[1]

By this time the Khalifate had begun to reveal signs of serious political decline. One of the causes of this decay was the rise of the Turkish soldiery, who played a part in the history of the Khalifate similar to that of the Prætorian guards in the Roman decline. They had been brought to Baghdād by Al-Ma'mūn (813-33) so as to counterbalance the influence of the Khurāsānī mercenaries,[2] and by the time of Al-Mu'taṣim (833-42) the entire standing army of the khalif comprised these soldiers, the Arabs, both officers and men, who had been displaced, having retired to their tribes, where they were to become "a chronic element of disturbance and revolt."[3] The Turks, whose numbers were ever on the increase, soon became masters of the Khalifate, and from the accession of Al-Mu'tazz (862) to the coming of the Buwaihids (945) the very succession to the Khalifate was determined by these people.[4] There can be but little doubt that the domination of these mercenaries contributed seriously to the decline of the political Khalifate.

Side by side with this military tyranny and political decadence, there was a revival of a bigoted orthodoxy in Islām that brought about a corresponding intellectual and artistic retrogression, which played no small part

[1] Ibn Khallikān, Biog. Dict., iii, 270.
[2] Muir, *Caliphate*, 511.
[3] Muir, *op. cit.*, 513.
[4] Muir, *op. cit.*, 531.

in the general decline. The first century of 'Abbāsid rule, as Professor R. A. Nicholson points out, was marked by a great intellectual agitation. Rationalism and free-thought were "in the air," and these ideas had official support from the time of Al-Ma'mūn (813-33). When Al-Mutawakkil (847-61) became khalif, orthodoxy was re-established, and all forms of heresy were suppressed with the utmost rigour and cruelty.[1] During the whole of this period practically, the Ḥanbalī sect dominated. A regular inquisition—spilling wine and destroying forbidden musical instruments, to say nothing of executions and imprisonments—was in full swing. Whilst the Khalifate was pampering "religious men without intelligence" as Abū'l-'Alā al-Ma'arrī would say, and persecuting "intelligent men without religion," the finest civilization of the Middle Ages was slipping away.

We have already seen that Al-Andalus in the West had claimed its own sulṭān, an Umayyad, since 755, and the disintegration of the Empire was to follow swiftly on this event, although not connected causally with it. First there came Idrīs, a great-grandson of Khalif 'Alī, who raised the Idrīsids of Morocco (788-985) to independence. The rest of North Africa accepted this lead when the Aghlabids (800-909) set up their kingdom at Qairawān near Tunis, who, in turn, were succeeded by the Fāṭimids (909-972). In Egypt and Syria, the Ṭūlūnids (868-905) took control, and were succeeded (save for a brief interval when the khalif asserted his authority) by the Ikhshīdids (935-969).

In the East, matters were almost as bad, for the various provinces, Khurāsān, Ṭabaristān, Persia, Transoxiana, and Jurjān, had become practically independent (making a mere nominal acknowledgment to the khalif) under the Ṭāhirids (820-72), 'Alīds (864-928), Ṣaffārids (868-903), Sāmānids (874-999), and the Ziyārids (928-976) respectively. Nearer home, 'Uman had long since acknowledged its own *imām*. Al-Yaman claimed its own rulers in the Ziyādids (819-1018) of Zabīd, and the Ya'furids (861-997) of Ṣan'a and Janad, whilst the

[1] Al-Ṭabarī, iii, 1389, *seq.*

Ḥamdānids ruled in Mesopotamia (929-91) and Syria (944-1003). By the end of the period under consideration all that was left to the khalif, save nominal allegiance, was the capital, and even here, as Muir remarks, how little was the authority of the "Commander of the Faithful." Still, he was the spiritual head of this loosely-held empire, and Baghdād was the centre of Islāmic culture in the East, although it was Cordova that counted in the West.

§ I

Al-Mutawakkil (847-61), the first khalif of the decline, opened his reign with an official return to orthodoxy, and Aḥmad ibn Ḥanbal, the founder of the narrowest and least spiritual of the four orthodox sects,[1] became the chief theologian. There then began the terrors of an inquisition, details of which may be read in Al-Ṭabarī and Ibn al-Athīr. The philosopher and music theorist, Al-Kindī, had his library confiscated, whilst the renowned physician, Bukht-Yishū', was despoiled of his possessions and banished. It is not surprising therefore "how comparatively small is the number of writers and scholars of eminence who flourished in Al-Mutawakkil's time." Among the few writers on music were Al-Kindī and Ibn Khurdādhbih. The practice of music, however, was scarcely interfered with, for the khalif was a great lover of the art, and gave constant public encouragement to its professors.[2] His son, Abū 'Īsā 'Abdallāh, was an accomplished musician who composed some three hundred songs.[3] His *wazīr*, Muḥammad ibn Faḍl al-Jarjarā'ī, was also "celebrated for his musical talents."[4]

The khalif built a gorgeous palace away from Sāmarrā, now the official capital, which he called the Ja'fariyya, after himself. It was "crowded with every means of enjoyment, *music*, *song*, and gay divertissement."[5] Here the khalif encouraged the *virtuosi*—Isḥāq al-Mauṣilī, Aḥmad ibn Yaḥyā al-Makkī, Muḥammad ibn al-Ḥārith,

[1] Browne, E. G., *Literary History of Persia*, i, 344.
[2] Al-Mas'ūdī, vi, 191.
[3] *Aghānī*, ix, 104.
[4] *Fakhrī*, 413
[5] Muir, *Caliphate*, 528. Cf. Al-Mas'ūdī, vii, 192.

'Amr ibn Bāna, 'Abdallāh ibn al-'Abbās al-Rabī'ī, Aḥmad ibn Ṣadaqa, 'Ath'ath al-Aswād, Al-Ḥasan al-Masdūd, and Ibn al-Māriqī, as well as the songstresses—'Uraib, Shāriyya, Farīda, and his favourite Maḥbūba. He was most generous to them all,[1] but, as Muir says, it " makes but sorry amends for a life of cruel tyranny, bigotry, and self-indulgence."[2]

Al-Muntaṣir (861-2) had but a short reign. He was both a poet and musician himself, and the words of his songs have been preserved in the great *Kitāb al-aghānī*, where a chapter is devoted to him.[3] His favourite minstrel at court was Bunān ibn 'Amr [al-Ḥārith], who sang his compositions. Another to whom he was partial was Al-Ḥasan al-Masdūd. We read of his singing-girls in the *Murūj al-dhahab* of Al-Mas'ūdī.[4]

Al-Musta'īn (862-66) has left no record of his musical tastes. One of his governors, however, Muḥammad ibn 'Abdallāh ibn Ṭāhir (d. 867), was a great patron of music. One day he was asked by Abū'l-'Abbās al-Makkī, just before a concert, what he considered was the best music (*samā'*). He replied, " The best music is that of the four strings [the *'ūd*] when it accompanies a good song rendered by a perfect voice."[5]

Al-Mu'tazz (866-69) was also a musician and a poet, as we know from the great *Kitāb al-aghānī* which registers some of his songs.[6] Among his favourite minstrels were : Bunān ibn 'Amr [al-Ḥārith] and Sulaimān ibn al-Qaṣṣār, the latter a fine ṭunbūrist. Shāriyya and Jahā'ī were his two special songstresses. His son 'Abdallāh, a most accomplished musician,[7] took part in the musical discussions at the court of Al-Wāthiq.[8] This prince wrote a book on the songstress Shāriyya, and a *Kitāb al-badī'* (Book of Poetics), the first treatise of its kind.[9] He was called to the throne in 908 on the death of Al-Muktafī, but was murdered the same day by the partisans of Al-Muqtadir.

Al-Muhtadī (869-70) was a son of the artistic Al-Wāthiq,

[1] Al-Mas'ūdī, vii, 276.
[2] Muir, *op. cit.*, 530.
[3] *Aghānī*, viii, 175-8.
[4] Al-Mas'ūdī, vii, 297.
[5] Al-Mas'ūdī, vii, 347.
[6] *Aghānī*, viii, 178.
[7] *Aghānī*, ix, 140.
[8] *Aghānī*, v, 97.
[9] *Aghānī*, xiv, 109.

but he inherited neither his father's culture nor his toleration. He took the pious Umayyad khalif 'Umar II as his model, and the court was speedily transformed. First of all he placed an interdict on music.[1] " Singing-girls and musicians were expelled ; beasts in the menagerie slaughtered, and hounds turned adrift . . . wine and games proscribed ; and a frugal household."[2] It mattered little, for he was murdered as were his four predecessors.[3]

Al-Mu'tamid (870-92), under the impulsion of his brother, Al-Muwaffaq, was the first of the khalifs of the decline to attempt to stem the tyranny of the Turkish faction. The removal of the court back to Baghdād helped to accomplish this to some extent. The khalif was a musician himself, and he brought the musicians and singing-girls back to the court now held in the Ma'mūnī palace, or as it was now called, the Ḥasanī, so eloquently described by Yāqūt.[4] This khalif, says Al-Mas'ūdī, was appassioned for musical instruments (*malāhī*). Ibn Khurdādhbih, the geographer and writer on music, was favoured by him, and it is to his oration on music before this khalif that we owe some of our knowledge of the early musical history of the Arabs and Persians,[5] and to a songstress of his court for a description of the dances and dance rhythms of the period.[6] Among the newcomers to be favoured among the court *virtuosi* was Muḥammad ibn Aḥmad ibn Yaḥyā al-Makkī. Shāriyya too was still in good graces at court.[7] It was Al-Mu'tamid who commanded that a collection of the songs of 'Uraib be made.[8] One of his own songs in the *khafīf thaqīl* rhythm, set to the words of Al-Farazdaq, is given in the great *Kitāb al-aghānī*.[9]

Al-Mu'taḍid (892-902), although strictly orthodox and a bigot who interdicted philosophical works, favoured music and intellectual culture. When he was a prince

[1] *Fakhrī*, 427. [2] Muir, *Caliphate*, 539.
[3] Al-Muntaṣir however, *may* have died a natural death.
[4] Yāqūt, i, 806-9.
[5] Al-Mas'ūdī, viii, 88-89. See my *Studies in Oriental Musical Instruments*, chap. v.
[6] Al-Mas'ūdī, viii, 100. [7] *Aghānī*, xiv, 113.
[8] *Aghānī*, xviii, 176. [9] *Aghānī*, viii, 186.

he was noted for his marvellous voice.[1] He had 'Ubaidallāh ibn 'Abdallāh ibn Ṭāhir as his " boon companion," and this latter was the author of a *Kitāb fī'l-nagham* (Book on the Notes).[2] He anathematized all who even mentioned the name of the Umayyads in ordinary public affairs, yet he would listen for hours to a song by the Umayyad khalif Al-Walīd II, when sung by his favourite minstrel Aḥmad ibn 'Abdallāh ibn Abī'l-'Alā'.[3] At the same time, he had the philosopher and music theorist Al-Sarakhsī put to death for a political offence.[4] Al-Mu'taḍid held splendid courts at the Firdaus and Thurayyā palaces, which had been built by him.

Al-Muktafī (902-08) was a son of the preceding. We know nothing of his musical preferences save that 'Ubaidallāh ibn 'Abdallāh ibn Ṭāhir still continued to be one of the " boon companions,"[5] an honour shared with another music theorist—Yaḥyā ibn 'Alī ibn Yaḥyā ibn Abī Manṣūr. The Baghdād hospital at this time was under the direction of the famous Abū Bakr Muḥammad ibn Zakariyyā al-Rāzī (Rhazes) who was also a music theorist. Under this khalif the Empire became more secure than it had been for many years.

Al-Muqtadir (908-32) was but "a weak voluptuary in the hands of women of the court and their favourites."[6] Baghdād was still in the control of the Turkish soldiery who held the khalif at their mercy, whilst the orthodox party terrorized all and sundry who disagreed with their opinions.[7] Yet the khalif maintained brilliant and pompous courts at his new palaces, the Shajara and Muḥdith, and possessed no fewer than 11,000 eunuchs.[8] Spending his days and nights with musicians and singing-girls,[9] he made no attempt to check the excesses of the lawless soldiery or the intolerant theologians, with the result that he left a legacy of anarchy to his successors. Miskawaihi says that he "avoided male companions—even minstrels."[10] On the other hand, several male

[1] *Aghānī*, viii, 196.
[2] *Aghānī*, viii, 44, 45.
[3] *Aghānī*, viii, 88.
[4] Al-Mas'ūdī, viii, 179.
[5] *Aghānī*, viii, 54.
[6] Muir, *Caliphate*, 565.
[7] Muir, *Caliphate*, 567-8.
[8] *Fakhrī*, 449.
[9] Muir, *op.cit.*, 566.
[10] *The Eclipse of the 'Abbāsid Caliphate*, i, 13.

minstrels are mentioned at his court in the great *Kitāb al-aghānī*, and among them—Jaḥẓa al-Barmakī, Ibrāhīm ibn Abī'l-'Ubais, Ibrāhīm ibn al-Qāsim ibn Zurzūr, Waṣīf al-Zāmir, and Kanīz.[1] One of his favourite singing-girls was Ṣalifa.

Al-Qāhir (932), Al-Rāḍī (934), Al-Muttaqī (940), and Al-Mustakfī (944-46) were the next khalifs. Little need be said of them. Mere puppets in the hands of the Turkish soldiery, worse even than their predecessors, they wielded little or no authority. Their elevation to the thone depended upon the whims of the mercenaries. Three of these khalifs were deposed by them and blinded. Al-Rāḍī, the only one who died as khalif, is generally spoken of as "the last of the real khalifs," i.e., the last to deliver the Friday orations, and to conduct the affairs of state like the khalifs of old. He was also the last khalif whose poetry has been preserved.[2]

Yet in spite of these trials and tribulations, music still flourished at the courts.[3] Al-Qāhir made a show of "orthodoxy," and forbade wine, male musicians, songstresses and *mukhannathūn*. These individuals were arrested and sent to Al-Baṣra and Al-Kūfa. At the same time, Al-Qāhir himself indulged in music, and had as many songstresses as he liked.[4]

So far the state of music at the Baghdād court, the hub of the Eastern world. Yet we cannot ignore the influence of the many independent dynasties, "whose courts often became *foci* for learning and literature [and music], more apt in many ways to discover and stimulate local talent than a distant and unsympathetic metropolis."[5] It was the Sāmānids of Transoxiana who protected the scientist and music theorist Muḥammad ibn Zakariyyā al-Rāzī (Rhazes), and later fostered Ibn Sīnā, as well as the minstrel Rūdakī, who is sometimes claimed as the first Persian poet. In Syria, the Ḥamdānids patronized the philosopher and music theorist

[1] *Aghānī*, v, 22.
[2] *Fakhrī*, 484. Muir, *op. cit.*, 571.
[3] *Aghānī*, xv, 99.
[4] *The Eclipse of the 'Abbāsid Caliphate*, i, 269.
[5] Browne, *Lit. Hist. of Persia*, i, 339-40.

Al-Fārābī, and in their dominions there flourished the music historians Al-Iṣfahānī and Al-Mas'ūdī. In Egypt the Ṭūlūnids were the first under the Arab domination to make the land famed for its art, and the court for its wealth and splendour. Khumārawaih married his daughter to the Khalif Al-Mu'tamid, and spent one million pieces of gold on the event. He had such an inordinate appreciation for music and singers that his palace was adorned with portraits of his songstresses, in spite of the ban of Islām against portraiture.[1] The Ikhshīdids who succeeded the Ṭūlūnids were equally favourable to music and *belles lettres* (witness Al-Mutanabbī). If the court of the regent (*ustād*) Abū'l-Misk Kāfūr was resplendent for its music and musicians so were the *fêtes* of the people. Al-Mas'ūdī who visited Al-Fusṭāṭ in 942, describes a *fête* in which he heard music on all sides, with singing and dancing.[2]

More important still perhaps was the culture influence of Al-Andalus in the West. Here, rulers were equally anxious to patronize music, literature and science. During the reigns of Muḥammad I (852-86), Al-Mundhir (886-88), and 'Abdallāh (888-912), we see the arts flourishing, and science in the ascendant.[3] The last named khalif was, however, prejudiced against music.

"The learned of Al-Andalus," says Ṣā'id ibn Aḥmad (d. 1069), "exerted themselves in the cultivation of science and laboured in it with assiduity, giving evident proofs of their acquisitions in all manner of learning."[4] In the science of music, the first-fruit of this was Ibn Firnās (d. 888).[5]

At the same time, independent dynasties had sprung up in Al-Andalus as in the East. These petty rulers, who gave mere nominal allegiance to the sulṭān at Cordova, vied with each other not only for temporal, but for artistic and cultural superiority. The *amīr*

[1] Al-Maqrīzī, *Al-Mawā'iẓ* (Būlāq edit.), 316, 317. S. Lane-Poole, *A Hist. of Egypt in the Middle Ages*, 74.
[2] Al-Mas'ūdī, *Prairies d'or*, ii, 364-5.
[3] Casiri, ii, 34.
[4] Al-Maqqarī, *Moh. Dyn.*, i, 140, and Appendix xl.
[5] Aḥmad Zākī Bāshā, *L'Aviation chez les Musulmans* (Cairo, 1912).

of Cazlona, 'Ubaidallāh ibn Umayya, was distinguished for his patronage of minstrelsy and the arts in general, whilst Ibrāhīm ibn al-Ḥajjāj (d. 900), who ruled at Seville, was the envy of the land on account of his poets and musicians. He brought scholars from Arabia and singing-girls from Baghdād, including the famous Qamar.[1]

The next sulṭān of Cordova, 'Abd al-Raḥmān III (912-61), put an end to the independence of the petty chiefs. His reign is cited as the most illustrious in the history of Al-Andalus,[2] and he was the first of its rulers to adopt the title of khalif. "Except perhaps Byzantium," says Stanley Lane-Poole, "no city in Europe could compare with Cordova in the beauty of her buildings, the luxury and refinement of her life, and the learning and accomplishments of her inhabitants."[3] The famous Ibn 'Abd Rabbihi, the author of the *'Iqd al-farīd*, which has been freely drawn upon in these pages, was court poet to this sulṭān.

§ II

We now come to a period when alien influences reveal themselves more clearly in Arabian music. Ever since the accession of the 'Abbāsids (750), the influx of Persian notions, especially those of Khurāsān, persisted in general culture. The rise of the Sāmānids further east, exercised additional weight in the balance in favour of Iranian art. From the opening of the "Decline" (847) Turkish ideas found slight acceptance in Al-'Irāq, and with the supremacy of the Ṭūlūnids (867) these were extended to Egypt. Equally important perhaps was the impression created by the great strides made in the translation of the ancient Greek writers on music. How far all this flux was to change the course of Arabian music we shall see. Yet we must remember that if the Arabs borrowed from the Persians, the Persians too owed a weightier debt to the Arabs, not only for Islām, but for their sciences, philosophy, and *belles lettres*. As Noeldeke says, "Hellenism never touched more than the surface of Persian life,

[1] Al-Maqqarī, *Analectes*, ii, 97.
[2] Dozy, *Hist. des musul.*, iii, 90.
[3] Lane-Poole, *The Moors in Spain*, 129, 139.

but Iran was penetrated to the core by Arabian religion and Arabian ways."[1]

During the opening of this period, science and philosophy were proscribed. Scientists were punished, libraries of suspected individuals were seized and even destroyed, and booksellers were forbidden to sell anything but orthodox literature. Precisely the same plague of intolerance swept over Al-Andalus, and although it raged here for a shorter spell, the damage to be assessed in the actual destruction of books is probably greater in the latter case. The practice, and perhaps the science of music, alone escaped the fury of the orthodox reaction, and only one of the khalifs had either the courage or inclination to hurl *anathema* at it, and that was Al-Muhtadī. The theologians, it would appear, dared not interfere with the pleasures of the court and the Turkish officers. It would have been almost as futile as asking them not to breathe as to suggest that they should not indulge in music. However, the tendency of the age is well expressed in the literature of Abū Bakr ibn 'Abdallāh ibn Abī'l-Dunyā (823-94), the tutor of Al-Muktafī. In his *Dhamm al-malāhī* (Disapprobation of Musical Instruments), which is a diatribe against music, he argues in effect that all dissipation begins with music and ends in drunkenness.[2] Soon indeed a veritable school arose who put forth quite a library of literature on this question as to whether *al-samā'* or " listening to music " was lawful or not. On the whole most of their threatenings went for naught, for, indeed, there was a far more interesting debate in progress.

In the days of Hārūn (786-809) the court musicians were divided into two hostile camps, led by Ibrāhīm al-Mauṣilī and Ibn Jāmi' respectively. On the death of these *virtuosi*, we find Isḥāq al-Mauṣilī and Prince Ibrāhīm ibn al-Mahdī, leading rival cliques at court. Both of these movements had their origin in the jealousy aroused by the unique position held by the Mauṣilī family at court. In the second case, however, it developed

[1] Quoted by Browne, *Literary History of Persia*, i, 6.
[2] *Berlin MS.*, 5504. Cf. Ḥājjī Khalīfa, No. 5824.

into an epic struggle between a classic and romantic school in music. Prince Ibrāhīm was the son and the brother of a khalif, and, indeed, had been an anti-khalif himself for a time. He was a spoilt child, petted and pampered by all he came in contact with, and so became a consummate egotist. The author of the great *Kitāb al-aghānī* tells us that in spite of his natural gifts and eminent merits, Prince Ibrāhīm would not conform to the proper interpretation of the ancient music, but would suppress notes and alter passages just as he thought fit, and would answer when reproved, " I am a king, and the son of a king ; I sing just as the whim of my fancy takes me." He was the first musician who introduced licences into the ancient song. The result of this independent attitude was that a crowd of *dilettanti*, ever enthusiastic for novelties, as well as a considerable number of the *virtuosi*, set out to defy all classical traditions. The struggle between the Classicists and Romanticists was waged with considerable vigour on both sides, and whilst Isḥāq al-Mauṣilī lived the victory remained with him, but after that, the principles of the new school gained the day.

Apparently the new art tendencies suited the general social and political drift of the period. At the same time, it is not easy to discern clearly what the precise innovations were that the Romanticists were concerned with. It is clear from the great *Kitāb al-aghānī* that an alteration took place in the rhythmic modes (*īqā'āt*). Isḥāq al-Mauṣilī had carefully classified these, but Prince Ibrāhīm challenged him in this respect,[1] and there are some interesting discussions on the subject, some of which have been preserved. The author of the great *Kitāb al-aghānī* himself contributed a treatise to this question, which, unfortunately, has not come down to us.

More serious still was the interference with the old melodic modes. This may have been due to the intro-

[1] Isḥāq could trace his traditions back through pupil to master up to the days of the *jāhiliyya* thus,—Isḥāq al-Mauṣilī, Siyyāṭ, Burdān, 'Azza al-Mailā', and Rā'iqa.

duction of the Khurāsānī scale of two *limmas* and a *comma*, as exhibited in the *ṭunbūr al-khurāsānī*. Possibly, this was the innovation in the scale from Persia which is mentioned in the early ninth century.[1] The author of the *'Iqd al-farīd* says:

"Mukhāriq (d. 845) and 'Allūyah altered the old [music], all of it, and had introduced Persian notes [or modes] (*naghamāt*) into it. And when the Ḥijāzian came to them with the *thaqīl awwal* he said, 'Your singing requires bleeding' (i.e., it is too full of notes)."[2]

According to the author of the great *Kitāb al-aghānī*, Isḥāq al-Mauṣilī considered it a crime that the old music should be rendered other than as it had been traditionally handed down. The other school, led by Ibrāhīm ibn al-Mahdī and his followers, such as Mukhāriq, Shāriyya, Raiq, and others, subjected the old music to their caprices. Our author was anxious to pillory the Romanticists for all time, and so he names those responsible for the alteration of the old Arabian traditional music as follows. Among the foremost, he says, of those who corrupted the old music were: the family of Ḥamdūn ibn Ismā'īl and his teacher, Mukhāriq, the pupils of Zaryāt (*sic*) a songstress of Al-Wāthiq, and the female slaves of Shāriyya and Raiq (written Zīq). He then gives the names of the Classicists who followed Isḥāq al-Mauṣilī, and they were: 'Uraib and her circle of singing-girls, Al-Qāsim ibn Zurzūr and his family, the circle of Badhl the songstress, the minstrels of the Barmakid family, and the progeny of Hāshim, Yaḥyā ibn Mu'ād, and Al-Rabī' [ibn Yūnus].[3]

Jaḥza al-Barmakī, who died in 938, said that in his day, so great had been the tampering with the old music that it was impossible to hear one of the old songs executed as it had been composed.[4] At the same time,

[1] It is still possible however that the Khurāsānī scale is later, and that the innovation mentioned concerns merely the Persian "middle finger" note (*wusṭa al-fars*) which had been adopted on the *'ūd* being placed between the Pythagorean and Zalzalian third.

[2] *'Iqd al-fārid*, iii, 190. Al-Wāthiq employed songstresses from Khurāsān whose melodies were called *fahlīdhiyyāt*. They received this name after the famous Persian minstrel called Fahlīdh (Bārbad).

[3] *Aghānī*, ix, 35. [4] The author of the *Aghānī* says the same (ix. 35).

both Yaḥyā ibn 'Alī ibn Yaḥyā ibn Abī Manṣūr (d. 912) and the author of the great *Kitāb al-aghānī* (d. 967) insist that even in their day the theoretical system of Isḥāq still obtained. The latter says: "All that we have mentioned of the genres (*ajnās*) of the songs follows the theory of Isḥāq al-Mauṣilī... seeing that his method is that which is accepted to-day, and not that of those who opposed him like [Prince] Ibrāhīm ibn al-Mahdī, Mukhāriq, 'Allūyah, 'Amr ibn Bāna, Muḥammad ibn al-Hārith ibn Buskhunr and those who agree with them . . . for what they say is now rejected and left behind, and people only recognize what Isḥāq taught."[1]

At the same time, interest in the new ideas did not flag, since we have 'Alī ibn Hārūn ibn 'Alī ibn Yaḥyā ibn Abī Manṣūr (d. 963), a nephew of Yaḥyā ibn 'Alī ibn Yaḥyā ibn Abī Manṣūr, a great protagonist of the theories of Isḥāq, writing a book on this subject entitled, *Kitāb risāla fī'l-farq bain Ibrāhīm ibn al-Mahdī wa Isḥāq al-Mauṣilī fī'l-ghinā'* (Treatise on the Difference between Ibrāhīm ibn al-Mahdī and Isḥāq al-Mauṣilī concerning Music).[2]

If the Romantic movement was responsible for the loss of much of the older music of Arabia, it can claim to its credit the introduction of some new ideas from Persia which were to lend additional colour to the music of the Semites, an influence which remains to this very day. Most noticeable were the new modal ideas, due as much to a novel scale that had been introduced as to anything else. The Persian scale did not supersede the Arabian and Pythagorean systems but found acceptance side by side with them. East of the Tigris and Euphrates the scale of the *ṭunbūr al-khurāsānī* already adverted to was favoured.

It is rather unfortunate that we get no information from either Al-Kindī or Al-Fārābī on the construction of the melodic modes, although they both describe the rhythmic modes fully. We know from the great *Kitāb al-aghānī*[3] and the *Risāla fī'l-mūsīqī* (or *Kitāb al-nagham*)

[1] *Aghānī*, i, 2. [2] *Fihrist*, i, 144.
[3] *Aghānī*, viii, 24-5.

of Yaḥyā ibn ʻAlī ibn Yaḥyā ibn Abī Manṣūr (d. 912)[1] that modes of nine and ten notes had recently been introduced, the latter by ʻUbaidallāh ibn ʻAbdallāh ibn Ṭāhir (d. 912) it would seem. In view of this we need not necessarily attribute the nine note modes that we find very popular later, such as that known as *Iṣfahān*, to alien influence. Of course, the melodic modes were of secondary importance to the rhythmic modes in these days, and this attitude continued until the late tenth or early eleventh century, when Persian and Khurāsānī ideas made a breach in Arabian musical art.[2] The same thing might be shown in Arabic poetry. Metre (*ʻarūḍ*) was of more count than rhyme (*qāfiya*). Although rhyme is a necessity to Arabic poetry, yet the peculiarity of the latter is that, with the exception of the *muzdawaj*, the same rhyme is continued throughout the poem.

I have remarked that the influence of the Greek theorists in music did not make any definite headway until the "Golden Age" had passed,[3] and therefore although the treatises of Al-Kindī (d. 874) were written during the latter period, impressions only showed themselves during "The Decline." Whether Al-Kindī derived his theories of Greek music from Greek originals or from Arabic translations is a question for future discussion. One or two passages point to a Syriac version or an Arabic version *via* Syriac.[4] On the other hand his terminology is quite different from that of Al-Fārābī, Ibn Sīnā, and later writers, and from this it may be assumed that the treatises which he consulted on Greek theory were not the same as those consulted by the other writers mentioned.[5] Many of Al-Kindī's opinions on the physical and physiological aspects of sound may, indeed, be quite original, notwithstanding the fact that Arabic translations of such works as Aristotle's *De anima*,

[1] *British Museum MS.*, Or. 2361, fol. 238-238 v.

[2] The rhythmic modes hold the field in the Ikhwān al-Ṣafā', but by the time of the Ibn Sīnā there are signs of change.

[3] See *ante* p. 105.

[4] For instance he writes *qīthūra* and not *qīthāra*. *Berlin MS.*, Ahlwardt, 5531, fol. 24. But cf. *Berlin MS.*, Ahlwardt, 5503, fol. 35 v.

[5] On the question of Al-Kindī and his knowledge of Greek see Leclerc, *Histoire de la médecine arabe*, i, 134 *et seq.*

Historia animalium, and the *Problemata*, as well as Galen's *De voce*, made by Ḥunain ibn Isḥāq (d. 873), were probably known to him.

Although the Arabs had long been acquainted with ratios in the fretting of their stringed instruments, and probably the *Kitāb al-nagham* of Al-Khalīl (d. 791) dealt with them,[1] the teaching of Al-Kindī on this subject must have been of considerable importance. Indeed, there can be little doubt that the Ikhwān al-Ṣafā' borrowed from this writer. This is not the place to discuss his Greek theories. Suffice it to say that he deals with sound (*ṣaut*), intervals (*ab'ād*), genres (*ajnās*), systems (*jumū'*) and species (*anwā'*), modes (*luḥūn*), tones (*ṭanīnāt*), mutation (*intiqāl*), and composition (*ta'līf*), following the Greeks. As previously remarked, however, Al-Kindī's account of the practical art, as known to the Arabs, is of highest interest and value in the history of the theory of Arabian music.

Al-Kindī is also helpful as evidence that the Arabian system of music was not merely Persian or Byzantine methods as some writers have assumed. Here is one extract: " The teaching [of the art of music] is of many sorts (*funūn*), that is to say, Arabian, Persian, Byzantine (*Rumī*), etc."[2] Another reads: " To every nation in regard to this instrument [the lute] is a method which no other people have. And their difference in that respect is like their difference in other things. Do you not see between the Arabs, the Byzantines, the Persians, the *Khazar*,[3] the Abyssinians, and other people, the greatest difference in their natures, intellects, opinions, and customs ? " He then goes on to mention the difference in the musical art between the celebrated modes (*ṭuraq*) of the Persians, the eight modes (*alḥān thamāniyya*= 'Οκτώηχος) of the Byzantine theorists (*astūkhūsiyya*), and the eight rhythmic modes (*uṣūl*) of the Arabs, in each of which these nations specialized respectively.[4]

[1] The pioneer mathematicians of the Arabs,—Abū Isḥāq al-Fazārī, Al-Nūbasht, and Jābir ibn Ḥayyān were all dead by 777.

[2] *Berlin MS*, Ahlwardt, 5530, fol. 30.

[3] See *Encyclopædia of Islām*, ii, 935.

[4] *Berlin MS.*, Ahlwardt, 5530, fol. 30.

What helped to counteract Persian influence was the ascendancy of the Greek scholiasts. We have already seen that the scholars of the *Bait al-ḥikma*, the College of Science at Baghdād, had been busy with the treatises of the Greeks on music which had been translated into Arabic. Among the Greek musical theorists who had been translated were Aristoxenos, Euklid, Ptolemy and Nikomachos. Aristoxenos was known by two books, the *Kitāb al-rīmūs* [? *ru'ūs*] (Book of Principles = ἀρχαί) and the *Kitāb al-īqā'* (Book of Rhythm = ῥυθμός).[1] In addition to his *Problemata*, Euklid (Pseudo-Euklid) was studied in two other musical works, a *Kitāb al-nagham* (Book of Notes = Εἰσαγωγὴ ἁρμονική ?) and a *Kitāb al-qānūn* (Book of the Canon = Κατατομὴ κανόνος ?).[2] Ibn al-Haitham (d. 1038) wrote a "commentary" on Euklid's contribution to the science of music, and Ibn Sīnā may have made a similar contribution.[3] Nikomachos appeared in Arabic script in a *Kitāb al-mūsīqī al-kabīr* (Opus Major on Music) and in several compendia (*mukhtaṣar* = ἐγχειρίδιον).[4] Ptolemy is also mentioned as the author of a *Kitāb al-mūsīqī* (Book of Music = 'Αρμονική).[5] Even a treatise on music by Pythagoras is recorded by the Arabic bibliographers.[6]

When these writings of the Greeks made their appearance in Arabic, music became one of the courses of scientific study and part of the *'ulūm riyāḍiyya* or mathematical arts. Al-Kindī (d. *ca.* 874), Al-Sarakhsī (d. 899), the Banū Mūsā (tenth century), Thābit ibn Qurra (d. 901), Muḥammad ibn Zakariyyā al-Rāzī (d. 923), Qusṭā ibn Lūqā (d. 932), and Al-Fārābī (d. 950) were writers after the Greek school. What the Arabs borrowed directly may be traced in technical nomenclature. The Arabic word *ghinā'* had stood for both "song" in particular and "music" in general. It now came to be applied to the practical art, whilst the theoretical art was represented by the word *mūsīqī* or *mūsīqā*

[1] *Fihrist*, i, 270. [2] *Fihrist*, i, 266. Ibn al-Qifṭī, 65.
[3] Casiri, i, 416. Ibn Abī Uṣaibi'a, ii, 98. Cf. below, p. 218.
[4] *Fihrist*, i, 269.
[5] *'Iqd al-farīd*, iii, 186. *Kitāb al-tanbīh*, 128.
[6] Wenrich, *De auct. graec.*, 88.

(μουσική). The names of a few musical instruments appeared in Arabic such as the *qītāra* (κιθάρα) and *qānūn* (κανών). More permanent were some of the names introduced into the "theory." The *interval* was called the *bu'd*, and each specific interval was also given a name. The *quarter-tone* was the *irkhā'*, the *semitones* were the *baqiyya* (λεῖμμα) and *infiṣāl* ἀποτομή), the *whole-tone* was the *ṭanīn* (τόνος), etc. The Greek devices of *genres* (γένη) and *species* (εἴδη) were adopted as the *ajnās* and *anwā'* respectively.[1]

Following the example laid down in the Umayyad period and the "Golden Age" by Yūnus al-Kātib, Yaḥyā al-Makkī, Isḥāq al-Mauṣilī, and others, both *virtuosi* and *dilettanti* became quite diligent in the study of the history of music and the lives of its professors. Al-Mas'ūdī (d. *ca.* 957) says that he found an abundance of literature dealing with music (*al-samā'*), its history among the Arabs and other nations, as well as biographies of celebrated musicians both ancient and modern.[2] Al-Iṣfahānī (d. 967) compiled his famous *Kitāb al-aghānī* (Book of Songs), which, in spite of its title, is practically a history of Arabian music and poetry from the days of Idolatry to the tenth century. Biographers of musicians abound, and among them Quraiṣ al-Jarrāhī, Jaḥẓa al-Barmakī, Abū Ḥashīsha, Al-Ḥasan al-Naṣibī, and Al-Madīnī.

From the *Kitāb al-aghānī* we are able to appreciate the type of vocal music that was current. We not only have the lighter *qiṭ'a*, which was more in keeping with the tastes of the period, but also the more serious pieces from the *qaṣā'id*. It was apparently about this time that the musical performance called the *nauba* became known. In the *Kitāb al-aghānī* we read in several places of a company of musicians being called a *nauba*.[3] The name probably originated from the circumstance that the performance of these musicians was given at certain specified

[1] See my *Facts for the Arabian Musical Influence*, chap. iv.
[2] Al-Mas'ūdī, viii, 103.
[3] *Aghānī*, iii, 184-5; v, 167; vi, 76; xxi, 233.

periods of the day, or that these musicians took turns in performance. In the course of time, however, the word was transferred from the performers to the performance, and we find the periodic playing of the khalif's military band at the five hours of prayer being called the *nauba*.

The military band had now become one of the most important emblems (*marātib*) of the sovereignty of the khalif. In the early days, as Ibn Khaldūn points out, the shrill trump (*būq*) and spirit-stirring drum (*ṭabl*) were unknown to the Islāmic armies.[1] It was the *duff* (square tambourine) and *mizmār* (reed-pipe) that sufficed in these days.[2] But when the stern Muslims of Al-Ḥijāz came in contact with the Arabs of Al-Ḥīra and Ghassān, the pomp and circumstance of war became the order of the day, and we find bands with the *surnāy* (reed-pipe) and *ṭabl*,[3] and then with the *būq al-nafīr* (large metal trumpet), the *dabdāb* (kettledrum), the *qaṣ'a* (shallow kettledrum),[4] as well as the *ṣunūj* (cymbals).

Instrumental music in general was considerably developed during this period, and the careful descriptions of musical instruments in the *Kitāb al-mūsīqī* of Al-Fārābī are extremely valuable.[5] The *'ūd* (lute) was still "the most generally used" instrument, and was still strung with four strings in the East, although in Al-Andalus it possessed five; that innovation having been introduced in the ninth century. A fifth string is certainly postulated by Al-Fārābī, but seemingly only as a theoretical makeshift, just as Al-Kindī had done in the previous century. An arch-lute or zither called the *shāhrūd* was invented by a certain Ḥakīm ibn Aḥwas al-Sughdī.[6] It had a compass of three octaves.

The *ṭunbūr* (pandore) became a special favourite with

[1] Ibn Khaldūn, *Prol.*, ii, 44. The *būq* was not a warlike instrument with the Arabs when Al-Laith ibn Naṣr (8th cent.) wrote, and in the following century Al Aṣma'ī only knows of it as a martial instrument of the Christians. Lane, *Lexicon*, s.v.

[2] *Aghānī*, ii, 175. Cf. Evliyā Chelebī, i, ii, 226.

[3] *Aghānī*, xvi, 139.

[4] *Fakhrī*, p. 30.

[5] Casiri says that the Madrid MS. of Al-Fārābī contains upwards of 30 designs of musical instruments. The statement has been often repeated, but it is erroneous.

[6] See my *Studies in Oriental Musical Instruments*, p. 7.

the *virtuosi*, contesting the supremacy of the *'ūd* as the instrument *par excellençe* for the accompaniment.[1] Ibn Khurdādhbih assures us that it was common to Persia, Al-Raiy, Ṭabaristān, and Al-Dailam.[2] The peculiar timbre of the instrument, due to the drum-like structure of the sound-chest (it was probably constructed with a skin belly at this time) gave it a noisy tone, and was therefore more acceptable for solo performance. Two kinds of *ṭunbūr* are described at length by Al-Fārābī, the old Pagan *ṭunbūr al-mīzānī*, now called the *ṭunbūr al-baghdādī*, and the *ṭunbūr al-khurāsānī* fretted with a scale of two limmas and a comma. At this time both these instruments were to be found in Syria, but Al-Fārābī says that the former was more common to the people of Baghdād and the lands to the West and Centre, whilst the latter instrument belonged especially to Khurāsān and the countries east and north of it.[3]

Harps and psalteries like the *jank* (*ṣanj*), the *salbāq* (= σαμβύκη),[4] the *mi'zafa* (?), and the *qānūn*, which had been improved by Al-Fārābī,[5] were in general use. For the first time we have positive proof of a stringed instrument being played with a bow.[6] The older lutes of the *mizhar* and *kirān* type are also mentioned during the period.

Among wind instruments, the *nāy*, the *suryānai*, the *mizmār*, and the *diyānai* or *mizmār al-muthannā*, represented the wood-wind, whilst the *būq* or clarion belonged to martial music together with drums (*ṭubūl*, sing. *ṭabl*) of various types, and perhaps the cymbals (plur. *ṣunūj*, sing. *ṣinj*). Both the pneumatic organ and the *hydraulis* were also known to the Arabs of these days.[7] Nearly all these instruments are mentioned by Al-Mas'ūdī on the authority of Ibn Khurdādhbih (d.*c.* 912),[8] and carefully described by Al-Fārābī.[9]

[1] *Aghānī*, viii, 184-5.
[2] Al-Mas'ūdī, viii, 91.
[3] Kosegarten, *Lib. Cant.*, 89 *et seq.* Land, *Recherches*, 107-121.
[4] See my article "Byzantine Musical Instruments in the Ninth Century," in the *Journal of the Royal Asiatic Society*, April, 1925, p. 301, *et seq.*
[5] Ibn Khallikān, *Biog. Dict.*, iii, 309.
[6] Kosegarten, *Lib. Cant.*, 77, line 4.
[7] See my *Organ of the Ancients: From Eastern Sources.*
[8] See my *Studies in Oriental Musical Instruments, p.* 53 *et. seq.*
[9] Kosegarten, *Lib. Cant.*, 76-115. Land, *Recherches*, 100-68.

The period of the Decline, in spite of the political decadence, the internecine strife, and the infirmity of the court at Baghdād, was almost as glorious an era for music as the "Golden Age." It was said of Al-Mutawakkal (847-61), who opened this epoch, that music and the dance reached a higher degree of excellence than before. The eloquent oration of Ibn Khurdādhbih on music at the throne of Al-Mu'tamid (870-92) amply discloses the ideals of the age. "Music (*ghinā'*)," he says, "sharpens the intellect, softens the disposition, and agitates the soul. It gives cheer and courage to the heart, and high-mindedness to the debased. With wine (*nabīdh*) it creates freshness and vivacity against the grief and care which afflict the body. It is to be preferred to speech, as health would be to sickness. . . . May the peace of Allāh fall on the sage who discovered this art, and on the philosopher who improved it. What a mystery he unveiled! What a secret he revealed."[1]

Similarly in Al-Andalus of the West we find the court poet Ibn 'Abd Rabbihi (d. 940) singing the praises of music. He calls it "the 'foraging ground' of hearing, the pasturage of the soul, the spring-grass of the heart, the arena of love, the comfort of the dejected, the companionship of the lonely, and the provision of the traveller. . . . Oftentimes, man only appreciates the blessings of this world and the next through beautiful music (*alḥān*), for it induces to generosity of character in the performance of kindness, and of observing the ties of kinship, and the defending of one's honour, and the overcoming of faults. Oftentimes man will weep over his sins through [the influence of] music, and the heart will be softened from its stubbornness, and man may picture the Kingdom of Heaven and perceive its joys through the medium of beautiful music."[2]

§ III

The *virtuosi* still thronged the courts, even though there were no outstanding figures as of old. Among the per-

[1] Al-Mas'ūdī, viii, 88. [2] *'Iqd al-farīd*, iii, 176.

formers, whether vocal or instrumental, there were no names that could be matched with a Ma'bad, Ibn 'Ā'isha, Ibn Suraij, or Mālik of the Umayyad days, nor with an Ibrāhīm al-Mauṣilī, Isḥāq al-Mauṣilī, Prince Ibrāhīm, or Ibn Jāmi' of the "Golden Age." Fresh conditions obtained. Something more than the talents of a *virtuoso* were demanded. To make headway at court and elsewhere, a minstrel had to possess other than executive musical accomplishments alone, and it will be observed that among the performers who will now be mentioned there were a goodly few who rose to celebrity because of their ability as poets, authors, story-tellers, chess players, and as agreeable "boon companions."

'Amr ibn Bāna[1] (d. 891), whose full name was 'Amr ibn Muḥammad ibn Sulaimān ibn Rāshid, was a freeman of Yūsuf ibn 'Umar al-Thaqafī. His father was in charge of one of the government offices and was a distinguished scribe, whilst his mother, from whom he took the name of Bāna, was a daughter of Rauḥ the secretary of Salama al-Waṣīf. 'Amr was a pupil of Isḥāq al-Mauṣilī and Prince Ibrāhīm, and he made his first public appearance at the court of Al-Ma'mūn (813-33). In the days of Al-Mu'taṣim (833-42) he was quite prominent, and on the accession of Al-Mutawakkil (847) he became the khalif's "boon companion." With Prince Ibrāhīm he was a great favourite, and one of his most reliable supporters in the Romantic movement. We are told, however, that although he was "an excellent singer and a good poet," he was, at bottom, but a mediocre musician. On one occasion, at a musical festival given by 'Abdallāh ibn Ṭāhir, he carried off the prize, a circumstance due, we are informed, to the importunacy of Prince Ibrāhīm, who was particularly solicitous that his *protégé* should have this honour. He was not an instrumentalist, and was quite ignorant of the art of accompaniment. His fame seems to have rested mainly on his *Kitāb mujarrad al-aghānī* (Book of Choice Songs), which, says Ibn Khallikān, was "a sufficient proof of his abilities." On the other hand, the author of the great *Kitāb al-*

[1] Cf. index of the *Nihāyat al-arab.*

aghānī in comparing Ibn Bāna's book with that of Isḥāq al-Mauṣilī, has small opinion of its worth.[1] "His haughtiness and pride were excessive," we are told. He died at Sāmarrā of leprosy.[2]

Abū Ḥashīsha or Abū Ja'far Muḥammad ibn 'Alī ibn Umayya, was a clever ṭunbūrist who flourished at the courts from the time of Al-Ma'mūn (813-33) to Al-Mu'tamid (870-92). He had some reputation also as a composer and musical *littérateur*. Several of his melodies are mentioned in the great *Kitāb al-aghānī*,[3] whilst two of his books, a *Kitāb al-mughannī al-majīd* (Book of the Glorious Singer) and a *Kitāb akhbār al-ṭunbūriyyin* (Stories of the Ṭunbūrists), are mentioned in the *Fihrist*. Among his pupils was the celebrated Jaḥẓa al-Barmakī.[4]

Aḥmad ibn Ṣadaqa ibn Abī Ṣadaqa was the son and grandson of famous musicians at the court of Hārūn, and he himself was one of the greatest performers on the *ṭunbūr* from the time of Al-Ma'mūn (813-33) to Al-Mutawakkil (847-61), hence his surname Al-Ṭunbūrī. He was besides an excellent composer in the *ramal*, *hazaj* and *mākhūrī* rhythmic modes.[5]

Bunān ibn 'Amr [al-Ḥārith][6] was an adroit musician at the courts of Al-Mutawakkil (847-61) and Al-Muntaṣir (861-2). It was this musician that the poetess Faḍl fell in love with, and of whom Al-Buḥturī (d. 897) wrote:

"The *'ūd* (lute) resounds with pleasing tune
Under the arm of Bunān,
Whilst Zunām's hand just as nimbly
Plays upon the *mizmār* (reed-pipe)."

With Al-Muntaṣir, Bunān was specially preferred.[7]

Abū'Alī al-Ḥasan al-Masdūd was the son of a

[1] *Aghānī*, v, 52.
[2] *Aghānī*, xiv, 52-55. *Fihrist*, 145. Ibn Khallikān, ii, 414.
[3] *Aghānī*, viii, 173. xi, 32. xiv, 54.
[4] *Aghānī*, xxi, 257. *Fihrist*, 145.
[5] *Aghānī*, xix, 137-9. xxi, 154.
[6] I have added al-Ḥārith following Al-Mas'ūdī. He is the Shaibān ibn al-Ḥārith al-'Awwādh mentioned by Von Hammer, iv, 744. The great *Kitāb al-aghānī* only refers to him as Bunān, or Bunān ibn 'Amr al-Mughannī.
[7] *Aghānī*, viii, 176-8, 184, 186; xvii, 8; xxi, 179, 184. Al-Mas'ūdī, vii, 294.

butcher of Baghdād. He was an admirable composer, and as a ṭunbūrist he was considered by Jaḥẓa al-Barmakī, the historian of the ṭunbūrists, as the foremost performer of his day. He, too, was surnamed Al-Ṭunbūrī on this account. He flourished at the courts of Al-Wāthiq (842-47), Al-Mutawakkil (847-61), and Al-Muntaṣir (861-2).[1] Ibn 'Abd Rabbihi says that he was "one of the ablest men in singing," and we read of him with Zunain (Aḥmad ibn Yaḥyā al-Makkī) and Dubais, at the house of Abū 'Īsā ibn al-Mutawakkil.[2]

'Abdallāh ibn Abī'l-'Alā' was a musician of Sāmarrā, and a pupil of Isḥāq al-Mauṣilī. He is praised in the great *Kitāb al-aghānī* for his superior talents.[3] It was of this minstrel that a poet wrote:

"When Ibn Abī'l-'Alā' is with us,
Then welcome be company and wine."

Aḥmad ibn 'Abdallāh ibn Abī'l-'Alā', son of the above, was also a fine musician. He flourished at the courts of Al-Mu'taḍid (892-902). Mukhāriq and 'Allūyah were his teachers.[4]

'Amr al-Maidānī was a famous singer and ṭunbūrist, who was born at Baghdād. Jaḥẓa al-Barmakī says, on the authority of Abū'l-'Ubais ibn Ḥamdūn, that whilst both Abū Ḥashīsha and Al-Ḥasan al-Masdūd[5] were considered to be the first among contemporary ṭunbūrists, 'Amr al-Maidānī really surpassed them both.[6]

Jirāb al-Daula was the name given to Abū'l-'Abbās Aḥmad ibn Muḥammad ibn 'Allūyah (?) al-Sajzī. He was a clever ṭunbūrist, although more celebrated perhaps as the author of a book of "rare and laughable stories" entitled the *Kitāb tarwīḥ al-arwāḥ wa miftāḥ al-surūr wa'l-afrāḥ* (Alleviation of the Spirits and the Key to Joy and Gladness).[7]

[1] *Aghānī*, xxi, 256-8.
[2] *'Iqd al-farīd*, iii, 191.
[3] *Aghānī*, xx, 114.
[4] *Aghānī*, viii, 88; ix, 34; xx, 114.
[5] The name is written Mastūrad in both the Būlāq and Sāsī editions of the *Aghānī*.
[6] *Aghānī*, xx, 66-7.
[7] *Fihrist*, 153.

Ibn al-Qaṣṣār or Abū Faḍl Sulaimān ibn 'Alī, was another good ṭunbūrist praised by Jaḥẓa al-Barmakī. He appears to have been the favourite accompanist to Al-Mu'tazz (866-69), who was himself a musician, and we are told that every time Ibn al-Qaṣṣār performed, this khalif gave him a hundred pieces of gold.[1]

'Abdallāh ibn al-'Abbās ibn al-Faḍl ibn al-Rabī'ī was a singer, poet and composer who was celebrated at the courts from the time of Hārūn (786-813) to Al-Muntaṣir (861-2)! He was a great admirer of Isḥāq al-Mauṣilī. Al-Mutawakkil was particularly partial to him. Two of his compositions were celebrated.[2]

Muḥammad ibn Aḥmad ibn Yaḥyā al-Makkī was the son and grandson of famous musicians, and a well-known singer at the court of Al-Mu'tamid (870-92). He became noted for his pupils.[3]

The Ziryāb family in Al-Andalus carried on the musical reputation of its founder, the illustrious Abū'l-Ḥasan 'Alī ibn Nāfi'. The latter had six sons and two daughters, " all of whom," says Al-Maqqarī, " sang and practised the art of music." Their names were: 'Abd al-Raḥmān, 'Ubaidallāh, Yaḥyā, Ja'far, Muḥammad, Al-Qāsim, and the daughters Ḥamdūna and 'Ulayya. 'Abd al-Raḥmān inherited his father's talents and carried on the music-school, but he displeased the aristocracy by the undue familiarity which he assumed. He was an extremely vain man, and in singing he asserted that he had no equal. Aḥmad had his father's poetic gifts, whilst Al-Qāsim was considered the finest singer of the family. The best all-round musician was 'Ubaidallāh. The daughter Ḥamdūna married the *wazīr* Hishām ibn 'Abd al-'Azīz, and Al-Maqqarī says that she " excelled in singing " and was more proficient than her sister 'Ulayya.[4]

Quraiṣ al-Jarrāhī, sometimes called Quraiṣ al-Mughannī (d. 936), was another contemporary musician of merit in the Baghdād Khalifate, and is called " one of the

[1] *Aghānī*, xii, 167-8.
[2] *Aghānī*, xvii, 121-41.
[3] *Aghānī*, vi, 17.
[4] Al-Maqqarī, *Analectes*, ii, 89.

clever ones of the musicians, and among the most learned of them." He wrote an important work entitled the *Kitāb ṣinā'at al-ghinā' wa akhbār al-mughanniyyin* (The Art of the Song and Stories of the Singers), which dealt with the songs in alphabetical order. He did not live to complete his work, but what was finished and given to the public, comprised about a thousand folios.[1]

Jaḥẓa al-Barmakī was the name generally given to Abū'l-Ḥasan Aḥmad ibn Ja'far ibn Mūsā ibn Khālid ibn Barmak (*ca.* 839-938). Ibn Khallikān says that he was " a man of talent and a master of various accomplishments." In the *Fihrist* we are told that he was " a poet and a singer, innate in poetry and clever in the art of singing to the *ṭunbūr*, and well educated." Al-Khatīb al-Baghdādī says that he was " the first singer of his time." He was taught the *ṭunbūr* (pandore) by no less a master than Abū Ḥashīsha. " He had met the learned and the narrators, and had studied under them, and had a great reputation in this respect." His books, a *Kitāb al-ṭunbūriyyin* (Book of Ṭunbūrists) and a *Kitāb al-nadīm* (Book of the Boon Companion) became famous. The author of the great *Kitāb al-aghānī* quotes from the former work, although he censures Jaḥẓa for calumniating several musicians, and insists that it is the duty of a biographer to bring out the best points in the life of a person, not the worst.[2] In spite of his talents, Jaḥẓa appears to have had a small mind, and even the author of the *Fihrist* speaks of his " meanness of soul." He was favoured at the courts of Al-Mu'taḍid (892-902) and Al-Muqtadir (908-32). It was 'Abdallāh ibn al-Mu'tazz that nicknamed him Jaḥẓa (" cross-eyed ").[3]

Among the lesser known musicians of the period were: 'Amīr ibn Murra,[4] Abū'l-'Ubais ibn Ḥamdūn,[5] Abū'l-'Anbas ibn Ḥamdūn,[6] Abū'l-Faḍl Radhādh,[7] 'Ath'ath

[1] *Fihrist*, 156.
[2] *Aghānī*, v, 161.
[3] *Aghani*, v, 32. See Guidi, 262. *Fihrist*, 145-6. Al-Mas'ūdī, viii, 261. Ibn Khallikān, *Biog. Dict.*, i, 118.
[4] *Aghānī*, xx, 35-6.
[5] *Aghānī*, xix, 118-19 ; xx, 10-11, 66.
[6] *Aghānī*, xii, 3 ; xiv, 162.
[7] *Aghānī*, xii, 32, 59.

al-Aswad,[1] and Ibn al-Māriqī,[2] all of whom were present at the court of Al-Mutawakkil (847-61). One of the principal men of state under this khalif, Ibrāhīm ibn al-Mudabbir, patronized several of these musicians.[3] Nashwān was a singer in the house of 'Abdallāh ibn al-Mu'tazz.[4] Ibrāhīm ibn Abī'l-'Ubais,[5] Kanīz, Al-Qāsim ibn Zurzūr,[6] Ibrāhīm ibn al-Qāsim ibn Zurzūr[7] and Waṣīf al-Zāmir,[8] were minstrels at the court of Al-Muqtadir (908-32).

Among the songstresses, some famous names have been preserved.

Maḥbūba (" Beloved ") was a half-caste born at Al-Baṣra who became the property of a man of al-Ṭā'if. She was given a fine education, and became a good singer and lutenist, but above all an exquisite poetess. 'Abdallāh ibn Ṭāhir purchased her as a gift for Al-Mutawakkil (847-61), and the khalif became so infatuated with her that he could not bear her out of his sight. After the assassination of Al-Mutawakkil, a number of court songstresses including Maḥbūba, passed into the hands of Waṣīf al-Turkī, the *wazīr*, and when she first appeared before him, she was still dressed in mourning for her late master, which the *wazīr*, at first, appeared to be amused at. When, however, he commanded her to sing she took her lute and sang some elegaic verses in memory of Al-Mutawakkil, which so enraged Waṣīf that he had her flung into prison. At the demand of the Turkish captain, Bughā', she was set at liberty on condition that she left Sāmarrā. She retired to Baghdād and died there in obscurity.[9]

Farīda was originally a singing-girl of 'Amr ibn Bāna the musician, but afterwards passed into the intimate circles of the court of Al-Wāthiq (842-47) and Al-Mutawakkil (847-61), where her performances were highly esteemed. She was a pupil of Shāriyya, and a great

[1] *Aghānī*, xiii, 30-2.
[2] *Aghānī*, vi, 20-1.
[3] *Aghānī*, xix, 114-27.
[4] *Aghānī*, ix, 143.
[5] *Aghānī*, v, 32.
[6] *Aghānī*, v, 32.
[7] *Aghānī*, viii, 44.
[8] *Aghānī*, v, 32.
[9] *Aghānī*, xix, 132-4. Al-Mas'ūdī, vii, 281-6.

admirer of the talents of Isḥāq al-Mauṣilī, whose reputation she defended when it was assailed.[1]

Mu'nisa was a singing-girl of Al-Ma'mūn (813-33),[2] but was later possessed by Muḥammad ibn Ṭāhir. There is an anecdote of her in the *Murūj al-dhahab* of Al-Mas'ūdī, as well as some of her verses.[3]

Among the lesser songstresses were: Ziryāb (*sic*) whom we find singing before 'Abdallāh ibn al-Mu'tazz,[4] and Ṣalifa, a singing-girl owned by the preceding, who is shown performing before Al-Muqtadir (908-32).[5] Shājī belonged to 'Ubaidallāh ibn 'Abdallāh ibn Ṭāhir, and she sang to Al-Mu'taḍid (892-902).[6] Bunān was another singing-girl who appeared before Al-Mutawakkil (847-61).[7]

In Al-Andalus there were also some famed songstresses.

Qamar was the name of a songstress who graced the court of Ibrāhīm ibn al-Ḥajjāj (d. 900), the *amīr* of Seville and Carmona. He purchased her for an immense sum from Abū Muḥammad al-'Udhrī, a grammarian of Al-Ḥijāz. She was noted for her eloquence, erudition, and her cleverness as a composer of music (*alḥān*).[8]

Ṭarab[9] was a singing-girl presented by a merchant to Al-Mundhir, a son of 'Abd al-Raḥmān II, who sent his donor in return a thousand gold pieces. She "excelled in music (*ghinā'*)."[10]

Uns al-Qulūb was one of the most famous of the singing-girls who shed lustre on the Zāhira palace of 'Abd al-Raḥmān III.[11]

Bazya was a singing-girl of 'Uthmān, the son of Muḥammad I (852-86).[12]

It has already been pointed out how musical literature had grown. Historians, biographers, and writers on the

[1] *Aghānī*, iii, 183-6. v, 95-6. viii, 166.
[2] Al-Mas'ūdī says that she was a slave of Al-Mahdī (775-85).
[3] *Aghānī*, vii, 36. xx, 57. Al-Mas'ūdī, vii, 387-93.
[4] *Aghānī*, ix, 142-3. She may be identical with the songstress Zaryāt (ix, 35) mentioned already (*ante* p. 148).
[5] *Aghānī*, v, 32.
[6] *Aghānī*, viii, 44-6. She is called Sājī in the *Nihāyat al-arab*, v, 66.
[7] *Aghānī*, xxi, 179.
[8] Al-Maqqarī, *Analectes*, ii, 97. Dozy, ii, 313-14.
[9] Called *Ṭarb* by Ribera.
[10] Al-Maqqarī, *Analectes*, ii, 391. *Moh. Dyn.*, i, 17.
[11] Al-Maqqarī, *Analectes*, i, 406
[12] Ibn al-Qūṭiyya, 80.

theory of music had sprung up on all sides, and among them were some of the foremost names in the annals of Arabic literature.

'Alī al-Iṣfahānī (897-967) or Abū'l-Faraj 'Alī ibn al-Ḥusain ibn Muḥammad al-Quraishī, was born at Iṣfahān, although he was an Arab who claimed descent from Marwān the last Umayyad khalif. Educated at Baghdād, he settled nominally at Aleppo under the patronage of the Ḥamdānids, although he led the life of the ordinary literary man in travel. He was a most painstaking collector of poetry and songs, and Al-Tanūkhī (d. 994) said of him: "I never found a person knowing by heart such a quantity as he did of poems, songs, etc."[1] At Aleppo, he compiled his famous *Kitāb al-aghānī* (Book of Songs), a work of the first rank among the literary productions of the Arabs.[2] It took a lifetime to compile, and the vast erudition displayed, to say nothing of the enormous industry and patience which it engendered, leaves one abashed at the productions which pass as "musical literature" to-day. Besides being a history of Arabian music from the days of Idolatry to the tenth century, it is a storehouse of information on almost every phase of the social life of the Arabs. Ibn Khaldūn calls it "the register (*dīwān*) of the Arabs," and the "final resource of the student of *belles lettres*." Saif al-Daula the Ḥamdānid sulṭān gave the author a thousand pieces of gold on account of this work, whilst the Andalusian sulṭān Al-Ḥakam II bestowed a similar amount.

The text of this monumental work was published by the Būlāq Press in twenty volumes in 1868, whilst a twenty-first volume was issued at Leyden in 1888 by Brünnow.[3] Guidi then followed with his invaluable *Tables alphabétiques du Kitāb al-aghānī* (1895-1900). A more correct edition of the *Aghānī* (known as the Sāsī edition) under the editorship of Aḥmad al-Shanqīṭī was afterwards issued at Cairo (1905-6), together with

[1] Ibn Khallikān, *Biog. Dict.*, ii, 249.
[2] Huart, *Arab. Lit.*, 185.
[3] Wellhausen, in the *Z.D.M.G.*, i, 145-51, also added fresh material. See *J.R.A.S.* (1927), 905-6, *re* a new edition of the Aghānī.

Guidi's tables amended in Arabic. Since then Muḥammad 'Abd al-Jawwād al-Aṣma'ī has issued his *Taṣḥīḥ kitāb al-aghānī* (Cairo, 1916), and now an entirely new edition of the "Songs" is being published. Both Quatremère[1] and Kosegarten[2] began translating the work, the former in French and the latter in Latin.

Al-Iṣfahānī was also the author of a *Kitāb al-qiyān* (Book of Singing-Girls),[3] *Kitāb al-imā' al-shawā'ir* (Book of Female Slave Poets), *Kitāb mujarrad al-aghānī* (Book of Choice Songs),[4] *Kitāb al-ghilmān cl-mughanniyyin* (Book of Slave Singers), *Kitāb akhbār Jaḥẓa al-Barmakī* (Book of Stories of Jaḥẓa al-Barmakī), and a *Kitāb al-ḥānāt* (Book of Taverns).[5]

Al-Mas'ūdī (d. *ca.* 957) or Abū'l-Ḥasan 'Alī ibn al-Ḥusain ibn 'Alī al-Mas'ūdī, came of a family of Al-Ḥijāz, one of his ancestors, Mas'ūd, having been a "Companion of the Prophet." He was born at Baghdād in the last years of the third century of the *Hijra*. From his earliest years he had a passion for travel, and in the year 912 we find him at Multān, and three years later in Fārs and Kirmān. He again penetrated India, journeying from there, possibly by the Deccan, to Ceylon, Madagascar and to the coast of 'Uman. It is not improbable that he even travelled as far as the Malay archipelago and the seaboard of China. We certainly know that he visited the shores of the Caspian and the Red Sea.

His great work, the *Akhbār al-zamān*, is a universal history from the "Creation of the world to the year 947." It was completed in thirty volumes, of which, but a solitary volume, now at Vienna, has been preserved. The *Murūj al-dhahab* and the *Kitāb al-awsāṭ*, are two other important works from his pen, the former being an ex-

[1] *Journal Asiatique* (1835).
[2] *Liber Cantilenarum Magnus* (*ca.* 1840-43).
[3] Thus in Ibn Khallikān, but Quatremère reads *Kitāb al-nabāt* (Book of Vegetation).
[4] It was an issue of the *Kitab al-aghānī*, without the historical or biographical material.
[5] Quatremère calls this a "*Recueil d'airs*" as though it were *Kitāb al-alḥān*, but cf. Kosegarten, *Lib. Cant.*, 196. For the life of Al-Iṣfahānī, see Ibn Khallikān, ii, 249-52. Wüstenfeld, *Die Geschichtschreiber der Araber, No.* 132.

tract from the *Akhbār al-zamān*, and the latter an abridgment of it.

It is in the *Murūj al-dhahab* (Meadows of Gold) that we find a section devoted to the early history of Arabian music, part of which was derived from an earlier authority, Ibn Khurdādhbih (d. *ca.* 912). The text of this work together with a translation in French was issued by Barbier de Meynard in 1861-77 under the title of *Les prairies d'or*. Al-Mas'ūdī was particularly interested in music, and he tells us in his *Murūj al-dhahab*, that in his other books he dealt " fully with the question of music, the various kinds of musical instruments (*malāhī*), dances, rhythms (*ṭuraq*, sing. *ṭurqa*),[1] and notes (*nagham*)," as well as " the kinds of instruments used by the Greeks, Byzantines, Syrians, Nabaṭaeans, and the people of Sind, India, Persia, etc." In his *Kitāb al-zulaf* he dealt with interval ratios (*munāsabat al-nagham lil'awtār*), as well as the influence of melodies on the soul. In his *Akhbār al-zamān* and *Kitāb al-awsāṭ*, he also gave some " curious details about the concerts and musical instruments of these peoples."[2] Al-Mas'ūdī is counted among the greatest of Arab historians, worthy of rank beside Al-Ṭabarī and Ibn al-Athīr. Ibn Khaldūn calls him " The imām of the historians."[3]

Ibn 'Abd Rabbihi (860-940) or Aḥmad ibn Muḥammad, was an Andalusian Arab known by his anthology the *'Iqd al-farīd* (The Unique Necklace). It contains twenty-five sections, each of which is named after a precious stone. One section (*kitāb al-yāqūtat al-thāniyya*) is devoted to " The Science of Melodies, and the Disagreement of People about them," which deals with a number of interesting topics, including the lawfulness of listening to music, the origin of the song, biographies of musicians, etc. Several editions of the text have been printed at Būlāq and Cairo,[4] but there is no translation at present.

[1] The text has *ṭarab* and Barbier de Meynard translates it as *rhythms*. For that reason I suggest that the word should be *ṭuraq*.

[2] Al-Mas'ūdī, ii, 322.

[3] *Prairies d'or*, avant-propos. Quatremère, *Journal Asiatique*, Ser. iii, Tome vii.

[4] Būlāq, A. H., 1293. Cairo, A. H., 1303, *et seq.*

The family of Abū Manṣūr al-Munajjim, famous as astrologers, poets, historians, and "Boon Companions" to the khalifs, were all keen musicians. The first of them, Yaḥyā ibn Abī Manṣūr, was a freeman of Al-Manṣūr (754-75), and was very intimate with Al-Ma'mūn (813-33). He died about the year 831. His two sons, Muḥammad and 'Alī, were both interested in music.

Muḥammad ibn Yaḥyā ibn Abī Manṣūr was a man "of eloquence and good education," says the *Fihrist.* He "had a knowledge of music and of the stars." Among his books was a *Kitāb akhbār al-shu'arā'* (Stories of the Poets).[1]

'Alī ibn Yaḥyā ibn Abī Manṣūr (d. 888) was especially noted as a poet, musician, and reciter (*rāwī*) of verses and stories, all of which he learnt from Isḥāq al-Mauṣilī. At first he attached himself to Muḥammad ibn Isḥāq ibn Ibrāhīm al-Muṣa'bī, the governor of Fārs, but finally he accepted service at the court of Al-Mutawakkil (847-61) and became his "Boon Companion." This position he held under successive khalifs down to the time of Al-Mu'tamid (870-92). The *Fihrist* says: "He used to sit in front of their thrones and they would impart to him their secrets." Ibn Khallikān says that "his skill lay particularly in music (*ghinā'*), which had been taught him by Isḥāq al-Mauṣilī, with whom he was personally acquainted." Among his books were: a *Kitāb al-shu'arā' al-qudamā' wa'l-Islāmiyya* (Book of Poets Ancient and Modern), and a *Kitāb akhbār Isḥāq ibn Ibrāhīm* (Stories of Isḥāq al-Mauṣilī). His two sons, Yaḥyā and Hārūn, became well-known authors.[2]

Yaḥyā ibn 'Alī ibn Yaḥyā ibn Abī Manṣūr (856-912) was "Boon Companion" to Al-Muwaffaq, the brother of Khalif Al-Mu'tamid (870-92). He was also a learned metaphysician of the Mu'tazalī school, an excellent poet, and a gifted music theorist, well acquainted with the writings of the Greeks. Specimens of his poetry delivered by him before Al-Mu'taḍid (892-902) and Al-Muktafī

[1] *Fihrist,* 143.
[2] *Fihrist,* 143. Ibn Khallikān, *Biog. Dict.,* ii, 312. *Wafayāt al-a'yān,* i, 506. Guidi, 500.

(902-08) have been preserved by Al-Mas'ūdī.[1] Among his books were: a *Kitāb al-bāhir* (Book of the Illuminating) on stories of the half-caste poets,[2] and a *Kitāb al-nagham* (Book on the Notes).[3] This latter is quoted in the great *Kitāb al-aghānī* as an important work. The British Museum has a solitary exemplar of a treatise from his pen entitled a *Risāla fī'l-mūsīqī* (Treatise on Music), which may be identical with the afore-mentioned book.[4] Apparently he was also the author of a work on singing.[5]

'Alī ibn Hārūn ibn 'Alī ibn Yaḥyā ibn Abī Manṣūr (890-963), a nephew of the preceding, was "a reciter of poetry and a poet; learned, witty, a metaphysician, and a religious writer (*ḥibrā'*)." He was "Boon Companion" to a number of the khalifs, and he wrote a musical work entitled *Kitāb risāla fī'l-farq bain Ibrāhīm ibn al-Mahdī wa Isḥāq al-Mauṣilī fī'l-ghinā'* (Treatise on the Difference between Ibrāhīm ibn al-Mahdī and Isḥāq al-Mauṣilī concerning music).[6] His verse set to music was very popular.[7]

Hārūn ibn 'Alī ibn Hārūn ibn Yaḥyā ibn Abī Manṣūr, a son of the preceding, was "a poet and learned man, pre-eminent in discourse, and acquainted with music." He was the author of a *Kitāb mukhtār fī'l-aghānī* (Book of Choice Songs).[8]

The family of Ṭāhir, which furnished generals, prefects, governors and statesmen for the Khalifate, were all keen patrons of music and many of them clever musicians to boot. The great Ṭāhir was the founder of the Ṭāhirid dynasty (820), and his son, 'Abdallāh ibn Ṭāhir (d. 844), was not only a generous supporter of music,[9] but a clever performer, who sang his own compositions before

[1] Al-Mas'ūdī, viii, 206, 222, 238.
[2] *Fihrist*, 143.
[3] *Aghānī*, viii, 26. *Kāmil*, viii, 57.
[4] *British Museum MS.* Or. 2361, fol. 236, v.
[5] A passage in the *British Museum MS.* runs,—"We have mentioned *in our book before this*, the description of the singer, and what sort of man he must be, and we have described what is requisite in him for that."
[6] *Fihrist*, 144.
[7] Ibn Khallikān, *Biog. Dict.*, i, 313.
[8] *Fihrist*, 144.
[9] *Aghānī*, xiv, 55.

Al-Ma'mūn. His two sons, Muḥammad and 'Ubaidallāh, were great enthusiasts for the art.[1]

'Ubaidallāh ibn 'Abdallāh ibn Ṭāhir (d. *ca.* 912) was a "Boon Companion" of Al-Mu'taḍid (892-902) and Al-Muktafī (902-08), and was Commander of the Police Guards at Baghdād. His life is given in the great *Kitāb al-aghānī*, where he is counted as "the first in the philosophy of music."[2] His book, the *Kitāb fī'l-nagham wa 'ilal al-aghānī al-musammā* (Book on the Notes and the Denominated Songs),[3] is placed among the *chefs d'œuvre* on the theoretical and practical science of music of the period.[4] We read of him and the sons of Ḥamdūn having correspondence with 'Abdallāh ibn al-Mu'tazz (who was also "clever in the science and art of music") on the question of certain notes in the ancient song.[5]

Manṣūr ibn Ṭalḥa ibn Ṭāhir, a cousin of the preceding, was also a musical theorist, and the author of a *Kitāb mu'nis fī'l-mūsīqī* (Companion Book on Music) according to the method of Al-Kindī.[6]

Ibn Khurdādhbih (d. *ca.* 912) or Abū'l-Qāsim 'Ubaidallāh [ibn 'Abdallāh] ibn Khurdādhbih, was of Persian origin, his grandfather being a Magian converted to Islām. His father was governor of Ṭabaristān, but 'Ubaidallāh was educated in Baghdād, being instructed in music and *belles lettres* by Isḥāq al-Mauṣilī. He was Director of the Posts in Al-Jabal (? Al-'Irāq), and was at Sāmarrā between 844 and 848, when he wrote his famous *Kitāb al-masālik wa'l-mamālik* (Book of Routes and Kingdoms). He afterwards became "Boon Companion" to Al-Mu'tamid (870-92), and "was intimate with him." It was before this khalif that he delivered his oration on music, which, as reported by Al-Mas'ūdī, gives us details of the earliest musical traditions of the Arabs.[7] Among his other books were: a *Kitāb adab al-samā'* (Book of Liberal

[1] Al-Mas'ūdī, vii, 347-8.
[2] *Aghānī*, viii, 44-46. Philosophy (*falsafa*) with the Arabs included mathematics (with music), logic, medicine, and the natural sciences.
[3] *Aghānī*, viii, 45.
[4] *Aghānī*, viii, 54.
[5] *Aghānī*, ix, 141.
[6] *Fihrist*, 117.
[7] For further information about this oration see my *Studies in Oriental Musical Instruments*, chap. v.

Education in Music), *Kitāb al-lahw wa'l-malāhī* (Book of Diversion and Musical Instruments), and a *Kitāb al-nudamā' wa'l-julasā'* (Book of Boon Companions and Associates). Only the second of these works has been preserved to-day, and a solitary exemplar is in the library of Ḥabīb Afandī al-Zayyāt of Alexandria.[1]

Abū'l-Qāsim 'Abbās ibn Firnās, who is identified with the poet of that name who died in 888,[2] was a man of considerable attainments in art, science, and literature. He is credited with being the "first who taught the *science* of music in Al-Andalus," and the first to introduce the science of prosody as laid down by Al-Khalīl.[3]

The family of Ḥamdūn were noted "Boon Companions" to the khalifs. The first of them was Ḥamdūn ibn Ismā'īl ibn Dā'ūd al-Kātib, who was a pupil of Mukhāriq in music, and a great admirer of the songstress Shāriyya.[4] His three sons were familiar figures at the courts and well known for their literary and musical talents. Aḥmad ibn Ḥamdūn was a chronicler of stories and the author of a *Kitāb al-nudamā' wa'l-julasā'* (Book of Boon Companions and Associates).[5] Abū'l-'Ubais ibn Ḥamdūn and Abū'l-'Anbas ibn Ḥamdūn were musicians at the court of Al-Mutawakkil (847-61).[6] The family supported the Romantic movement of Prince Ibrāhīm ibn al-Mahdī.[7]

Al-Ḥasan ibn Mūsā al-Naṣibī was the author of two musical works, a *Kitāb al-aghānī 'alā'l-ḥurūf* (Book of Songs in Alphabetical Order) and a *Kitāb mujarradāt al-mughanniyyin* (Book of Abstracts of the Singers). The former book was written for Al-Mutawakkil (847-61), and it is praised in the *Fihrist* because it contains information about the songs which had not been mentioned by Isḥāq al-Mauṣilī nor by 'Amr ibn Bāna. It gave the names of the singers both male and female in the Days of Idolatry as well as in Islāmic times.[8]

[1] *Fihrist*, 149. Ḥājjī Khalīfa, v, 509 (cf. the name,—Khurdādbih). De Goeje, *Bibl. Geog. Arab.*, vi, prefacc. *Hilāl*, xxviii, 214.

[2] Al-Maqqarī, *Moh. Dyn.*, i, 426.

[3] Al-Maqqarī, *Moh. Dyn.*, i, 148. See *L'aviation chez les Musulmans*, by Aḥmad Zākī Bāshā (Cairo, 1912).

[4] *Aghānī*, viii, 168. ix, 35. xiv, 111.

[5] *Fihrist*, 144.

[6] *Aghānī*, xii, 3. xx, 10-11.

[7] *Aghānī*, ix, 35.

[8] *Fihrist*, 145.

Ḥammād ibn Isḥāq al-Mauṣilī was a son and grandson of two of the most famous musicians in Islām. He was a pupil and disciple of Abū 'Ubaida and Al-Aṣma'ī, and studied music under his father, who also taught him the sciences. Al-Ṣūlī says: " He was a learned traditionist and shared with his father much of his [ability in] music." He wrote a number of books, mostly biographies of the poets.[1]

Al-Madīnī, or Abū Ayyūb Sulaimān ibn Ayyūb ibn Muḥammad al-Madīnī, belonged, as his name tells us, to Al-Medīna. According to the *Fihrist*, he was " one of the ingeniously learned, acquainted with music (*ghinā'*) and with the stories of the singers." Among his books were: a *Kitāb akhbār 'Azza al-Mailā'* (Stories of 'Azza al-Mailā'), *Kitāb Ibn Misjaḥ* (Book of Ibn Misjaḥ), *Kitāb qiyān al-Ḥijāz* (Book of the Singing-Girls of Al-Ḥijāz), *Kitāb qiyān Makka* (Book of the Singing-Girls of Mecca), *Kitāb ṭabaqāt al-mughanniyyin* (Book of the Ranks of the Singers), *Kitāb al-nagham wa'l-īqā'* (Book of Notes and Rhythm), *Kitāb al-munādimīn* (Book of Boon Companions), *Kitāb akhbār Ibn 'Ā'isha* (Stories of Ibn 'Ā'isha), *Kitāb akhbār Ḥunain al-Ḥīrī* (Stories of Ḥunain al-Ḥīrī), *Kitāb Ibn Suraij* (Book of Ibn Suraij), and a *Kitāb Al-Gharīḍ* (Book of Al-Gharīḍ).[2]

Ibn Tarkhān, or Abū'l-Ḥasan 'Alī ibn Ḥasan, was a good singer and *littérateur*, and among his books was one entitled *Kitāb akhbār al-mughanniyyin al-ṭunbūriyyin* (Book of Stories of the Singers of the Ṭunbūrists).[3]

Ibn Al-Dubbī (d. 920), or Abū'l-Ṭayyib Muḥammad ibn al-Mufaḍḍal ibn Salama al-Dubbī, was an eminent Shāfi'ī doctor of Baghdād and a renowned philologist who had studied under Ibn al-A'rābī, who had been a pupil of his father. Among his books is a *Kitāb al-'ūd wa'l-malāhī* (Book on the Lute and Musical Instruments), a solitary copy of which exists at Cairo.[4]

One of the outstanding features of the period was the contribution of the Greek Scholiasts to the theoretical art

[1] *Fihrist*, 142-3.
[2] *Fihrist*, 148.
[3] *Fihrist*, 156.
[4] Ibn Khallikān, *Biog. Dict.*, ii, 610. *Hilāl*, xxviii, 214.

as has already been stressed. Following in the footsteps of the scholars of the *Bait al-ḥikma*, the Banū Mūsā, and Al-Kindī, there came Al-Sarakhsī, Thābit ibn Qurra, Qusṭā ibn Lūqā, Muḥammad ibn Zakariyyā al-Rāzī, and Al-Fārābī.

Al-Sarakhsī (d. 899) or Aḥmad ibn Muḥammad ibn Marwān al-Sarakhsī,[1] who was also called Aḥmad ibn al-Ṭayyib, was the greatest pupil of Al-Kindī, and was even known as Tilmīdh al-Kindī (pupil of Al-Kindī). He was born at Sarakhs in Khurāsān, and became tutor to the son of Al-Muwaffaq, afterwards Khalif Al-Muʿtaḍid (892-902), who made him a member of his suite and Director of Weights and Measures in Baghdād. Unfortunately, the choler of the khalif was aroused against this eminent scientist on account of a secret having been betrayed. He was put to death and his property confiscated.[2] Al-Sarakhsī, like his teacher, was learned in most of the sciences, including mathematics, logic, astronomy, music, and philosophy, and he left more than thirty works on these subjects. Among his theoretical works on music were: a *Kitāb al-madkhal ilā ʿilm al-mūsīqī* (Introduction to the Science of Music), *Kitāb al-mūsīqī al-kabīr* (Opus Major on Music), *Kitāb al-mūsīqī al-ṣaghīr* (Opus Minor on Music). Unlike a number of the scientific writers on music at this period, he was also keenly interested in the practical side of the art, as we are told in the great *Kitāb al-aghānī*, and he wrote such works as: *Kitāb al-lahw wa'l-malāhī fī'l-ghinā' wa'l-mughanniyyin* . . . (Book of Joy and Diversion in the Song and the Singers, etc.), a *Kitāb nuzhat al-mufakkir al-sāhī fī'l-mughanniyyin wa'l-ghinā' wa'l-malāhī* (Book of Diversion for the Perplexed Thinker concerning the Singers, the Song, and Musical Instruments), and a *Kitāb al-dalālat ʿalā asrār al-ghinā'* (Book of Guidance in the Secrets of Singing).[3]

[1] Collangettes, *Journal Asiatique*, Nov.-Dec. 1904, p. 382, and Rouanet, *Encyclopédie de la musique* (Lavignac), v, 2679, both write Sarshārdhī.

[2] Arrested in 896, he languished in prison until his execution in 899.

[3] *Fihrist*, 149, 261. Ibn Abī Uṣaibiʿa, i, 214. Al-Masʿūdī, viii, 179. *Aghānī*, viii, 54. xix, 136. Casiri, i, 406. Ḥājjī Khalīfa, v, 161. Ahlwardt, *Verz.* No. 5536 (2).

Thābit ibn Qurra Abū'l Ḥasan (836-901) was a Ṣabian of Ḥarrān in Mesopotamia. He was one of the most brilliant of the scholars of his day who studied the "exact sciences" including music. Owing to his rationalism, he was persecuted, and was finally driven into retirement at Kafartūthā. Here he met Muḥammad ibn Mūsā ibn Shākir, who brought him to Baghdād,[1] where he was given the opportunity to devote himself to scientific study. He became the greatest mathematician of his day, and was the first to apply algebra to geometry. Among his music books were the following: *Kitāb fī 'ilm al-mūsīqī* (Book on the Science of Music), *Maqāla fī'l-mūsīqī* (Discourse on Music), *Kitāb al-mūsīqī* (Book of Music), and a *Kitāb fī ālat al-zamr* (Book of the Wind Instrument).[2] Ḥājjī Khalīfa mentions a work entitled *Kitāb fī'l-mūsīqī* in fifteen sections, which is probably identical with one of the above.[3] Some of these works were known to the practical musicians of the period.[4]

Qusṭā ibn Lūqā al-Ba'albakī (d. 932) was a Melchite Christian of Ba'albak in Syria. We are told that he "greatly excelled in the science of medicine, philosophy, geometry, arithmetic, numerals, and *music*," and was the author of several translations from the Greek as well as of many original treatises. He was employed by Al-Musta'īn (852-66), and was alive in the reign of Al-Muqtadir (908-32), hence his death is given as 932. On the other hand Suter places his death about 912, whilst an earlier date (890 or 900) is even suggested.[5] Casiri mentions a *Liber de musica* by Qusṭā ibn Lūqā, which in the Arabic text is really a *Kitāb al-qarasṭūn* (Book of the Steelyard), and has nothing to do with music. His Greek translations were of inestimable benefit to succeeding generations.[6]

[1] He is said to have introduced Thābit to Khalif Al-Mu'taḍid (892-902), but this cannot be correct if Muḥammad ibn Mūsā died in 873.

[2] Probably a treatise on some type of organ. See my *Studies in Oriental Musical Instruments*, Chap. iii.

[3] *Fihrist*, 272. Casiri, i, 390-1. Ibn Khallikān, *Biog. Dict.*, i, 288. Ibn Abī Uṣaibi'a, i, 216. Ḥājjī Khalīfa, v, 161. Ibn al-Qifṭī, 115.

[4] *Aghānī*, viii, 54.

[5] Suter, *Die Mathematiker u. Astronomen der Araber*, 41. *Ency. of Islām*, ii, 1081.

[6] *Fihrist*, 295. Casiri, i, 420. Ibn Abī Uṣaibi'a, i, 244. Ibn al-Qifṭī, 262.

Abū Bakr Muḥammad ibn Zakariyyā al-Rāzī (d. 923) was born at Al-Raiy. Abū Dā'ūd ibn Juljul says of Al-Rāzī that he was a practical musician who "in his youth played on the *'ūd* (lute) and cultivated music." In his twentieth year, however, he abandoned these arts and came to Baghdād to study the sciences. Here, he became the pupil of 'Alī ibn Sahl ibn Rabban, the personal physician to Al-Mu'taṣim (833-42). Later, Al-Rāzī became director of the Baghdād hospital, and was considered the greatest medical authority of his time. For centuries the works of Rhazes, as he was called in Latin, were the text-books for European doctors. Finally, he rose to be a court dignitary with the Sāmānid prince Al-Manṣūr ibn Isḥāq, to whom he dedicated his great medical treatise the *Manṣūrī*.[1] Although Kiesewetter says that he left no work on music, Leclerc, the medical historian, mentions a "Compendium on Music."[2] This probably refers to the *Kitāb fī jumal al-mūsīqī* (Book of the Summings Up of Music) mentioned by Ibn Abī Uṣaibi'a. Works in the Paris *Bibliothèque Nationale* have been wrongly attributed to him, as I have pointed out elsewhere.[3]

Sa'īd ibn Yūsuf (892-942), better known as Saadia ben Joseph the Gaon, was a Jew born in Egypt. Emigrating to Palestine in 915, he became famous by his controversy with the Qaraites and the celebrated Ben Meir. In 928 he was appointed Principal (Gaon) of the Sura Academy in Al-'Irāq, but owing to trouble with the Exilarch he was deposed two years later, and was not reinstated until 938. During the interim, which was spent in literary activity in Baghdād, Saadia wrote some of his most important works, for the greater part in Arabic, which was the language of polite literature among the Jews.[4] Among his works is *Kitāb al-amānāt wa'l-i'tiqādāt* (Book of Philosophical Doctrines and Religious Beliefs), which was translated

[1] *Fihrist*, 299. Ibn Abī Uṣaibi'a, i, 309. Ibn Khallikān, iii, 311. Ibn al-Qifṭī, 271.

[2] Leclerc, *Hist. de la médecine arabe*, i, 353.

[3] See my article,—*Some Musical MSS. Identified* in the *Journal of the Royal Asiatic Society*, Jan., 1926. Cf. Collangettes, *Journal Asiatique*, Nov.-Dec., 1904, p. 384, and Lavignac's *Encyclopédie de la musique*, v, 2679.

[4] See Malter, *Saadia Gaon: His Life and Works* (Philadelphia, 1921).

into Hebrew by Judah ben Tibbon (d. 1190). At the end of the tenth section (*maqāla*) of this work there is an interesting discussion on music and its influence, which appears to have considerable affinity with Arabian notions. It is on this account especially that Saadia is given a place here. The Arabic text of this work was issued by Landauer (Leyden, 1880), whilst the Hebrew text was edited by Slucki (Leipsic, 1864).[1]

Al-Fārābī (*ca.* 870-950), or in full Abū Naṣr Muḥammad ibn Tarkhān, was of Turkish origin, and was born at Fārāb in Transoxiana. Coming to Baghdād he studied philosophy under Abū Bishr Mattā ibn Yūnus, and later went to Ḥarrān to prosecute studies under Yūḥannā ibn Khailān. Having mastered the sciences of the Greeks, he soon surpassed his contemporaries.[2] We are informed that he was "a perfect and erudite musician,"[3] and "an excellent performer on the *'ūd* (lute)."[4] His fame in music led Saif al-Daula the Ḥamdānid ruler to invite him to settle in Aleppo. Here, the great philosopher and music theorist attracted pupils from all parts, who thronged to his lectures, which were held in the delightful gardens on the outskirts of the city. He wrote on logic, ethics, politics, mathematics, alchemy, philosophy, and *music.* Many of these works were translated into Latin, and Alpharabius, as he was called in the West, had an immense influence on the culture of Mediæval Europe. He has been called "the Second Master" (i.e., Second to Aristotle), and "the greatest philosopher the Arabs ever produced."[5]

Among his musical writings were: the *Kitāb al-mūsīqī al-kabīr* (Grand Book on Music), *Kilām fī'l-mūsīqā*

[1] Steinschneider gave another reading from a Bodleian MS. in "Beth O'çar haṣṣpharoth," Year I, xxx. See also the same writer's *Jewish Literature,* pp. 154, 337, and Malter, *op. cit.*, pp. 259, 369.

[2] Soriano-Fuertes, *Historia de la mûsica Española,* i, 82; and Saldoni, *Diccionario . . . de musicos Españoles,* s.v., would make him an Andalusian Arab. Lichtenthal, *Dizionario e Bibliographia della Musica,* s.v., and S. M. Tagore, *Universal Hist. of Music,* 101, make him a khalif ! !

[3] Abū'l-Fidā', *Annales Moslem.*

[4] Ibn Ghaibī, *Sharḥ al-adwār MS.*

[5] Ibn Khallikān, *Biog. Dict.*, iii, 146. 307. *Fihrist,* 263. Ibn al-Qifṭī, 277. Ibn Abī Uṣaibi'a, ii, 134. Casiri, i, 189.

(*sic.* Styles in Music), *Kitāb fī iḥṣā' al-īqā'* (Book on the Classification of Rhythm), and *Kitāb fī'l-nuqra (? nuqla) muḍāf ilā al-īqā'* (Book of Supplementary Enquiry concerning Rhythm).[1] Of these, only the first-named appears to have survived, and three copies are preserved at Madrid, Leyden, and Milan. The Madrid copy, which dates from prior to 1138, appears to have been made for the celebrated Ibn Bājja (Avenpace).[2] The Milan example dates from 1347,[3] and that of Leyden from 1537, being copied from one dated 1089.[4] Portions of this monumental treatise, both in text and translation have been given by Kosegarten in his *Alii Ispahanensis Liber Cantilenarum Magnus* (*ca.* 1840-43), and in the *Zeitschrift für d. Kunde d. Morgenlandes*, v. (1850). Soriano-Fuertes, in his *Mûsica Arabe Española y Conexión de la mûsica con la astronomía, medicina y arquitectura* (1854), and Land in his *Recherches sur l'histoire de la gamme arabe* (1884), also gave extracts.[5]

Al-Fārābī also wrote a second volume to this *Kitāb al-mūsīqī al-kabīr*, which has not come down to us. It comprised four chapters (*maqālāt*), in which he says he examined and commented on the theories of the Greeks.[6] It was suggested by Kosegarten, Land, and Tripodo,[7] that the manuscript alluded to by Toderini, entitled the *Majāl al-mūsīqī* (Arena of Music), preserved in the 'Abd al-Ḥamīd Library at Constantinople, was perhaps, the lost second volume of the *Kitāb al-mūsīqī al-kabīr*.[8] But the title given by these writers was clearly

[1] Steinschneider, *Al-Fārābī*, 79.

[2] Robles, *Catálogo de los MSS. Arabes . . . Bibl. Nac. de Madrid.* No. 602. Derenbourg, in *Homenaje á D. Franc. Codera*, 612.

[3] Hammer-Purgstall, *Catalogo dei Codici arabi, persiani e turchi della Biblioteca Ambrosiana* (Bibl. Ital., T. xciv), No. 289.

[4] *Catalogus Codicum Orientalium Bibliothecae Academicae Lugduno Batavae*, No. 1423.

[5] It has been said that Jerome of Prague made a translation of part of the *Kitāb al-mūsīqī al-kabīr*, but see my *Arabian Influence on Musical Theory*, 15-16.

[6] *Zeitschrift f. d. Kunde d. Morgenlandes*, v. 150, 159. Munk, *Mélanges*, 350.

[7] Kosegarten, *Zeit. f. d. Kunde d. Morg.*, v. 150, but cf. *Lib. Cant.*, 35. Land, *Recherches*, 43, but cf. his *Remarks on the Earliest Development of Arabic Music* (*Trans. Inter. Congress of Orientalists*, 1892). Tripodo, *Lo stato degli studii sulla Musica degli Arabi*, 13.

[8] Toderini, *Letteratura Turchesca* (1787), i, 233.

an error for *Madkhal al-mūsīqī*,[1] of which copies exist in the 'Abd al-Ḥamīd Library,[2] as well as in other collections in Constantinôple,[3] and elsewhere.[4] Munk, too, was of opinion that the lost work was the one referred to by Andrés in his *Dell' origine, progressi . . . d'ogni Letteratura.*[5] This was also incorrect, since Andrés says that his information was based on particulars obtained from Casiri concerning a MS. in the Escurial, from which we know that it was the first volume of the *Kitāb al-mūsīqī al-kabīr* that was under discussion.[6]

Al-Fārābī also deals with music in his *Kitāb fī iḥṣā' al-'ulūm* (Classification of the Sciences). This work was translated into both Latin and Hebrew and is frequently quoted by Mediæval writers, under its Latin title, *De scientiis*,[7] as was another work of Al-Fārābī's, known as *De ortu scientiarum.*[8] Another work attributed to Al-Fārābī, but not mentioned under this title by his biographers, is a *Kitāb al-adwār* now in the Library of Aḥmad Taimūr.[9]

['Alī ibn Sa'īd al-Andalusī is the name of the author of a *Tract on Musical Composition* mentioned in an old catalogue of Oriental manuscripts.[10] Search for the identity of the writer and the location of the manuscript has been in vain. There is an 'Alī ibn Mūsā al-Maghribī called Ibn Sa'īd (1214-74 ?), who might conceivably be the same individual,[11] but it is more likely that the above writer should be identified with the 'Alī ibn Sa'īd al-Uqlīdisī (early tenth cent.) mentioned in the *Fihrist.*[12]]

[1] The original Italian edition of Toderini (as above) has *Medchalul Musikī*, which was clearly intended for what we would transliterate *madkhal al-mūsīqī*.

[2] Ḥājjī Khalīfa, vii, 520.

[3] Ḥājjī Khalīfa, vii, 318, 400, 453.

[4] *British Museum MS.*, Or. 2361, fol. 238, v.

[5] Munk, *Mélanges*, 350.

[6] See Toderini, i, 248-52.

[7] Farmer, *Arabian Influence on Musical Theory*, p. 15.

[8] *Beiträge z. Geschichte d. Philosophie d. Mittelalters*, xix.

[9] *Hilāl*, xxviii, 214.

[10] *Catalogue of Oriental Manuscripts purchased in Turkey, belonging to Dr. Lee*, 1830. Printed by R. Watts, London, 1831. Second Part, 1840. See my *Arabic Musical Manuscripts in the Bodleian Library*, p. 16.

[11] Cf. Brockelmann, i, 313, and 336.

[12] *Fihrist*, 285. Andalusī and Uqlīdisī could very easily be confused by a scribe.

CHAPTER VII

THE 'ABBĀSIDS

(The Fall; 945-1258)

"The soul of man derives many benefits from the song . . . and among them the calmness that it brings in the hour of care or pain."
Al-Ḥusain Ibn Zaila (d. 1048).

ALTHOUGH this chapter covers nominally the Khalifate of Baghdād from the coming of the Buwaihids to the fall of the city before the hordes of Hūlāgū in 1258, it also includes, as in the previous chapters, a survey of the history of the art in other Arabian lands, and specifically that of Al-Andalus up to the rout of the Muwaḥḥids (1230), and that of Egypt until the Mamlūk period (1250).

The break-up of the Baghdād Khalifate continued apace, and with it much of the culture that had made it illustrious. The intellectual and artistic decline only made itself felt however, in Al-'Irāq and the capital. Elsewhere, the independent kingdoms made up for what was being lost through the inactivity of Baghdād. During the Buwaihid (945-1055), Saljūqid (1055-1184), and Khwārizmian (1184-1231) "protection," some improvement in the cultural situation resulted to Al-'Irāq and the capital. Not that either of the first two had any particular gifts of refinement to offer. The coming of these "protectors" simply meant a wider patronage to general culture. Indeed, in most respects the "protectors" imitated the tastes of the "protected."

These were days as great and as glorious for Arabian culture as for Arabian polity, although both refer to lands that were outwith the Baghdād Khalifate,—that is to say,—Al-Andalus, Egypt, and Syria. The superiority of the Umayyad arms in the West, and of the Ayyūbids and Zangids in the East, from the tenth to the twelfth century, was only to be matched by their surpassing culture. This too broke through the walls of Western Mediæval civilization, and gave birth to the Renaissance. Elsewhere I have shown that music played an important part in this cultural conquest of Western Europe.[1]

§ I

By the mid-tenth century, the situation in Al-'Irāq and the capital was desperate, and the conquest of the land by the Buwaihids was, to some extent, a timely one. The conquerors themselves were Iranians from Al-Dailam. Since 933 they had been gradually advancing westward, wresting provinces from the khalif,—'Irāq 'Ajamī, Kirmān, Fārs, and Khuzistān. Their occupation of Baghdād checked for a time the lawless domination of the Turkish soldiery which had been a menace to the state for a century. Further, the Buwaihids, being of the Shī'a sect, curbed the orthodox fanatics. Scientific and philosophic speculation which had long been silent were given freedom once more, whilst music and the arts generally enjoyed a liberty that had been denied them under the Ḥanbalī rigours.

The khalifs of the Buwaihid period were Al-Muṭī' (946-74), Al-Ṭā'ī' (974-91), Al-Qādir (991-1031), and Al-Qā'im (1031-75), but the "Commander of the Faithful" exercised as little authority as he did under the Turkish soldiery the previous century. With "a mere pittance doled out for his support, the office was shorn of every token of respect and dignity."[2] Yet Le Strange says that at this period "the palaces of the khalifs may be considered to have attained their utmost extent and splendour."[3] Here, the same musical extravagance appears to have been carried on as in the days of the great khalifs. The group of philosophers and music theorists

[1] See my *Arabian Influence on Musical Theory* (1925), and *Facts for the Arabian Musical Influence* (1929).
[2] Muir, *The Caliphate*, 578.
[3] Le Strange, *Baghdād*,

known as the Ikhwān al-Ṣafa, and the bibliographer Muḥammad ibn Isḥāq al-Warrāq lived under these rulers.

Not only in the palaces of the khalifs were music, *belles lettres*, and learning generally patronized, but also in the palaces of the Buwaihids. One of the criticisms levelled against 'Izz al-Daula (967-77) was that he spent too much time with musicians and buffoons.[1] 'Aḍud al-Daula (977-82), who built the 'Aḍudī hospital which for three centuries was famous as a school of medicine,[2] was also interested in music.[3] Bahā' al-Daula (989-1012) had a *wazīr*, Fakhr al-Mulk, who protected the song collector Al-Maghribī, whilst another *wazīr*, Sābūr ibn Ardashīr, founded the Karkh academy with a library of 10,400 books.[4] Musharrif al-Daula (1020-25) made Al-Maghribī his *wazīr*. Mu'ayyid al-Daula (976-83) of Iṣfahān had a *wazīr*, Ibn 'Abbād, who possessed a library of 140,000 volumes.[5] Shams al-Daula (997—*c.* 1021) of Hamadhān was a patron of the scientist and music theorist Ibn Sīnā.

Whilst the various Buwaihids ruled the Baghdād Khalifate, i.e., Al-'Irāq (which included Khuzistān and Kirmān), 'Irāq 'Ajamī (which embraced the Caspian provinces), and Fārs,—Syria, Mesopotamia, and the whole of Arabia proper were in the hands of Arab rulers. The Ḥamdānids were established at Al-Mauṣil (929-91) and at Aleppo (944-1003). At the latter city was called forth one of the most important artistic and literary movements of the century.[6] The 'Uqailids (966-1096) succeeded to the lands of the Ḥamdānids of Al-Mauṣil whilst the Mirdāsids (1023-79) followed the Aleppo family. Contemporary with these dynasties were the Marwānids (990-1150) of Diyār-Bakr, and the Mazyādids (1012-1150) of Al-Ḥilla.

These Arab dynasties form one of the outstanding features of the period, and in spite of the fact that they

[1] *The Eclipse of the 'Abbāsid Caliphate*, ii, 234.
[2] Le Strange, *op. cit.*, 318.
[3] *The Eclipse of the 'Abbāsid Caliphate*, iii, 41, 68.
[4] Margoliouth, *Letters of Abū'l-'Alā*, xxiv. *Journal Asiatique*, July, 1838, p. 50.
[5] *Journal Asiatique*, July, 1838, p. 49. Another library at Al-Baṣra at this period numbered 10,000 volumes.
[6] Huart, *Arab. Lit.*, 90.

did not succeed in re-establishing a purely Arab polity[1] within the Khalifate (and the Ḥamdānids occupied Baghdād for a while), yet they were mainly responsible for a restoration of the indigenous arts and literature.[2] It was the Ḥamdānids, as we have seen, who sheltered Al-Fārābī the music theorist, and the music historians Al-Iṣfahānī and Al-Mas'ūdī. The 'Uqailids had the song-collector Al-Maghribī as their *wazīr*. In the peninsula itself,—Al-Yaman, Al-Ḥijāz, and 'Uman, needless to say, the Arabs held undisputed sway.

After a century of beneficent rule by the Buwaihid *umarā'*, the Saljūqid Turks became masters of the lands of the Khalifate. They came from Jand in Bukhārā, and had been pushing Westward since 1037, when they drove the Ghaznawids from Khurāsān and Ṭabaristān. In 1055 they conquered 'Irāq 'Ajamī and entered Baghdād, finally subjugating Syria and Asia Minor, claiming dominion from the Caucasus mountains to the borders of Afghānistān. The Saljūqids were of the Sunnī persuasion, *i.e.*, Orthodox Muslims, and they granted considerable freedom to the khalif, whom they acknowledged as spiritual head, and accepted investiture at his hands.

Al-Qā'im (1031-75) was the khalif at the Saljūqid conquest, and he was succeeded by Al-Muqtadī (1075-94), Al-Mustaẓhir (1094-1118), Al-Mustarshid (1118-35), Al-Rāshid (1135-36), Al-Muqtafī (1136-60), Al-Mustanjid (1160-70), and Al-Mustaḍī (1170-1180). There is little difference between their reigns. Some of them tried their hand at gaining independence but with small success. Others were content to be mere figure-heads, and spent their treasury on keeping up courtly surroundings. Only the last two khalifs occupied anything like an independent position. Every one of them appears however, to have exercised his right to distribute patents of authority to tributary *malik, sulṭān, amīr* or *atābag*.

The Saljūqids divided their dominions among their family,—the "Great Saljūqids" of Khurāsān (1037-1157) controlling Al-'Irāq, whilst others ruled in Kirmān

[1] Jurjī Zaidān, 264.
[2] *Ibid.*, 262.

N

(1041-1187), Asia Minor (1077-1300), and Syria (1094-1117). The earliest of the "Great Saljūqids" resided at Baghdād as well as at Nīsābūr, and one cannot fail to recognize that the protection which they gave to art and letters was greater even than that bestowed by the khalifs. It was Malik Shāh who patronized 'Umar al-Khayyām, whilst his *wazīr*, Niẓām al-Mulk, founded the Niẓāmiyya colleges at Baghdād and Nīsābūr. Sanjar (1117-57), the last of the "Great Saljūqids," was particularly attached to music, and his court minstrel, Kamāl al-Zamān, was far-famed. The 'Irāqian Saljūqid Maḥmūd (1117-31) protected the music theorist and scientist Abū'l-Ḥakam al-Bāhilī.

The Saljūqid *atābags* or provincial governors soon became independent rulers in their various districts. The first of these were the Anūshtigīnids of Khwārizm (1077–1231). Then came the Sukmānids of Armenia (1100–1207), the Urtuqids of Diyār-Bakr (1101-1408), the Būrids of Damascus (1103-54) the Zangids of Mesopotamia and Syria (1127-1250), the Īldigizids of Adharbaijān (1136-1225), the Bagtigīnids of Arbela (1144-1232), and the Salgharids of Fārs (1148-1287). This decentralization, as elsewhere, helped rather than retarded general culture. Towns which hitherto had mere provincial standing, now began to flourish as centres of government where courts were maintained with pomp and ceremony. Music theorists like Fakhr al-Dīn al-Rāzī, Muḥammad ibn Abī'l-Ḥakam, and Ibn Man'a, were patronized by the Anūshtigīnids, Zangids, and Bagtigīnids respectively.

Although the authority, both temporal and spiritual, of the Khalifate of Baghdād was wider under the Saljūqids than under the preceding "protectors," yet the real rulers were the Saljūqids, and they were "foreigners." Arabia itself however, was still left quite undisturbed in Arab hands. Al-Yaman was ruled at Zabīd by the Najāḥids (1021-1159) and Mahdīds (1159-73), and at Ṣan'ā by the Ṣulaiḥids (1037-98) and the Ḥamdānids (1098-1173), when the Egyptian Ayyūbids became masters. Al-Ḥijāz prospered under the Hāshimids until 1202, whilst 'Uman was still content with its *imāms*. In Al-Yaman the Najāḥid

Sa'īd al-Aḥwal (1080-89) favoured music and singing.[1] and the names of some of the Najāḥid songstresses have come down to us. Under the first of the Mahdīds,—'Alī ibn Mahdī (1159) who himself possessed an excellent voice, singing and wine were forbidden.[2] The Ṣulaiḥid Al-Mukarram Aḥmad ibn 'Alī (1080-91) and other rulers were particularly attached to music.[3]

It is still necessary to follow the developments political and cultural in the extreme East, for we must not forget that Islām was a world in itself. What is more, Iranians and Turanians were to be found everywhere in the lands of the Arabs, even in Al-Yaman, where the Ghuzz managed to gain a footing. At the Eastern extremity of the old Khalifate the Sāmānids' dominions had fallen to the Īlak Khāns (*c.* 932—*c.* 1165) of Turkestan, and to the Ghaznawids (962-1186) of Afghānistān. The latter became the leaders of Persian culture just as the Sāmānids had been. The literary, artistic, and scientific activity of the Ghaznawid rulers throws all the other contemporary Islāmic courts into the shade.[4] In the mid-twelfth century, the Ghūrids superseded the Ghaznawids, and their sulṭāns were not a whit behind their predecessors in the patronage of culture. Among their *protégés* was the music theorist 'Abd al-Mu'min ibn Ṣafī al-Dīn.

In 1180, the Khalifate fell to Al-Nāṣir (1180-1225) whose set purpose was to restore his office "to its ancient rôle among the nations."[5] Four years later, chafing at the Saljūqid yoke, he invited the Shāh of Khwārizm to rid him of his irksome suzerain. The shāh complied, and entering Al-'Irāq in 1184, he exterminated the Saljūqids. The next khalifs—Al-Ẓāhir (1225-26) and Al-Mustanṣir (1226-42)—were the son and grandson respectively of Al-Nāṣir. This period was one of comparative quiet. Under Al-Nāṣir "learning flourished" and "schools and libraries were patronized."[6] whilst the famous Al-

[1] Kay, *Yaman, Its Early Mediæval History*, 84, 108, 116.
[2] *Ibid.*, 124.
[3] *Ibid.*, 40, 51, 54.
[4] Browne, *Lit. Hist. of Persia*, ii, chap. ii.
[5] Muir, *The Caliphate*, 587.
[6] *Ibid.*, 589.

Mustanṣiriyya college at Baghdād, built by his successor, accumulated a library of 80,000 books. But the sands of the Khalifate were running low.

Al-Musta'ṣim (1242-58) was the last khalif of Baghdād. During his reign, much of the ancient pomp and dignity of the Khalifate were restored. He was not merely a patron of culture, but lived the life of a literary man and bibliophile. The author of the *Fakhrī* says that he spent many of his leisure hours listening to music.[1] One of the most celebrated musicians of Arabian history,—Ṣafī al-Dīn 'Abd al-Mu'min, was his chief minstrel.

In the year 1219, Chingiz Khān and his Mughal hordes conquered the Eastern lands of the Khwārizmian empire. His son Ugdai completed the conquest in 1231 which resulted in the death of the last Shāh of Khwārizm. In 1256, Hūlāgū, a grandson of the former, crossed the Oxus to chastise the Ismā'īlī. This having been accomplished, the khān marched on Baghdād, and in the beginning of 1258, the "City of Peace" was invested, stormed and taken. Then followed weeks of massacre, pillage and burning, the details of which make the fall of Baghdād the most awful and frightful episode in history. Out of over two million inhabitants says Ibn Khaldūn, one million six hundred thousand were put to the sword or otherwise perished,[2] including the khalif and every member of his family on whom hands could be laid. Palaces, mosques, and colleges were burned or destroyed after having been ransacked. Learned men, professors, literary men, and *imāms*, were slaughtered as ruthlessly as whole libraries of books, the treasures of centuries, were committed to the flames or the Tigris.[3] "The loss suffered by Muslim learning," says the late Professor E. G. Browne, "defies description and almost surpasses imagination: not only were thousands of priceless books utterly annihilated, but owing to the number of men of learning who perished or barely escaped with their lives, the very tradition of accurate scholarship and original research, so conspicuous

[1] *Fakhrī*, 571. Howorth, *op. cit.*, iii, 113, 117.

[2] The figures differ in the various accounts.

[3] Ibn Sa'īd al Maghribī (d. 1274 or 1286) who was at Baghdād just before this, visited thirty-six libraries in the city.

in Arabic literature before this period, was almost destroyed."[1] So ende.. the Khalifate of Baghdād.

We have now to turn our attention to other important centres of Arabian polity and culture,—Al-Andalus and Egypt.

In Al-Andalus, the arts, literature and science flourished with such brilliance that their light was reflected to all parts, not only of the world of Islām, but of Western Europe. At the opening of this period "the torch of science" says Ṣā'id ibn Aḥmad (d. 1069) "shone brighter than ever," in Al-Andalus. The Greek sciences were especially studied. The fame of its people has been expressed in a panegyric of Ibn Ghālib (d. 1044) who likens them to the Indians "in their love of learning, as well as their assiduous cultivation of science," and to the Greeks "in their knowledge of the physical and natural sciences."[2] Ibn al-Ḥijārī (d. 1194) says that during the reign of the Umayyads in Al-Andalus (eighth to eleventh century), "students from all parts of the world flocked . . . to learn the sciences of which Cordova was the most noble repository, and to derive knowledge from the mouth of the doctors and *'ulamā'* who swarmed in it."[3]

Al-Ḥakam II (961-76) was the khalif who succeeded the great 'Abd al-Raḥmān III. Like his predecessor, he was a liberal patron of culture. Being a zealous bibliophile he dispatched emissaries to Cairo, Baghdād, Damascus and other cities, to procure books, and in this way collected a library of some 600,000 volumes.[4] He sent 1,000 pieces of gold to the author of the great *Kitāb al-aghānī*, so as to be one of the first to obtain a copy of his *magnum opus*.[5]

Hishām II (976-1009) was a weakling who was ruled by his minister Al-Manṣūr and the theologians. While the

[1] Browne, *Lit. Hist. of Persia*, ii, 463.

[2] Curiously enough, this writer says that all this superiority of the Andalusians was due to planetary influence. According to him their musical gifts were due to Venus and their love of learning and science to Mercury.

[3] Al-Maqqarī, *Moh. Dyn.*, i, 30, 117-8, 140, and Appendix xl.

[4] The number given by Casiri (i, 38) is 600,000, but Al-Maqqarī (*Moh. Dyn.*) says 400,000.

[5] Al-Maqqarī, *op. cit.*, ii, 169.

wazīr led his victorious armies against the Christians in the North, the theologians made war on heresy in Islām. The special aversion of the theologians was Greek science, and works on natural philosophy and astronomy especially were seized and destroyed.[1] The sciences actually fell into desuetude for a time on this account.

After the death of Al-Manṣūr in 1002, the Prætorian guards became masters of the situation. These were Slavs (hence their name *ṣaqāliba*) and Berbers, and precisely the same turn of affairs that happened to the Baghdād Khalifate now came to that of Cordova. In less than thirty years, no fewer than nine khalifs occupied the throne, some of them twice. The first of these puppet khalifs was Muḥammad II *al-Mahdī* (1009-10). He gave offence to the orthodox by reason of his indulgence in music and wine. His palace resounded with a hundred lutes (*'īdān*) and as many reed-pipes (*mazāmīr*).[2] Al-Mustakfī (1024-27) had a daughter Wallāda who was a famous poetess and musician. The last of these puppet khalifs was Hishām III (1027-31), and on his fall the House of Umayya ceased in Al-Andalus. In a year or two Cordova became a republic.

The land then became split up under numerous " Party Kings " (*mulūk al-ṭawā'if*), who set up courts at Malaga (Ḥammūdids, 1016-57), Algeciras (Ḥammūdids, 1039-58), Seville ('Abbādids, 1023-91), Granada (Zairids, 1012-90), Cordova (Jahwarids, 1031-68), Toledo (Dhū'l-Nūnids, 1035-85), Valencia ('Āmirids, 1021-1085), Saragossa (Tujibids, 1019; Hūdids, 1039-1141), Denia (Mujāhids, 1017-75) and others. " The cause of science and literature " says Al-Shaqandī (d. 1231), " instead of losing, gained considerably " by the break-up of Al-Andalus into petty states.[3] These rulers " delighted to do honour to learning and *belles lettres* and made their courts the homes of poets and musicians."[4]

The 'Abbādids of Seville, who for a time ruled Cordova, were the most important of these kings. Al-Shaqandī

[1] Al-Maqqarī, *Moh. Dyn.*, i, 141
[2] Dozy, *Hist. des Mus. d'Espagne*, iii, 284.
[3] Al-Maqqarī, *Moh. Dyn.*, i, 35. See also i, 37, 40, 42, 53, 67.
[4] S. Lane-Poole, *The Moors in Spain*, 176.

avers that the 'Abbādids " showed a greater passion for literature than was even shown by the Ḥamdānids in Aleppo,"[1] and Seville had long been famed for its cultivation of art and science.[2] Al-Mu'tamid (1068-91) the last 'Abbādid ruler, says a contemporary poet Ibn al-Kattā (b. 1041), made his court " the meeting-place of the learned . . . the resort of poets and literary men."[3] This monarch was a singer and a performer on the *'ūd* and his son, 'Ubaidallāh al-Rashīd, was also a cultured musician and poet who performed on both the *'ūd* and *mizhar*.[4] His inordinate passion for music offended his subjects.[5] The songs of the court poet 'Abd al-Jabbār ibn Ḥamdīs, a Sicilian Arab, were the rage of the Sevillian musicians.[6] One of the 'Abbādids used to carry a copy of the great *Kitāb al-aghānī* about with him on his itineraries.[7] According to Al-Shaqandī, Seville was famous for its manufacture of musical instruments, in which it had an export trade,[8] and Ibn Rushd (d. 1198) testifies that it was the centre of this industry.[9]

At Toledo, the splendour and extravagance of the entertainments of the Dhū'l-Nūnids gave rise to the proverb,—" Like a Dhū'l-Nūnid banquet."[10] It was this city that boasted of the celebrated musician Abū'l-Ḥusain ibn Abī Ja'far al-Waqshī. The *amīr* Yaḥyā al-Ma'mūn (d. 1074) fostered the study of the mathematical sciences,[11] and it was through the portals of Toledo that many of the Latin translations from the Arabic of the sciences found their way into Christian Europe.[12]

Other petty rulers were just as keen in their patronage of music. Indeed, the gallant Cid himself censured them

[1] Al-Maqqarī, *op. cit.*, i, 36.
[2] Al-Maqqarī, *op. cit.*, i, 59. It was the home of science in Gothic days, i, 26.
[3] Al-Maqqarī, ii, 301.
[4] For music under the 'Abbādids, see *Scriptorum Arabum loci de Abbadidis*, edited by Dozy (1846-52), i, 394, 422 ; ii, 40, 62, 71.
[5] Al-Maqqarī, *op. cit.*, ii, 254.
[6] His songs were published by Schiaparelli in his *Il Canzoniere di Ibn Hamdīs* (Rome, 1897).
[7] Ḥājjī Khalīfa, i, 367.
[8] Al-Maqqarī, *Moh. Dyn.*, i, 58-9. [9] *Ibid.*, i, 42.
[10] Dozy, *Hist. des Mus. d'Espagne*, ii, 255.
[11] Al-Maqqarī, *Moh. Dyn.*, i, 384.
[12] Haskins, *Studies in Mediæval Science*, 12-13.

for dabbling so much with "wine, woman, and song."[1] A certain Aḥmad ibn Muḥammad al-Yamanī testifies to the inordinate taste for music by the inhabitants of Malaga in 1015. He heard the sounds of the *'ūd* (lute), *ṭunbūr* (pandore,) *mizmār* (reed-pipe), and other instruments on every side.[2] Al-Shaqandī (d. 1231) remarks on the fondness of the people of Ubeda near Jaen for music and dancing, and the fame of this town for its dancing-girls.[3] Saragossa boasted of a great mathematician and music theorist in Abū'l-Faḍl Ḥasdāy.

In Al-Andalus, music and poetry belonged, not so much to a special class as in the East, but to the people at large. Zakariyyā al-Qazwīnī (d. 1283) mentions in his *Āthār al-bilād* that at Shilb in Portugal almost every inhabitant displayed an interest in literature, and that one could find even ploughmen capable of improvising in verse.[4]

In the second half of the eleventh century, the Christians began to seriously threaten the Muslim states, and when Toledo fell in 1085, the Andalusians petitioned their co-religionists the Murāwids of North Africa to extend their help. The latter entered Al-Andalus in 1086 and defeated the Christian army at Zallāqa near Badajoz. Like all "protectors," the Murāwids had their price, and that was Al-Andalus. The petty kingdoms were broken up and the whole land became part of the empire of Morocco.

The new masters were fanatics, and with them the *faqīh* (theologian) possessed an enormous influence. "Freethought became impossible," whilst "culture and science faded away."[5] Even the *Iḥyā 'ulūm al-dīn* of Al-Ghazālī was interdicted. Poets and musicians were scarcely looked on with favour publicly. One of the great names however that stand out during this period is that of the celebrated Ibn Bājja the philosopher and music teacher, known in Western Europe as Avenpace. It is

[1] *Primera crónica general.* (*Nueva Biblioteca de Autores Espan.* 1906), i, 589. Quoted by Ribera.
[2] *Hadīqat al-afrāḥ* (Cairo Edit.) p. 127.
[3] Al-Maqqarī, *Moh. Dyn.*, i, 54.
[4] Al-Qazwīnī, *Āthār al-bilād* (Wüstenfeld Edit.), 364.
[5] Nicholson, *Lit. Hist. of the Arabs*, 431.

the life of Ibn Bājja that shows us that the Murāwids were not so averse to the fine arts after all. At any rate they kept their singing-girls as did their predecessors, as we know from a story told of the Murāwid *amīr* of Saragossa Ibn Tīfalawīt.[1] The Murāwids were soon to find masters themselves.

In 1130 a new power arose in North Africa. This was the Muwaḥḥids. Attacking the Murāwids in Morocco and Al-Andalus (1144-5) they practically exterminated them. The Muwaḥḥids ruled Al-Andalus and North Africa for nearly a century. Like the Murāwids, the Muwaḥḥids were Berbers, but they were "far more enlightened and favourable to culture than the Murāwids had been."[2] During their *régime* some of the greatest names of Arabian culture became world-famous, and among them,—Ibn Ṭufail, Ibn Rushd (Averroës) Mūsā ibn Maimūn (Maimonides), and Ibn Sab'īn, all of whom however, were persecuted on account of their philosophical opinions.

The Muwaḥḥids eventually suffered the fate of their predecessors. In 1228, the Ḥafṣids of Tunis claimed their independence, and by 1230, the Christians had driven the Muwaḥḥids from Al-Andalus back to North Africa. The final blow to the Muwaḥḥids came in 1269 when the Marīnids of Morocco ousted them from their very stronghold. The disastrous rout of the Muwaḥḥids was not however, the end of the Arabs in Al-Andalus. Granada gave shelter to the surviving Arab population, and here the Naṣrid dynasty (1232-1492) held the banner of Islām aloft against the Christians of the peninsula.

Egypt, at the opening of this period, was ruled by the Ikhshīdids (938-69), but in the latter year they were ousted by the Fāṭimid khalifs from the West. The newcomers removed their capital from Al-Mahdiyya near Tunis to Al-Qāhira (Cairo) a new quarter of Fusṭāṭ, which was soon to become the centre of Arabian culture for the Near East. The Fāṭimids, claiming descent from Fāṭima the daughter of the Prophet, assumed the title of khalif,

[1] Ibn Khaldūn, *Prol.*, iii, 426-7.
[2] Nicholson, *Lit. Hist. of the Arabs*, 432. Al-Marrākushī, 159, 170-5.

and were recognized as such by the Shī'a world of Islām, dispensing patents of regality to their spiritual subjects as far off as Delhī.[1] Naturally, a magnificent court was maintained at Cairo, where every effort was made to outdo the prestige of the Baghdād Khalifate. Art, science, and letters were promoted under their ægis, whilst music and musicians were encouraged with prodigality.

Al-Mu'izz (953-75) was the first Fāṭimid khalif to rule in Egypt, and he is described as "an accomplished scholar, well versed in science and philosophy and a munificent patron of arts and learning."[2] His son Tamīm was an accomplished poet and like his father, a keen devotee to music.[3] During this reign the Fāṭimids extended their power to Syria and Al-Ḥijāz, completed the conquest of Sicily, and broke the power of the *Qarāmiṭa* (Carmathians).

Al-'Azīz (975-96) accomplished the conquest of Syria and of a considerable part of Mesopotamia. The Fāṭimid empire now extended from the Euphrates to the Atlantic. The khalif's court indulged in the most inordinate luxury and unheard-of splendour.[4] He founded the college at the Azhar, which had been built in the previous reign.

Al-Ḥākim (996-1021) ascended the throne as a child under the tutelage of his Slav *ustād* Barjawān. This tutor is recorded as having lavished too much attention upon musicians, and in this way neglected the proper attention to his ward.[5] After the assassination of Barjawān, the young khalif revealed himself a bigot and barbarian. He forbade all public amusements, and musicians were threatened with banishment if they dared follow their vocation.[6] At the same time he gave encouragement to the historian and song collector Al-Musabbiḥī, and patronized the physicist and music theorist Ibn al-Haitham. The literature and science of

[1] Al-Badā'ūnī, i, 94, 310. *Ṭabaqāt al-nāṣirī*, ii, 616.
[2] Syed Ameer Ali, *A Short Hist. of the Saracens*, 597.
[3] Ibn Khallikān, *Biog. Dict.*, iii, 494.
[4] Wüstenfeld, *Gesch. der Fat.-Chal.*, 162. S. Lane-Poole, *A Hist. of Egypt in the Middle Ages*, 120-3.
[5] S. Lane-Poole, *op. cit.*, 125.
[6] Ibn Khallikān, *Biog. Dict.*, iii, 451.

music were not counted among the *malāhī* in the same way as "listening to music" was. He built colleges and observatories in both Egypt and Syria, including the famous *Dār al-ḥikma* (Hall of Science), erected in 1005.

Al-Zāhir (1021-36), unlike his father, cultivated an immoderate taste for the *malāhī* or forbidden pleasures. He was an accomplished amateur in music and spent fabulous sums of money on his female singers.[1] He became completely engrossed in a sybaritic life, in which "his love of music and dancers was combined with a savage cruelty."[2]

Al-Mustanṣir (1036-94) was similarly appassioned for musicians and singing-girls, and an estate near the Nile known as the *Arḍ al-ṭabbāla* (Demesne of the Female Drummer) was a gift to a favourite singing-girl.[3] He ignored many of the precepts of Islām, and his *wazīr* Al-Yāzurī had pictures painted of dancing-girls.[4] The khalif had a pavilion with a pond of wine constructed in imitation of the *Zamzam* building and well at Mecca. Here he passed his hours drinking and feasting to the music of stringed instruments and singers, saying,—"This is pleasanter than staring at a black stone, listening to the drone of the *mu'adhdhin*, and drinking bad water!"[5] It was during this reign that the Persian traveller Nāṣir-i Khusrau visited Egypt and wrote so enthusiastically about the Fāṭimid splendour, including its military music.[6] Of all the Fāṭimid khalifs, Al-Mustanṣir was the richest, and his reign is certainly the most splendid, in spite of anarchy, famine, and pestilence. The inventory of his treasures, as recorded by Al-Maqrīzī, reads, as Stanley Lane-Poole says,[7] "like a fable in *The Thousand*

[1] Al-Maqrīzī, *Al-Mawā'iẓ*, 355.
[2] S. Lane-Poole, *op. cit.*, 136.
[3] *Ibid.*, 139. Al-Maqrīzī, *op. cit.*, 338.
[4] *Ibid.*, 111.
[5] S. Lane-Poole, *op. cit.*, 145. This refers to the sacred stone built into the wall of the *Ka'ba* at Mecca, and the *Zamzam* well opposite it, whose waters the pilgrims drink. The *mu'adhdhin* is he who chants the call (*adhān*) to prayer.
[6] Nāṣir-i Khusrau, *Safar nāma* (Paris, 1881), pp. 43, 46, 47.
[7] S. Lane-Poole, *op. cit.*, 147.

and One Nights." His library housed over 100,000 volumes.[1]

Al-Musta'lī (1094-1101) and Al-Āmir (1101-1131) were the next khalifs. The latter, like most of his predecessors, was addicted to pleasure and music. He patronized Abū'l-Ṣalt Umayya the scientist, composer, and music theorist. During this period the real decline of the Fāṭimid Khalifate asserted itself. The loss of Syria and Palestine to the Crusaders was a serious blow to its prestige.

Al-Ḥāfiẓ (1131-49) was deeply interested in astrology,[2] and it was for him that a court physician made a special drum whose notes were supposed to cure a malady from which he suffered. It was constructed of seven different metals "welded at the exact moment when the southing of each of the seven planets promised fortunate results."[3] This instrument was preserved in the palace until the time of Salāḥ al-Dīn when it was accidentally broken by one of his soldiers.[4]

Al-Ẓāfir (1149-54) is blamed for having given more attention to music than to arms and politics.[5] A copy of the great *Kitāb al-aghānī* that was made for this monarch is still preserved.

Under the next two khalifs,—Al-Fā'iz (1154-60) and Al-'Āḍid (1160-71), the Fāṭimid dynasty was hurried to its close. The end came when the two Zangid generals Shīrkūḥ and Salāḥ al-Dīn entered the capital in 1169. Two years later the last of the Fāṭimid khalifs died, and Salāḥ al-Dīn better known as Saladin, the first of the Ayyūbids, became the ruler of Egypt.

[1] *Ibid.*, 149. Some writers put the total of this Khalifate library at *two million* books. It was pillaged during his reign by the Turkish soldiery, yet when Salāḥ al-Dīn took control in 1171, there were still 120,000 volumes in the khalif's library. They eventually passed into the possession of the Fāḍiliyya college. It is said that this library contained 6,500 works on the *quadrivium* alone. See the figures given in the *Journal Asiatique*, July, 1838, p. 55 *et seq.*, *Encyclopædia of Islām*, ii, 1045, and Leclerc, *Histoire de la Médecine arabe*, i, 583.

[2] Al-Maqrīzī, *Al-Mawā'iẓ*, 357.

[3] This was prompted by the astro-musical theories which held a place in therapeutics. See my brochure *The Influence of Music: From Arabic Sources* (1926).

[4] S. Lane-Poole, *op. cit.*, 169.

[5] *Ibid.*, 171.

Although the Fāṭimid period is one of the most brilliant for intellectual culture in Arabian history, and in science alone the *Dār al-ḥikma* (Hall of Science) and such names as Isḥāq al-Isrā'īlī, Ibn Riḍwān, and Ibn al-Haitham, known to Western Europe as Isaac Israeli, Rodoam, and Alhazen, enable us to appreciate to some extent what this amounts to, yet it is in the fine arts probably that their great patronage was most fruitful. Not only in their architecture but in their encouragement of the industrial arts, the Fāṭimids have left a glorious record.

Under the Ayyūbids (1171-1250), Egypt returned to the Sunnī or Orthodox faith, and the Shī'a creed was tabooed. The name of the 'Abbāsid khalif of Baghdād was re-inserted in the *khuṭba*[1] in place of that of the Fāṭimid, and in return the khalif created Ṣalāḥ al-Dīn a *sulṭān*. The Ayyūbids extended their dominions to Mesopotamia, Syria, Palestine, Tripoli, and Al-Yaman, and dynasties were set up in Mesopotamia (1200-44), Damascus (1186-1260), Aleppo (1186-1260), Ḥama (1178-1341), Ḥimṣ (1178-1262), and Al-Yaman (1173-1228).

Music and the arts in general flourished under these sulṭāns. Ṣalāḥ al-Dīn (1171-93) and Al-'Azīz (1193-98) were the patrons of scholars. The famous Mūsā ibn Maimūn was employed by them, and the scientists and music theorists Abū Zakariyyā al-Bayāsī and Abū Naṣr ibn al-Maṭrān were favoured. "Of the cultivated tastes" of 'Ādil (1199-1218), Al-Kāmil (1218-38), and Al-Ṣāliḥ (1240-49), says Stanley Lane-Poole, "we have contemporary evidence from Ibn Khallikān, Ibn al-Athīr, and Bahā' al-Dīn Zuhair."[2] Although Al-Ashraf Mūsā (1250-52) was named in the *khuṭba*, the rule of the Ayyūbids in Egypt ended with Tūrānshāh (1249-50), when the Turkish Baḥrī Mamlūks took the reins of government.

Under the Ayyūbids a new phase of culture is said to have been developed, which, so far as the court and society is concerned, is claimed to have been due in some

[1] The Friday oration delivered in the mosque. It comprises praise to Allāh, blessing on the Prophet and his descendants, and prayer for the Khalif.

[2] S. Lane-Poole, *op. cit.*, 240.

respects to Turkish ideas.[1] How music was affected we shall see later.

§ II

In spite of political adversity in both the East and West, the Muslim states still held their own in the battle throng, in art, in science, and in philosophy. One has but to mention such names as Salāḥ al-Dīn (Saladin), the Alcazar at Seville, Ibn Sīnā (Avicenna), and Ibn Rushd (Averroës), and the truth of this is as palpable as the noon-day sun. No serious change had come to the social life of the Arab in these days of "the fall." Music was still "the one thing needful" where joy was concerned, and was as fully appreciated as ever it had been, although, strange to say, the stricter Muslims were even more insistent on its condemnation. Indeed, the polemical writings concerned with the lawfulness of music help us to understand the temper of the age, for it would seem that this descanting on the "sin of listening," just as much as the pessimistic poetry of the period, was nurtured, as much by the introspective state of minds created by the political events as anything else. The curious point about this debate is that, after Al-Ghazālī (d. 1111), music came to play an important part in the dervish (*darwīsh*) and marabout (*murābiṭ*) fraternities. The cue for this had been given by *ṣūfī* teaching and practice.[2]

We have already seen how the opposition to music arose, and a landmark in the controversy is the *Dhamm al-malāhī* (Disapprobation of Musical Instruments) of Ibn Abī'l Dunyā (d. 894). Since the Ḥanbalī governance, the discussion seems to have become more acute in Al-'Irāq, and by the twelfth century a literature specially devoted to this subject abounded. The legal position was regularized by such authoritative writers as the Shāfi'ī Al-Māwardī (d. 1058) and the Ḥanafī Al-Marghīnānī (d. 1197) whose *Hidāya* became the most widely read compend of Muslim law.[3] Opinions however, were to a

[1] *Encyclopædia of Islām*, i, 223.
[2] See Chapter II, p. 35.
[3] Al-Māwardī's works however, were not published during his lifetime.

great extent controlled by the teaching of the great philosopher Al-Ghazālī (d. 1111). As Principal of the Niẓāmiyya colleges at Baghdād and Nīsāpūr, he exercised an enormous influence, and his defence of music (*al-samā'*) in his monumental *Iḥyā 'ulūm al-dīn* (Revivification of the Religious Sciences), so widely read, must have served as a balm to the consciences of many on this subject.[1] His brother who succeeded him as Principal of the Niẓāmiyya college at Baghdād,—Abū'l-Futuḥ Majd al-Dīn Aḥmad ibn Muḥammad ibn Muḥammad al-Ṭūsī, was also a strong champion of music, which is testified by his *Kitāb biwāriq al-asmā'* preserved at the Staatsbibliothek at Berlin.[2] Another writer of the period in Al-'Irāq, 'Abd al-Laṭīf al-Baghdādī (d. 1232), also wrote a *Kitāb al-samā'*.[3]

In Syria, we see the problem handled by Tāj al-Dīn al-Sarkhadī (d. 1275), a Ḥanafī professor at the Nūriyyī college at Damascus, who wrote a *Tashnīf al-asmā'* (Condemnation of Listening to Music), and by the Shāfi'ī *muftī* 'Abd al-Raḥmān ibn Ibrāhīm al-Firkāḥ (d. 1291), the author of a *Kashf al-qinā' fī ḥall al-samā'* (Lifting the Veil in the Solution of Listening to Music).[4]

In the West, as early as the tenth century, we have seen Ibn 'Abd Rabbihi reproving those who argued that listening to music was sinful.[5] At the same time there were legists who were influencing opinion that music was to be condemned.[6] By the close of the eleventh century, the fanatical Murāwids were masters in the land, and the pleadings of the partisans of *al-samā'* were hushed, the *Iḥyā 'ulūm al-dīn* of Al-Ghazālī being among the works interdicted. By the twelfth century we have Abū Bakr ibn al-'Arabī (d. 1151), a celebrated *qāḍī* of Seville, defend-

[1] The text of the *Iḥyā* was issued at Cairo in the year A.H. 1326. The 7th section of the 2nd *rub'*, which deals with the question under discussion, was translated by Professor D. B. Macdonald in the *Journal of the Royal Asiatic Society* (1901-2) under the title of " Emotional Religion in Islām as Affected by Music and Singing."

[2] Ahlwardt, *Verz.*, No. 5505.

[3] *Ibid.*, No. 5536, 8.

[4] Ahlwardt, *Verz.*, No. 5536, 9.

[5] *'Iqd al-farīd*, iii, 176.

[6] Aljoxani, *Historia de los Jueces de Córdoba*, 255.

ing music against the strictures of the extremists.[1] A townsman of his, Aḥmad ibn Muḥammad al-Ishbīlī (d. 1253) was the author of a *Kitāb al-samā' wa aḥkāmuhu* (Book of Listening to Music and its Ordinances).[2]

The *'ulamā'* or *fuqahā'* (legists) could rail as they pleased, for it made little difference in the long run. The *ṭabl khāna* (military band) still cheered the soldiers; the *mughannī* (professional musician) still found unlimited patronage in public and private festivities; the *qaina* (singing-girl) was yet an adornment of the *ḥarīm*; and the *darwīsh* (dervish) was beginning to regulate his *dhikr* (ritual) by means of music. The poets still sang in praise of music, musicians, and musical instruments.[3] Perhaps the musicians themselves did not hold quite the same social position that we see them enjoying in the great *Kitāb al-aghānī* or in the earlier stories of the *Alf laila wa laila*, but they were still people of importance. Even the Ikhwān al-Ṣafā', Ibn Sīnā and Ibn Zaila, refer their readers to the rules of the practitioners when they consider it necessary. The important position of Ṣafī al-Dīn 'Abd al-Mu'min at the Baghdād court is, perhaps, no criterion, since he was first of all the court librarian and scribe, but the fact that eminent scientists and men of letters like Abū'l-Ṣalt Umayya, Ibn Bājja, Abū'l-Ḥakam al-Bāhilī, and Abū'l-Majd Muḥammad ibn Abī'l-Ḥakam all boasted of being performers on the *'ūd* (lute) shows that the art of music was still "respectable." There were of course, certain reasons besides art and mere diversion that made music necessary, for as one of the characters says in the *Alf laila wa laila*,[4]—" To some people music is meat, and to others medicine."

The doctrine of the " influence of music " was given a fresh lease of life by contact with the Greek notions of the *ēthos*. As for the doctrine of the Harmony of the Spheres, the Ikhwān al-Ṣafā' say,—" It is clear that to the move-

[1] Ibn al-'Arabī's work does not appear to have come down to us, but it is freely quoted in the *Kitāb al-imtā' wa'l-intifā'* in the National Library at Madrid (Robles, *Catálogo*, No. 603.).

[2] Ahlwardt, *Verz.*, No. 5536, 7.

[3] Al-Nuwairī, *Nihāyat al-arab*, v, 113-22.

[4] *Alf laila wa laila*, ii, 87.

ment of the spheres and stars are notes (*naghamāt*) and melodies (*alḥān*)." In this doctrine was found the "first cause" fōr all music in the world of "generation and corruption." They taught that "the temperaments of the body are of many varieties, and the animal natures of many kinds. And to every temperament and every nature is a note resembling it and a melody befitting it." For that reason, music was employed in the hospitals because "it lightened the pain of disease and sickness from the afflicted."[1] Every genre (*jins*) and tone (*tamdīd*) in music, as well as every melodic and rhythmic mode had its particular ethical value.[2] Ibn Sīnā says that certain modes should be allocated to particular periods of the day and night. He says,—"It behoves that the musician should tune the time of the false dawn (*ṣubḥ al-kādhib*) with the [mode] *Rāhawī*, and the time of the true dawn (*ṣubḥ al-ṣādiq*) with the *Ḥusain*, and the rising of the sun with the *Rāst*, and the time of the forenoon (*ḍuḥā*) with the *Būsalīk*[3]; and the time of midday (*niṣf al-nahār*) with the *Zankūlā*, and the time of noon (*ẓuhr*) with the *'Ushshāq*, and between the prayers with the *Ḥijāz*, and the time of the afternoon (*'aṣr*) with the *'Irāq*, and the time of sunset (*ghurūb*) with the *Iṣfahān*, and the time of nightfall (*maghrib*) with the *Nawā*, and after the evening prayer (*'ashā'*) with the *Buzurk*, and the time of sleep with the *Mukhālif* (= *Zīrāfkand*)."[4]

His disciple Al-Ḥusain ibn Zaila devotes considerable attention to the ethical aspect of this question.[5] Ṣafī al-Dīn 'Abd al-Mu'min says that "every mode (*shadd*) has an influence on the soul, only that it is of different kinds. Some influence courage and simplicity, and these are three,—the *'Ushshāq*, *Abū Salīk*, and *Nawā*. . . . And as for the *Rāst*, *Naurūz*, *'Irāq*, and *Iṣfahān*, then they pacify the soul with a pleasant pacification, delightful. And as for the *Buzurk*, *Rāhawī*, *Zīrāfkand*,

[1] Ikhwān al-Ṣafā' (Bombay Edit.), i, 87, 92, 100-1.
[2] *Mafātīḥ al-'ulūm*, p. 243-4.
[3] =*Abū Salīk*.
[4] *British Museum MS.*, Or. 2361, fol 201 v.
[5] *British Museum MS.*, Or. 2361, fol. 226 v.

Zankūla, Husainī, and *Ḥijāzī,* they influence grief, lassitude."[1]

After the period covered by the great *Kitāb al-aghānī,* which takes us to the opening of the tenth century, we have little information concerning the type of verse used in the vocal music of these days, the works of writers of the same class as Abū'l-Faraj al-Iṣfahānī having been lost. The names of four important eleventh to thirteenth century poets, whose verses were set to music, have been preserved. They are Al-Bayādī (d. 1076), Ibn Ḥamdīs (d. 1132) of Seville, Abū 'Abdallāh al-Abla (d. *ca.* 1138) of Baghdād, and Taqī al-Dīn al-Sarūqī (d. 1294) of Cairo. In the British Museum there is a MS. dating from the thirteenth century, which contains the words of songs, each superscribed with the name of the mode in which it was sung.[2] From Al-Andalus and North Africa there have come down to us the words of the classical *naubāt,* even though the music may be questioned.[3] It was in Al-Andalus that the popular verse-forms—the *zajal* and *muwashshaḥ*—came. These became the more general vehicles for songs.[4] Popular verse, when set to music caught the public taste, as we know from Ḍiyā' al-Dīn Ibn al-Athīr (d. 1239).[5]

'Abd al-Qādir ibn Ghaibī (d. 1435) who deals at length with the various art-forms that were current in his day tells us that in olden days the recognized vocal forms were the *nauba, nashīd,* and *basīṭ.* The last-named was a *qiṭ'a* which had to be set to one of the *thaqīl* rhythms.[6]

As of old, melodies could be either set to rhythm (*īqā'*) or not. The technical terms for these two features were *naẓm al-naghamāt* (arrangement of the notes) and *nashr al-naghamāt* (dispersion of the notes).

Among the melodies that were set to the rhythmic modes were those known as the *dastānāt* (sing. *dastān*),[7]

[1] *Kitāb al-adwār,* faṣl xiv. For further information on this question see my brochure *The Influence of Music : From Arabic Sources.*

[2] *British Museum MS.,* Or. 136, fols. 40-55 v.

[3] *Majmū' al-aghānī wa'l-alḥān.* (Algiers, 1904).

[4] Ibn Khaldūn, *Prol.,* iii, 422, 436, 441. Hartmann, *Das Muwaššah.* Schack, *Poesie und Kunst der Araber in Spanien und Sizilien.*

[5] *Al-mathal al-sā'ir* (Būlāq, A. H., 1282), 46.

[6] *British Museum MS.,* Or. 2361, fol. 215 v.

[7] *Ibid.,* fol. 233.

the origin of which has been ascribed to Bārbad the minstrel of the Sāsānian monarch Khusrau Parwīz (d. 628).[1] Eight rhythmic modes are given by Ibn Sīnā[2] and Al-Ḥusain ibn Zaila,[3] and they are quoted not only on the authority of Al-Kindī and Al-Fārābī, but also according to the contemporary practitioners. Agreement between them is lacking, and it is difficult even to make them conform to the rules of the *Mafātīḥ al-'ulūm* and the Ikhwān al-Ṣafā'. In the days of Ṣafī al-Dīn ' Abd al-Mu'min only six of these rhythmic modes were current. This author informs us that the Persians had several rhythmic modes that were unknown to the Arabs, and *vice versâ*.[4] In Al-Andalus, according to Ibn Sīda (d. 1066) the rhythmic modes were similar (at least in name) to the Eastern school.[5] As for the songs and instrumental pieces that were not set to rhythm, they were known by the general name of *rāwisīn* (sic).[6] The *ghazal* or love-song was sung in this way in the thirteenth century, whilst the *nashīd* exhibited both the rhythmical and unrhythmical features.[7]

The most important class of composition appears to have been the *nauba* (pl. *naubāt*). We have reference to this as early as the ninth century,[8] although we know little of its character. Apparently it was a *suite*, i.e., a number of movements played in succession (*suite*) hence the term. It was chamber music and must not be confused with the *nauba* of the *ṭabl khāna* or military band. In the *Alf laila wa laila* we read of an entire *nauba* being performed, and also a portion (the *dārij*) of a *nauba*,[9] but we cannot be sure of the dates of these stories. It is not until the time of 'Abd al-Qādir ibn Ghaibī (d. 1435) that we get any reliable particulars concerning the *nauba*. According to this *virtuoso* and theorist the *nauba* was of ancient origin, and in his day it comprised four move-

[1] *Mafātīḥ al-'ulūm*, p. 238. Cf. *ante* p. 49.
[2] *Al-shifā'*, maqala v.
[3] *British Museum MS.*, Or. 2361, fol. 227 *et seq.*
[4] *Bodleian MS.*, March 115, fol. 52. *British Museum MS.* Or. 135, fol. 37 v.
[5] *Kitāb al-mukhaṣṣaṣ* (Būlāq edit.), xii. i, 11.
[6] *British Museum MS.*, Or. 2361, fol. 233.
[7] *Ibid.*, fol. 215.
[8] See *ante* p. 153.
[9] *Alf laila wa laila* (Macnaghten edit.), ii, 54, 87 ; iv, 183.

ments (*qiṭa'*) called the *qaul, ghazal, tarāna,* and *furū dāsht.* But in the year 1379, Ibn Ghaibī, whilst at the court of the Jalāyrid sulṭān of Al-'Irāq, Jalāl al-Dīn al-Ḥusain, introduced a fifth movement which he named the *mustazād.*[1] That the ancient *nauba* only contained four movements is specifically mentioned.

In Al-Andalus the *nauba* received special attention, every mode being used by the composers, hence the misnomer,—" the twenty-four *naubāt.*"[2] The Andalusian *nauba,* according to modern writers, had five distinct movements quite irrespective of a *dā'ira* or vocal prelude, a *mustakhbir* or instrumental prelude, and a *tūshiya* or overture. These five movements, each of which is preceded by an introductory *karsī,* are called the *maṣdar, baṭaiḥ, darj, inṣirāf,* and *khalāṣ* (or *mukhlaṣ*).[3] The *nauba* was the classical type of Andalusian music.[4]

In the science of music, save for two Persian documents—the *Bahjat al-rūḥ* of 'Abd al-Mu'min ibn Ṣafī al-Dīn,[5] and the *Jāmi' al-'ulūm* of Fakhr al-Dīn al-Rāzī,[6] all the works that we know of during this period are in Arabic. This was still the language of science and of polite society throughout Islāmic lands, from Afghanistān to Al-Andalus, and so, whatever theoretical treatises on music were studied, had to be read for the most part in the language of the *Qur'ān.* Of course, the scientific (mathe-

[1] *Bodleian MS.,* fol. 95 *et seq. British Museum MS.,* Or. 2361, fol. 215 v. *et seq.*

[2] Rafael Mitjana, *Le monde oriental* (1906), p. 215. Lavignac's *Encyclopédie de la musique,* v, p. 2846.

[3] *Majmū' al-aghānī wa'l-alḥān* (Algiers, 1904). See also Delphin et Guin, *Notes sur la poësie et la musique arabes,* p. 63 *et seq.*

[4] The examples of the *nauba ṣīka* and *nauba jārka* given in the first-named work cannot be earlier than the 16th century, and they are not Andalusian.

[5] The author of the *Bahjat al-rūḥ* (Bodleian Library, Ouseley, 117) is 'Abd al Mu'min ibn Ṣafī al-Dīn ibn 'Izz al-Dīn Muḥyī al-Dīn ibn Ni'mat ibn Qābūs Washmgīr Jurjānī. The work appears to have been written in Afghanistan during the reign of Muḥammad Ghūrī, Mu'izz al-Dīn (1173-1206). The work quotes both Greek and native authorities,—Plato, Hermes, Fakhr al-Dīn Ṭā'ūs Marwī, and Diyā' al-Dīn Muḥammad Yūsuf.

[6] Fakhr al-Dīn al-Rāzī (1149-1209) was born at Raiy and resided in Khurāsān, Khwārizm, and Transoxiana, dying at Herat. The Khwārizmī shāh, 'Alā' al-Dīn, for whom he wrote his *Jāmi' al-'ulūm,* accorded him high honours. There are two copies of this latter work in the British Museum (Or. 2972, and Or. 3308).

matical) side of Arabian theory was derived from the Greeks of old as we have seen, yet the practical art always had reference to purely Arabian models. Even Ibn Sīnā and Al-Ḥusain ibn Zaila, both of whom were probably Iranians, register Arabian methods in dealing with the practical art.

In Al-'Irāq and the East up to the first half of the eleventh century we have ample information concerning the state of both the science and the practical art of music in the works of Abū'l-Wafā' al-Būzjānī, the Ikhwān al-Ṣafā', Muḥammad ibn Aḥmad al-Khwārizmī, Ibn Sīnā, and Al-Ḥusain ibn Zaila, all of which, save that of the first-named, have come down to us. In Egypt, Ibn al-Haitham was the representative theorist, although his works have perished, whilst in Al-Andalus, the interest of Al-Majrīṭī in the treatises of the Ikhwān al-Ṣafā', enables us to gauge the opinions of the Western theorists.

The second half of the eleventh century is almost sterile of music theorists. In Al-'Irāq and the East, this may be accounted for by the Saljūqid conquests, which probably retarded intellectual activities for a time. In Al-Andalus, the fall of the House of Umayya, and the relegation of Cordova to provinciality, may also explain the gap in the West.

The twelfth century, however, opens brilliantly with Ibn Bājja in Al-Andalus, and he is followed by Muḥammad ibn al-Ḥaddād, Ibn Sab'īn, and Muḥammad ibn Aḥmad al-Raqūṭī. In Egypt and Syria several important names occur, and among them: Abū'l-Ṣalt Umayya, Abū'l-Majd ibn Abī'l-Ḥakam, Kamāl al-Dīn ibn Man'a, and 'Alam al-Dīn Qaiṣar. In Al-'Irāq we have Ibn al-Naqqāsh, Abū'l-Ḥakam al-Bāhilī and Ṣafī al-Din 'Abd al-Mu'min. Unfortunately, with the exception of two treatises by the last-named, no works of any writer after Al-Ḥusain ibn Zaila, have been spared for us.[1]

By this time the Arabs were able to delve deeper still into the treatises of the Greeks of old. A new school of translators had also appeared in Yaḥyā ibn 'Adī (d. 975),

[1] A work by Ibn Sab'īn has indeed, been preserved, but it is in private hands and not accessible.

'Īsā ibn Zar'a (d. 1007), and others. The Ikhwān al-Ṣafā' reveal themselves as thorough-going Aristotelians in philosophy. In music, whilst they follow Euklid and Nikomachos so far as mathematics is concerned, they deal with the practical art, in most respects, just as they found it. Their contribution to the question of sound is certainly an advance on the Greeks.[1] The *Mafātīḥ al-'ulūm* of Muḥammad ibn Aḥmad al-Khwārizmī (tenth cent.) is of considerable value because it helps us with precise definitions. Here, too, we get a marked influence from the Greek writers.

With Ibn Sīnā (d. 1037) we are introduced to a theorist who is profoundly interested in Greek theory, and especially in Euklid. His biographers even claim that he dealt with questions that had been neglected by the Greeks. As valuable as this part of both the *Shifā'* and *Najāt* may be, it is really of subsidiary importance to what he has preserved for us of the practical musical art of the eleventh century. Ibn al-Haitham (d. 1039) was also interested in Euklid (or Pseudo-Euklid) and wrote commentaries on the two treatises on music that are attributed to the latter. Ibn Zaila (d. 1048), a disciple of Ibn Sīnā, follows his master rather slavishly in many respects, although in some cases his information regarding the practical art is additional to that recorded by Ibn Sīnā.

After Ibn Zaila, as already remarked, we have a blank of two centuries so far as theoretical documents are concerned. Nothing has been spared us from the East until we reach the thirteenth century in the works of Ṣafī al-Dīn 'Abd al-Mu'min (d. 1294). This author, says the late Professor Collangettes, " n'y invoque l'autorité ni des Grecs ni des Persans. Il prétend bien faire œuvre purement arabe. Ce qui n'empêche pas les mots persans d'y figurer à tout instant, surtout pour la désignation des modes. On s'est dégagé de l'influence grecque, mais pour subir celle de la Perse. Quels que soient du reste les élements de ce style composite, l'œuvre finale est sans contredit l'expression de l'art arabe au XIIIe siècle."[2]

[1] See my *Facts for the Arabian Musical Influence*, appendix 33.
[2] *Journal Asiatique*, Nov.-Dec., 1904, p. 379.

The influence of this *virtuoso* and savant was far-reaching. His "authority" is quoted by most of the later theorists, for as Ḥājjī Khalīfa says, he is one of those "taking the front rank" in this question.[1] Quṭb al-Dīn al-Shīrāzī (d. 1310), Muḥammad ibn Maḥmūd al-Amūlī (fourteenth cent.), the author of the *Kanz al-tuḥaf* (fourteenth cent.), 'Abd al-Qādir ibn Ghaibī (d. 1453), Muḥammad ibn 'Abd al-Ḥamīd al-Lādhiqī (fifteenth cent.), and the author of the *Muḥammad ibn Murād MS.* (fifteenth cent.), all prostrate themselves before the authority of Ṣafī al-Dīn 'Abd al-Mu'min, even when they have to disagree with him.

A notation has already been referred to as being used by both the theorists and the practitioners.[2] The idea was borrowed from the Greeks. It is used or mentioned by both Ibn Sīnā and Ibn Zaila. By the time of Ṣafī al-Dīn 'Abd al-Mu'min we find it being used for recording melodies.[3]

We know from Ibn Sīnā (d. 1037) that there were twelve principal modes, some of them bearing Persian names.[4] The old modes which had been named after the fingers or *aṣābi'*, had in time become known by more fanciful names, and others of a more complex nature, due to fresh scales, Zalzalian and Persian, had been added. These latter, as we know from the *Shifā'* of Ibn Sīnā, were very popular, especially two named *Iṣfahān* and *Salmakī*.[5] Here the modes are referred to under the generic name of the *jamā'āt al-mashhūra* (sing. *jamā'a* "assembly"). By the time of Ṣafī al-Dīn 'Abd al-Mu'min (d. 1294), these principal modes were called the *maqāmāt* (sing. *maqāma*). There were also six secondary modes called *awāzāt* (sing. *awāz*), which are stated to be of later origin than the principal modes.[6]

[1] Ḥājjī Khalīfa, vi, 255.
[2] See *ante* p. 108
[3] See my *Facts for the Arabian Musical Influence*, chap. vi.
[4] *British Museum MS.*, Or. 2361, fol. 201 v.
[5] *India Office MS.*, No. 1811, fol 174. We must not conclude from these names that Persian modes were favoured rather than Arabian. In the *Gulistān* of Sa'dī (d. 1292) *Ṣifāhān* (= *Iṣfahān*) and *Ḥijāz* are mentioned as though they were the commonly performed modes.
[6] *Bodleian MS.*, Marsh, 521, fol. 171.

How far the branch modes named *shu'ab* (sing. *shu'ba*) or *furū'* (sing. *far'*), which later became so popular,[1] were practised by the Arabs at this period, we have no evidence, in spite of their appearance in the Persian *Bahjat al-rūḥ*,[2] the *Durrat al-tāj* of Al-Shīrāzī (1236-1310),[3] and elsewhere.[4] Here are the names of the *maqāmāt* and *awāzāt* according to the *Kitāb al-adwār* of Ṣafī al-Dīn 'Abd al-Mu'min[5]:

MAQĀMĀT.—*'Ushshāq, Nawā, Abū Salīk, Rāst, 'Irāq, Zīrāfkand, Buzurk, Zankūla, Rāhawī,*[6] *Husainī,* and *Ḥijāzī.*

AWĀZĀT.—*Kuwāsht, Kardāniyya, Naurūz, Salmak, Māya,* and *Shahnāz.*

In Al-Andalus and North Africa the modal system appears to have been different from that practised in the East. We have little information that enables us to form an opinion concerning its origin, but if contemporary nomenclature and modern practice can tell us anything it would appear to have been of indigenous growth. According to the *Ma'rifat al-naghamāt al-thamān* treatise,[7] there were four principal modes (*uṣūl*), viz., *Dīl, Zaidān, Mazmūm,* and *Māya.* From these were derived a number of branch modes (*furū'*) as follows:

DĪL.—Ramal al-dīl, 'Irāq al-'arab, Mujannab al-dīl, Raṣd al-dīl, and *Istihlāl al-dīl.*[8]

ZAIDĀN.—Ḥijāz al-kabīr, Ḥijāz al-mashriqī, 'Ushshāq, Ḥiṣār, Iṣbahān, and *Zaurankand* (*sic.*).

MAZMŪM.—Gharībat al-ḥusain, Mashriqī, and *Ḥamdān.*

[1] Ibn Ghaibī, *Bodleian MS.*, Marsh, 282, fol. 41. *British Museum MS.*, Or. 2361, fol. 198 v.
[2] *Bodleian MS.*, Ouseley, 117, fol. 7 v.
[3] *British Museum MS.*, Add. 7694.
[4] *Bodleian MS.*, March, 521, fol. 171, and marginal notes in British Museum MS., Or. 136, fol. 21.
[5] *British Museum MS.*, Or. 136. For a critical account of the scales of these modes see my *Facts for the Arabian Musical Influence*, Appendix 49. The names given by Carra de Vaux in his *Traité des rapports musicaux*, p. 62, do not agree with those in the MSS. consulted by the present writer.
[6] Also written *Rahāwī*.
[7] *Madrid MS.*, No. 334 (2). See also 334 (3).
[8] Six branch modes are mentioned but only five are named in the text.

MĀYA.—Ramal al-māya, Inqilāb al-ramal, Ḥusain, and *Raṣd.*

There was also another principal mode called the *Gharībat al-muḥarra,* but this had no branch modes. In all there were twenty-four modes.

Notwithstanding the fairly considerable Persian nomenclature that obtained in Arabian music we must not too hastily assume that it was Persian music that prevailed. On the contrary we know from the Ikhwān al-Ṣafā' that different types of music were to be found in the two countries. The Ikhwān say, "Consider each nation, and the melodies (*alḥān*) and modes [or notes] (*naghamāt*) which they enjoy and are pleased with, which others do not enjoy nor are pleased with, for example, the music of the Dailamites, the Turks, the Arabs, the Kurds, the Armenians, the Æthiopians, the Persians, the Byzantines, and other nations who differ in language, nature, morals and customs."[1] In another place they say concerning the rhythmic modes (*īqā'āt*),—"These are the eight kinds (*ajnās*) which, as we have said, are a basic principle and are canons to the music (*ghinā'*) and melodies (*alḥān*) of the Arabs. And as for other people like the Persians, Byzantines, and Greeks, there are to their melodies and music other canons, *different from these.*"[2] Ibn Zaila also refers specifically to melodies known as the *dastānāt* of Khurāsān and Iṣfahān which were alien to Arabian practice.[3] In the time of Ṣafī al-Dīn 'Abd al-Mu'min, as already remarked, the rhythmic modes of the Arabs and Persians were different, although the Persians were singing the *nauba* in Arabic as late as the fifteenth century.[4]

As for the scale, the *Mafātīḥ al-'ulūm* shows the Pythagorean system in use, with the addition of both the Zalzalian and Persian systems which have already been adverted to.[5] The Ikhwān al-Ṣafā' only refer to the

[1] Ikhwān al-Ṣafā', i, 92-3.
[2] *Ibid.*, i, 116.
[3] *British Museum MS.*, Or, 2361, fols. 232 v, 233.
[4] *Bodleian MS.*, Marsh, 282, fol. 95.
[5] *Mafātīḥ al-'ulūm,* 238-9.

Pythagorean system.[1] Ibn Sīnā and Ibn Zaila demonstrate that the practitioners used both the Zalzalian and Pythagorean scales, although they refer to the latter as the " Old Persian " system.[2]

By the time of Ṣafī al-Dīn 'Abd al-Mu'min (d. 1294) a new scale had been adopted. We have no precise information concerning its designer, but probably it ought to be attributed to the above theorist. It is certainly not mentioned by his immediate predecessors, Fakhr al-Dīn al-Rāzī (d. 1209),[3] and Naṣīr al-Dīn al-Ṭūsī (d. 1273).[4] This scale, which proceeded by steps of two *limmas* and a *comma*, was clearly founded on the old *ṭunbūr al-khurāsānī* scale, and nominally, at any rate, embraced the Pythagorean, Zalzalian, and Persian systems. The theorists who built up this system have been designated by European authors the " Systematists."[5]

What scale system was used in Al-Andalus and North Africa at this period we have no direct evidence. No ratios are mentioned in the *Ma'rifat al-naghamāt al-thamān* treatise. We can only assume that the old system, already mentioned, was maintained,[6] although we know that the Pythagorean Ikhwān al-Ṣafā' treatise was favoured in the late tenth century. We are told, however, that North Africa was deeply influenced in the arts by Al-Andalus.[7] In music, the impression made by Abū'l-Ṣalt Umayya,[8] and Ibn Bājja[9] is openly acknowledged. The influence of the Andalusians in Africa was especially marked after the fall of Seville (1248), when 400,000 of its people went into exile.

The *ṭabl-khānāh* or military band has been lightly

[1] Ikhwān al Ṣafā', i, 98.

[2] *India Office MS.*, 1811, fol. 173. *British Museum MS.*, Or. 2361, fol. 235v.-36.

[3] *British Museum MS.*, Or. 2972, fol. 151 v.-155.

[4] *Paris Bibl. Nat. MS.*, Arabe, 2466, fol. 197 v.

[5] This theory was misunderstood by European writers until J. P. N. Land wrote his *Over de Toonladders der Arabische Musiek* (1880) and *Recherches sur l'histoire de la gamme arabe* (1884). See my *Facts for the Arabian Musical Influence*, Append. 49.

[6] See my *Facts for the Arabian Musical Influence*, Appendix 38

[7] Al-Maqqarī, *Moh. Dyn.*, i, 119.

[8] Al-Maqqarī, *Anal.*, i, 530.

[9] Ibn Khaldūn, iii, 422.

touched upon in previous chapters. During this period, however, it is lifted into such prominence that we must afford it detailed notice. Petty rulers were springing up, and all and sundry among them were clamouring for the privilege of the *ṭabl-khānāh* and the *nauba* (periodic musical performance) as part of their patent of royalty. Hitherto such honours had been reserved for the khalif alone. In the year 966, Al-Muṭī' had granted leave to a general to have kettledrums (*dabādib*, sing. *dabdāb*) played at prayer-times during a campaign, a privilege which appears to have been retained on his return.[1] The Buwaihid *amīr* Mu'izz al-Daula also begged this concession from the khalif, but, strange to say, it was refused.[2] Indeed, the Arab historians condemn such as presumption on the *amīr's* part, which, they aver, amounted to a usurpation of the sovereign attributes of the khalif.[3] In 979, however, Al-Ṭā'ī' conferred on 'Aḍud al-Daula the much-sought privilege, and it is claimed that he was the first monarch who obtained this.[4] This, however, was the three-fold *nauba*[5] and not the five-fold one which was still the prerogative of the khalif. Yet in 1000, under Al-Qādir, a minister was allowed to beat a *ṭabl* (drum) for the five-fold honour,[6] and in 1017 Sulṭān al-Daula beat this same *nauba*.[7]

Under the Saljūqids these privileges continued to be extended, although specific distinctions as to the class of *nauba*, and the number and type of instruments to be used, were introduced. Khalif Al-Muqtadī (1075-94), in appointing a governor to a province, conferred on him the great kettledrums called *kūsāt* (sing. *kūs*), and was permitted to sound the five-fold *nauba* within the limits of his province, but in the camp of the sulṭān he was to confine himself to the three-fold *nauba*.[8] A similar distinction was made at the peace treaty between the

[1] *The Eclipse of the 'Abbāsid Caliphate*, ii, 264.
[2] *Ibid.*, v, 435, note.
[3] Quatremère, *Histoire des Mongols*, 418.
[4] *The Eclipse of the 'Abbāsid Caliphate*, ii, 396.
[5] At daybreak (*subḥ*), sunset (*maghrib*), and nightfall (*'ashā'*).
[6] *The Eclipse of the 'Abbāsid Caliphate*, iii, 345.
[7] Quatremère, *loc. cit.*
[8] Quatremère, *op. cit.*, 419.

two Saljūqid princes Barkiyārūq and Muḥammad in 1101, when the former took the title of *sulṭān* and the latter that of *malik*. with the five-fold and three-fold *nauba* respectively.[1] The last Shāh of Khwārizm Jalāl al-Dīn Mankubartī (d. 1231), who boasted of playing the *nauba* of Alexander the Great (Dhū'l-qarnain), had it performed on twenty-seven drums of gold encrusted with pearls, the players at its inception being the sons of subject monarchs.[2] Ghiyāth al-Dīn (d. 1202), the Ghūrid, had great kettledrums of gold, which were carried on a chariot.[3] The Fāṭimid khalifs also dispensed musical honours to subject rulers when conferring patents of regality (*marātib*).[4] When Al-'Azīz (d. 996) marched into Syria he had five hundred clarions (*abwāq*, sing. *būq*).[5] We read of the *nauba* under the Fāṭimids being performed by a large military band.[6]

Nāṣir-i Khusrau refers to the *būq* (clarion), the *surnā* (reed-pipe), *ṭabl* (drum), *duhul* (drum), *kūs* (kettledrum), and *kāsa* (cymbal) among the Fāṭimid martial display.[7] With the 'Uqailids the *būq* (clarion) and *dabdāb* (kettledrum) were favoured,[8] whilst in Al-Yaman we read of the *būq* and *ṭabl*.[9] Nūr al-Dīn, the Zangid at Damascus, sounded the five-fold *nauba*, whilst his *amīr*, the famous Salāḥ al-Dīn only had the three-fold honour.[10]

In Al-Andalus we read of the gold-mounted clarions (*būqāt*) of Al-Ḥakam II.[11] The Muwaḥḥids reserved the drums (*ṭubūl*) for royalty alone, and the band was formed into a separate company with the standard-bearers and called the *sāqa*.[12]

The names of musical instruments, including many new ones, crowd upon the scene during this period. The *'ūd qadīm* or classical lute of four strings still con-

[1] *Ibid.* [2] Al-Nasawī, 21.
[3] *Ṭabaqāt al-nāṣirī*, i, 404.
[4] *Ibid.*, ii, 616. Al-Badā'ūnī, i, 94, 310.
[5] Ibn Khaldūn, *Prol.*, ii, 45.
[6] Quatremère, *op. cit.*, 420.
[7] Nāṣir-i Khusrau, *Safar nāma*, pp. 43, 46, 47.
[8] *Journal of the Royal Asiatic Society* (1901), 755, 785.
[9] Kay, *op. cit.*
[10] Quatremère, *op. cit.*, 419.
[11] Al-Maqqarī, *Moh. Dyn.*, ii, 158.
[12] Ibn Khaldūn, *Prol.*, ii, 52.

tinued to be favoured,[1] in spite of the introduction of the *'ūd kāmil* or perfect lute of five strings, which was fretted according to the "Systematist" scale. The lute is fully described by all the theorists, and the Ikhwān al-Ṣafā' give measurements,[2] whilst we have a design in one of the works of Ṣafī al-Dīn 'Abd al-Mu'min.[3] It was made in various sizes, and in some MSS., instruments of considerable dimensions are depicted.[4]

The *shāhrūd* was an arch-lute or zither. In the early fifteenth century it was certainly an arch-lute, and is described as being twice the length of the lute.[5] Two new instruments of the lute class were the *qūpūz* and the *awzān*, both apparently of Turkish origin, and introduced into Egypt under the Ayyūbids.[6] The former had a large sound-chest, and possessed five double strings.[7] The latter had three strings and was played with a wooden plectrum.[8]

The *ṭunbūr* (pandore) family also held its own. The *ṭunbūr al-baghdādī* was still to the fore at the close of the tenth century.[9] The two and three-stringed instruments are described by Ṣafī al-Dīn 'Abd al-Mu'min, but they are both given the scale of the "Systematists."[10]

The *qītāra*,[11] presumably a flat-chested instrument, was used in Al-Andalus. Since it was identified with the *murabba'*, it was probably quadrangular.[12] Other instruments of the lute, guitar, or pandore family were the *mizhar*, *awṭaba*, *kinnīra* or *kinnāra*, *kirān*, *barbaṭ* and *mi'zaf* (?).

Among psalteries there were the *qānūn* and the *nuzha*. The latter was the invention of Ṣafī al-Dīn 'Abd al-

[1] It was still in use in the 15th century. *Bodleian MS.*, Marsh, 282, fol. 77.
[2] Ikhwān al-Ṣafā', i, 97.
[3] See my *Arabic Musical MSS. in the Bodleian Library*, front.
[4] *Der Islām*, iii, fig. 6 in article entitled,—"*Beiträge zu einer Geschichte des Planetendarstellung im Orient und im Okzident.*"
[5] *Bodleian MS.*, Marsh, 282, fol. 79. *See frontispiece.*
[6] *Qūpūz rūmī* (Byzantine *qūpūz*) is mentioned in the above cited Bodleian MS.
[7] *Bodleian MS.* as cited, fol. 77 v.
[8] *Ibid.*
[9] *Mafātīḥ al-'ulūm*, p. 237.
[10] *Kitāb al-adwār*, faṣl. 7.
[11] Also written *qīthāra*, and in other forms.
[12] *Kitāb al-imtā'*, Madrid MS., No. 603.

Mu'min.[1] There was also the *mughnī*, another instrument invented by this *virtuoso*.[2] It is described as a type of *qānūn* on the one hand,[3] but is delineated as a lute on the other.[4] The *jank* (*ṣanj*) or harp was still in use. We have no particulars of its structure until the fourteenth century,[5] although in the mid-thirteenth century we read of instruments of 36 and 72 strings being used at the khalif's court at Baghdād.[6]

The *rabāb* or rebec, appears to have been specially favoured in Khurāsān,[7] although it must have had considerable support in Arab lands, since it passed for a national instrument.[8] The term *rabāb* covered several types of bowed instruments with the Arabs, and perhaps it was the flat-chested form that was considered the national type.[9] In a similar way, the Persians gave the term *kamānja* (*kamān* = a bow) to their bowed instruments. One particular type was the *ghishak* (= Arab *shaushak* (?)).[10] The use of the bow is inferred from the Ikhwān al-Ṣafā', Ibn Sīnā, and Ibn Zaila.[11]

Among wood-wind instruments we read of the *mizmār* or *zamr*, the *surnā* or *surnāy*, the *nāy*, the *shabbāba*, the *ṣaffāra*, the *yarā'*, the *shāhīn*, the *zummāra*, the *zulāmī*, the *qaṣaba*, the *būq* [*bi'l-qaṣaba*], and the *mauṣūl*. Brass instruments were represented by the *būq* and *nafīr*. Other wind instruments were the *urghanun* (organ) and the *armūnīqī* (pan-pipes).

Drums were to be found in the *kūs* or great kettledrum, the *naqqāra*, *dabdāb*, or *ṭabl al-markab* the ordinary kettledrum, the *qaṣa'* or shallow kettledrum, and the *nuqaira* or small kettledrum, the *ṭabl ṭawīl* or ordinary long drum,

[1] See my *Arabic Musical MSS. in the Bodleian Library*, front, and *Studies in Oriental Musical Instruments*, pp. 12-14, *Kanz al tuḥaf*, maq. 3.

[2] *Kanz al-tuḥaf*, maq. 3.

[3] *Bodleian MS.*, Marsh, 282, fol. 78.

[4] *Kanz al-tuḥaf*, maq. 3.

[5] *Kanz al-tuḥaf*. There is a 13th century design in Riano's *Notes on Early Spanish Music*, fig. 52.

[6] Bretschneider, *Notes on Mediæval Travellers*, 84.

[7] *Mafātīḥ al-'ulūm*, p. 237.

[8] *Berlin MS.* (Ahlwardt) 5527, fol. 47 v.

[9] *Bodleian MS.*, Marsh 282, fol. 78 v.

[10] This form occurs in the Ikhwān al-Ṣafā', i, 97, as *shaushal*.

[11] See my *Studies in Oriental Musical Instruments*, chap. viii.

as well as the *kūba* or *ṭabl al-mukhannath* the hour-glass-shaped drum. Tambourines were represented by the *duff*, *ghirbāl*, *bandair*, *ṭār*, *mazhar*, *tiryāl*, and *shaqf*. Then there were the cymbals, castanets, etc., in the *ṣunūj*, *kāsāt*, *muṣāfiqāt*, and *qaḍīb*

§ III

One noticeable feature of this period is the absence of names of the *virtuosi*. This is due to the fact that there were no historians of music of the calibre of the author of the great *Kitāb al-aghānī*. We certainly have Al-Maghribī and Al-Musabbiḥī in the East, and Yaḥyā [ibn] al-Khudujj al-Mursī in the West, who wrote works of this type, but these writings have not come down to us. Apart from this, however, a great change had come over the land. In the past, a composer's or singer's biography, his special compositions and accomplishments, were acceptable to the *élite* of society in Baghdād and other cities in close touch with the capital. It was necessary to be conversant with these topics since the songs and melodies of famous musicians like Ma‘bad, Ibn Suraij, or Ibrāhīm al-Mauṣilī belonged to the *répertoires*.

With the decline of the Khalifate, culture centres arose elsewhere, and the necessity for information about the traditional music of a distant metropolis became less apparent. Further, the strictures of the Ḥanbalī sectaries must have contributed to some extent to the diminution if not cessation of this type of literature, which dealt specifically with people who made the *malāhī* their living. Yet, as Collangettes says,—"Si la période suivante n'a pas eu son Al-Iṣfahānī pour nous narrer ses chroniques, rien ne nous autorise à croire à une décadence."[1]

A few names among the Andalusian *virtuosi* have been handed down.

‘Abd al-Waḥḥāb al-Ḥusain ibn Ja‘far al-Ḥājib was one of the most famous musicians of Al-Andalus at this period. Al-Maqqarī calls him "the unique one of his

[1] *Journal Asiatique*, Nov.-Dec. (1904), p. 378.

generation in pleasant music (*ghinā'*), delightful learning, fine poetry, and beautiful expression . . . the most capable of mankind in playing the *'ūd*, and in the different modes (*ṭarā'iq*) played on it, and in composing melodies (*luḥūn*). And he would often utter fine sentiments in beautiful verses, and mould them upon delightful melodies . . . out of his own invention and cleverness." So great was his reputation that no musician came from the East without first seeking to make his acquaintance, since he was recognized as "the one who had attained the highest excellence in the profession." His bounty and hospitality to other musicians were proverbial, and although his income was quite a considerable one, he was frequently poor on account of this generosity. All his family were musicians.[1]

Abū'l-Ḥasan [ibn al-Ḥasan] ibn al-Ḥāsib was a celebrated teacher of music (*mūsīqī*) at this time, and is known as the tutor of the next mentioned *artiste*.[2]

Abū'l-Ḥusain ibn Abī Ja'far al-Waqshī was the son of a *wazīr* of Toledo. He is called "a miracle of Allāh in sagacity . . . gifted with a taste . . . [for music], together with a wonderful voice more to be desired than the cup of the wine-bibber."[3]

Abū'l-Ḥusain 'Alī ibn al-Ḥamāra was a poet and musician of Granada. He surpassed all others as a composer of melodies (*alḥān*), and was a skilful performer on the *'ūd*. He also appears to have been the inventor of a special type of lute.[4]

Isḥāq ibn Sim'ān was a Jew of Cordova and a friend of Ibn Bājja, and famous as a composer of melodies in all styles.[5]

Yaḥyā ibn 'Abdallāh al-Bahdaba was a physician who wrote *zajal* melodies.[6]

Wallāda, one of most esteemed poetesses of her day, was the daughter of Al-Mustakfī (1024-27), one of the last of the Andalusian khalifs. Her *salon* was the centre of attraction for *artistes* and *littérateurs*. Her love affair

[1] Al-Maqqarī, *Analectes*, i, 119.
[2] *Ibid.*, ii, 516. [3] *Ibid.*, ii, 515-16.
[4] Al-Maqqarī, *Analectes*, ii, 517.
[5] Ribera, *La Música de las Cantigas*, 72. [6] *Ibid.*, 72.

with the poet Ibn Zaidūn has become a commonplace in Andalusian history. She was a musician and has been compared with 'Ulayya the musical step-sister of Hārūn al-Rashīd.[1]

Hind was a singing-girl of Abū Muḥammad 'Abdallāh ibn Maslama al-Shāṭabī. She excelled as a performer on the *'ūd,* and Abū 'Āmir ibn Yannaq (d. 1152) once addressed verses to her expressing his longing to hear the notes (*naghamāt*) of her *'ūd* in the *thaqīl awwal* rhythm.[2]

Bishāra al-Zāmir was " one of the cleverest of pipers from the East." He played for 'Abd al-Waḥḥāb al-Ḥusain.[3]

Nuzha al-Wahabiyya was another famous songstress of these days.[4]

In the East, the names of celebrated *virtuosi* are rarer.

Abū 'Abdallāh Muḥammad ibn Isḥāq ibn al-Munajjim (d. 1000) appears to have belonged to the family mentioned in the last chapter. It is said of him that there was no singer or lutenist who equalled or even approached him in ability. He died at Shīrāz.[5]

Kamāl al-Zamān was the chief court minstrel of the Saljūqid sulṭān Sanjar (1117-58). There is a story related by Minhāj-i-Sarāj concerning the effect of his *'ūd*-playing on his master.[6]

Umm Abī'l-Jaish was an accomplished songstress at the court of the Najāḥid ruler Al-Manṣūr ibn al-Fātik (1109-23 [?]) of Al-Yaman.[7]

Warda was a famous singing-girl of the Najāḥid *wazīr* 'Uthmān al-Ghuzzī.[8]

If we have but few names and details of the *virtuosi* there is ample information concerning the theorists and *littérateurs.*

Abū 'Abdallāh Muḥammad ibn Aḥmad ibn Yūsuf

[1] Al-Maqqarī, *op. cit.*, ii, 565.
[2] *Ibid.*, ii, 634. Cf. *Mohammadan Dynasties*, i, 166.
[3] Al-Maqqari, *Analectes*, i, 119. [4] Ibn al-Abbār, *Takmila*, ii, 745.
[5] Minhāj-i-Sarāj, i, 153-4.
[6] Ibn Khallikan, *Biog. Dict.*, iii, 401. A similar story is told of Rūdakī. See *Journal of the Royal Asiatic Society* (1899), p. 68.
[7] Kay, H. C., *Yaman, its early Mediæval History*, p. 98.
[8] *Ibid.*, p. 104-111.

al-Khwārizmī (*fl.* 976-97) was the author of a very important work entitled the *Mafātīḥ al-'ulūm* (Keys of the Sciences), the first of those abridged encyclopædias which afterwards became so common in the East. It was composed, between the years 976 and 991, for Abū'l-Ḥasan 'Ubaidallāh al-'Uṭbī, the *wazīr* of the Sāmānid *amīr* Nūḥ II (976-97). Manuscripts of this work are to be found in several libraries, the Leyden copy (dated 1160), the most perfect, having been edited by Van Vloten who issued the text in 1895.[1] The work is divided into two chapters (*maqālāt*) on (1) The Native Sciences, and (2) The Foreign Sciences. These are again divided into various parts (*abwāb*), the seventh part of the second chapter being on music (*mūsīqī*). It is practically a dictionary of music in which we have not only the explanation of musical terms, but their proper vocalization (pronunciation).

The Ikhwān al-Ṣafā' (Brothers of Purity) were a group of philosophers, scientists, mathematicians, and *littérateurs*, who flourished at Al-Baṣra during the second half of the tenth century. Five of them we know by name,—Abū Sulaimān Muḥammad ibn Mushīr (or Ma'shar) al-Bayustī, Abū'l-Ḥasan 'Alī ibn Hārūn al-Zanjānī, Abū Aḥmad al-Mihrajānī, Al-'Awfī, and Zaid ibn Rifā'a.[2] From these names we see that almost every corner of the Khalifate was represented,—two Persians, a Palestinian, and two Arabs apparently.[3] Ibn al-Qifṭī says that they belonged to a brotherhood for the furtherance of holiness, purity, and truth, maintaining that since the religious law had been corrupted through ignorance, it needed purifying.[4] This could only be done, said the Ikhwān al-Ṣafā', by combining science and philosophy with religion, and more especially Greek philosophy.[5] To this end the "Brothers" compiled fifty-one (or fifty-two) tracts (*rasā'il*) which may be said to cover the whole *gamut* of science (including music) and philosophy known to the

[1] Van Vloten, *Liber Mafātīh al-Olūm* (Leyden, 1895).
[2] For these names see Brockelmann, *Gesch. der Arab. Lit.*, i, 213-14. Nicholson, *Lit. Hist. of the Arabs*, 370.
[3] Browne, *Lit. Hist. of Persia*, i, 378.
[4] See Goldziher, *Muh. Stud.*, on the meaning of the word *ikhwān*.
[5] Ibn al-Qifṭī, 83.

Arabs.[1] These tracts are said to have been written about the year 961,[2] but it may have been later. Manuscripts of these *rasā'il* are to be found in many libraries, and the text has been printed several times and also edited,[3] whilst the mathematical portion (including music) has been translated by Dieterici in *Die Propaedeutik der Araber* (1865).

Abū'l-Faraj Muḥammad ibn Isḥāq ibn Abī Ya'qūb al-Nadīm al-Warrāq al-Baghdādī, was the author of a book called the *Fihrist* (Index). Of its author we have little information save that he was born at Baghdād, that he was a bookseller or copyist (*warrāq*), that he was in Constantinople in 988, and that he died about 995-6.[4] The preface of this monumental work tells us that it is "the index of all the books of all peoples, including the Arabs and others, which exist in the Arabic language and writing, in every branch of knowledge, together with information of the writers, and the classes of the authors, their genealogies, dates of birth, careers, times of death, domiciles, and their merits and demerits, from the time of the origin of each science down to the present time," *i.e.* the year A.H. 377 (A.D.987-8).

The work is divided into ten chapters (*maqālāt*) each of which is subdivided into sections (*funūn*). Three of the chapters give us valuable *data* concerning the early works on music and musicians, not only of the Arabs, but also of the Greeks which were known in Arabic translation. The third section, third chapter contains,—"*Stories of the Boon Companions, Favourites, Men of Letters, Musicians* (*mughanniyyūn*), *Jesters, Buffoons, and the titles of their books.*"[5] The first section, seventh chapter, gives us,—"*Stories of the Natural Philosophers and Logicians* [*including Music Theorists*], *and the titles of their books, with*

[1] For a list of the various subjects dealt with in the *risāla* on music see my *Arabic Musical Manuscripts in the Bodleian Library.*

[2] The preface to the Bombay edition says the *middle* of the 10th century. Professor Nicholson says the *end* of the 10th century. See *Der Islām,* iv., 324.

[3] The best texts are those of Bombay (1887-89), and Dieterici (*Die Abhandlungen der Ichwan es-Safa,* 1886).

[4] It has been suggested that he was related to Isḥāq al-Mauṣilī. See *Fihrist,* xi, and Nicholson, *op. cit.* 362.

[5] *Fihrist,* 140-56.

the various translations and commentaries on the same, such as are still in existence or are no longer extant."[1] The second section, seventh chapter, deals with,—"*Stories of Geometricians, Arithmeticians, Music Theorists (mūsīqiyyūn), Accountants, and Engineers.*"[2] Most of the books mentioned in this "Index" have probably disappeared, and possibly only a half-dozen out of some one hundred musical books are extant to-day. The holocausts of Hūlāgū, Tīmūr, and Ximenes in the thirteenth and fifteenth centuries brought about the destruction of the great libraries which probably contained, in many cases, solitary exemplars of the works mentioned in the *Fihrist*. The text of this work was published by Flügel, Roediger, and Müller in 1871-2, and the former had already analysed the work in the *Z.D.M.G.* in 1859.

Abū'l-Wafā' al-Buzjānī (940-98), one of the greatest of Arabian mathematicians, was born in Khurāsān, but before his twentieth year he had settled in Baghdād. It was due to his genius that improvements were made in spherical trigonometry. Several of his mathematical works have been preserved but not his commentaries on Euklid nor his *Mukhtaṣar fī fann al-īqā'* (Compendium on the Science of Rhythm), a work not mentioned in the ordinary biographies, but is referred to in the *Irshād al-qāṣid* of Al-Akfānī (d. 1348) in company with other important treatises on music which include those of Al-Fārābī, Ibn Sīnā, Ṣafī al-Dīn 'Abd al-Mu'min and Thābit ibn Qurra.[3]

Maslama al-Majrīṭī or Abū'l-Qāsim Maslama ibn Aḥmad al-Majrīṭī (d. 1007) belonged, as his name tells us, to Madrid in Al-Andalus. He was a famed mathematician and astronomer who flourished during the prosperous reigns of Al-Ḥakam II (961-76) and Hishām II (976-1009).[4] His writings were translated into Latin under the name of Moslema or Albucasim de Magerith, and had

[1] *Fihrist*, 238-65.
[2] *Fihrist*, 265-85.
[3] *Bibliotheca Indica*, 1849, p. 93. See my article "Some Musical MSS. Identified" in J.R.A.S., Jan., 1926. For the life of Abū'l-Wafā', see the *Fihrist*, 266, 283. Ibn al-Qifṭī, 287. Ibn Khallikān, *Biog. Dict.* iii, 320.
[4] Ibn Abī Uṣaibi'a, ii, 39. Al-Maqqarī, *Analectes*, ii, 134.

considerable circulation in Western Europe.[1] Maslama revised the astronomical tables of Muḥammad ibn Mūsā al-Khwārizmī, the astronomer of Al-Ma'mūn (813-33), and is credited with having added the *tangent* function.[2] The *rasā'il* of the Ikhwān al-Ṣafā' appear to have been introduced into Al-Andalus by him, and two copies in the Bodleian Library carry his name.[3]

Abū'l-Ḥasan 'Alī ibn Abī Sa'īd 'Abd al-Raḥmān ibn Yūnus (d. 1009), popularly known as Ibn Yūnus, was a famous astronomer and mathematician at the court of the Fāṭimid khalif Al-Ḥākim (996-1021), celebrated for his contributions to spherical trigonometry and his *Kitāb al-zīg al-Ḥākimī* (Ḥākimite Tables).[4] He was an excellent poet, and a work entitled *Al-'uqūd wa'l-su'ūd fī awṣāf al-'ūd* (The Necklaces and Felicities in the Praises of the Lute) stands in the name of Ibn Yūnus.[5]

Al-Maghribī or Abū'l-Qāsim al-Ḥusain ibn 'Alī al-Maghribī (981-1027) claimed descent from the Persian musical king Bahrām Ghūr (430-38). He was born at Cairo, and at an early age entered the service of the Fāṭimid khalif Al-Ḥākim. He was then employed by Fakhr al-Mulk, the famous literary *wazīr* of the Buwaihid *amīr* Bahā' al-Daula at Baghdād. Later he became *wazīr* to the 'Uqailids at Al-Mauṣil and re-entered the service of the Buwaihids as *wazīr* to Musharrif al-Daula. He died at Mayyāfārikīn under the protection of the Marwānids. Ibn Khallikān speaks highly of his erudition, " of which, even an inferior portion would suffice for any *kātib*." Al-Maghribī has a place here as the author (or compiler) of a *Kitāb al-aghānī* (Book of Songs).[6]

Al-Musabbiḥī, or 'Izz al-Mulk Muḥammad ibn 'Ubaidallāh ibn Aḥmad al-Ḥarrānī al-Musabbiḥī al-Kātib (977-1029), belonged to Egypt, and served the Fāṭimid khalif Al-Ḥākim. He rose to be a provincial governor

[1] Steinschneider, *Die europ. übersetzungen aus dem Arabischen*, i, 34, 49, 74.
[2] Cajori, *History of Mathematics* (2nd edit.), 104.
[3] Farmer, *Arabic Musical MSS. in the Bodleian Library*, 4, 6. See also Suter, *Die Math. u. Astron. der Araber*, p. 76.
[4] Ibn Khallikān, *Biog. Dict.*, ii, 365. Abū'l-Fidā', *Annal. Musl.*, ii, 619.
[5] Ahlwardt, *Verz.*, No. 5536, 31.
[6] Ibn Khallikān, *Biog. Dict.*, i, 450. Ḥājjī Khalīfa i, 357.

and one of Egypt's great historians. To his credit stands a collection of songs entitled the *Mukhtar al-aghānī wa ma'ānīhā* (Selections from the Songs with Explanations of the Verses).[1]

Ibn Sīnā, or Abū 'Alī al-Ḥusain ibn 'Abdallāh ibn Sīnā (980-1037), was born at Afshana near Bukhārā. Shortly after this event his father settled in the latter city, and here Ibn Sīnā or Avicenna as he is generally called, was educated. At the age of seventeen he was appointed physician to the Sāmānid Nūḥ II (976-97) at Bukhārā. In this position he had access to the unique library of this monarch which contained solitary exemplars of the scientific works of the "Ancients" (the Greeks). At the age of eighteen, Ibn Sīnā claimed to have mastered all the sciences. After the death of his father, four years later, the young scientist began the life of a wandering scholar. He then settled at Al-Raiy, where the *amīr* Majd al-Daula was the nominal ruler, but later entered the service of Shams al-Daula (997-1021) at Hamadhān, who appointed him his *wazīr*. During this period he wrote numerous works, besides teaching a crowd of pupils, which however, did not prevent him from spending his nights with singers and musicians. When Samā' al-Daula (1021) succeeded as *amīr*, Ibn Sīnā became dissatisfied with his position, and fled to 'Alā al-Daula at Iṣfahān, where he spent the last ten or twelve years of his life.[2] Here he wrote, among other things, upon the theory of music (*mūsīqī*), in which subject says Ibn Al-Qifṭī, he was able to throw light on the negligence of the "Ancients" (the Greeks) in several questions.[3]

Besides his famous *Qānūn fī'l-ṭibb* (Canon of Medicine) which became one of the text-books for physicians throughout the civilized world, Ibn Sīnā was noted for his contributions to science and philosophy. Three of his works at least deal with the theory of music at some

[1] Ibn Khallikān, *Biog. Dict.*, iii, 87. Ḥājjī Khalīfa, i, 367. Cf. his name and the title of his book in these writers.

[2] Ibn al-Qifṭī, 413 *et seq.* Ibn Khallikān, *Biog. Dict.*, i, 440. Ibn Abī Uṣaibi'a, ii, 2. Abū'l-Fidā', *Annal. Musl.*, iii, 93.

[3] It has been assumed by Casiri (i, 271) and Wenrich (189) that this work on music was an abridgement of a work by Euklid, but the text does not actually say this.

length. His most important work on this subject is that contained in the *Shifā'*, which has been printed at Teheran (A.H. 1313), and is to be found in manuscript in several libraries in this country.[1] According to the preface of the *Najāt*, this work also contains a section on the science of music (*'ilm al-mūsīqī*), which came at the end of the chapter on the mathematical sciences (*'ulūm riyāḍiyya*). Yet strange to say, neither the printed edition (Cairo, A.H. 1331), nor the manuscript in the British Museum (Add. 9613), nor the old Latin version (Rome, 1593), contain this section on music. At the same time, it is to be found separately in two MSS. in the Bodleian Library.[2] Ibn Abī Uṣaibi'a says that Ibn Sīnā also wrote a *Madkhal ilā ṣinā'at al-mūsīqī* (Introduction to the Art of Music), which, we are expressly told, was different from that in the *Najāt*. In the Persian *Dānish nāma*, written for the Kākwaihid 'Alā' al-Daula, Ibn Sīnā's last patron, there is also a section on music. This is practically identical with the treatise in the *Najāt*, and appears to have been written after Ibn Sīnā's death by his disciple Al-Jūzjānī.[3] Minor chapters on the science of music, with mere definitions, also occur in his *Risāla fī taqāsīm al-ḥikma* (Treatise on the Divisions of the Sciences) and similar works.[4]

For an account of the subjects dealt with by Ibn Sīnā on the theory of music in his *Shifā'* and *Najāt* the reader is referred to my *Arabic Musical MSS. in the Bodleian Library*. Ibn Sīnā, who was known as "The Chief Teacher" (*al-shaikh al-ra'īs*), had a tremendous influence on Arabian and Persian musical theorists for many centuries.

Ibn al-Haitham, whose full name was Abū'l-'Alī al-Ḥasan ibn al-Ḥasan (or al-Ḥusain) ibn al-Haitham (*c.* 965-1039) was one of the most brilliant mathematicians and physicists that the Arabs produced. He was born at

[1] *Bodleian Library MS.*, Pocock, 109 and 250. *India Office MS.*, 1811. *Royal Asiatic Society MS.*, 58.

[2] *Bodleian Library MSS.*, Marsh, 161 and 521.

[3] *British Museum MS.*, Add 16830. See also Add. 16659 and Or. 2361.

[4] See the *Rasā'il fī'l-ḥikma wa'l-tabi'iyyāt* (Constantinople, A.H. 1298), and the *Leyden MS.*, Or. 985, fol. 170 v.

Al-Baṣra, where he rose to the post of *wazīr*, but was invited to the court of the Fāṭimid khalif Al-Ḥākim. Here he was given a position in the administration, the duties of which Ibn al-Haitham could not, or would not, perform. This roused the ire of the khalif and he was compelled to conceal himself until the khalif's death (1021), when he was able to devote himself publicly to literary and scientific pursuits. Ibn Abī Uṣaibi'a gives the titles of some 200 treatises on mathematics, physics, medicine, and philosophy of which Ibn al-Haitham was the author. Euklid was especially studied by this savant and he wrote a *Sharḥ qānūn Uqlaidis* (Commentary on the Canon of Euklid) and a *Sharḥ al-*[*a*]*rmūnīqī* [*li-Uqlaidis*] (Commentary on the Harmonics [of Euklid]) but alas ! neither of these commentaries have come down to us.[1] Another work of his that appears to have perished is the *Risāla fī ta'thīrāt al-luḥūn al-mūsīqī fī'l-nufūs al-ḥayawāniyya* (Treatise on the Influences of Musical Melodies on the souls of Animals).

Abū Manṣūr al-Ḥusain ibn Muḥammad ibn 'Umar ibn Zaila (d. 1048), referred to as Al-Ḥusain ibn Zaila, is evidently the same individual mentioned by Ibn Abī Uṣaibi'a as Abū Manṣūr ibn Zailā, one of the most distinguished pupils of Ibn Sīnā.[2] He was the author of a lengthy and valuable treatise on music entitled the *Kitāb al-kāfī fī'l-mūsīqī* (Book of Sufficiency in Music), a copy of which (the only one that appears to have survived) is preserved in the British Museum.[3]

Abū'l-Ḥakam 'Umar . . . al-Karmānī (d. 1066) was born at Cordova of a Carmona family, and died at Saragossa. He was distinguished as a mathematician and physician, and had studied in the East, notably at Ḥarrān, the home of the Ṣabians. He popularized the *rasā'il* of the Ikhwān al-Ṣafā'.[4]

Ibn Nāqīyā was the more general name by which

[1] Ibn al-Qifṭi, 168. Ibn Abī Uṣaibi'a, ii, 90.

[2] Ibn Abī Uṣaibi'a, ii, 19. See also *British Museum MSS.* Add. 16659, fol. 332, and Add. 23403, fol. 106.

[3] *Brit. Mus. MS.*, Or. 2361, fol. 220, *et seq.*

[4] Ibn Abī Uṣaibi'a, ii, 40. Al-Maqqarī, *Analectes*, ii, 232. *Mch. Dyn.*, i, 150. The latter claims him to have *introduced* the writings of the Ikhwān al-Ṣafā' into Al-Andalus.

Abū'l-Qāsim 'Abdallāh ibn Muḥammad (1020-92) was known. He was a poet of Baghdād who was interested in music, playing the *mizhar* (pre-Islāmic lute).[1] It is as the author of an abridgment of the great *Kitāb al-aghānī* however, that he finds a place here.[2]

Abū'l-Faḍl Ḥasdāy ibn Yūsuf ibn Ḥasdāy belonged to an old Jewish family of Saragossa in Al-Andalus. The dates of his birth and death are denied us, but he was a young man in 1066. He was not only celebrated as a mathematician and astronomer, but displayed much talent in rhetoric and poetry, and was learned in the science of music (*mūsīqī*).[3]

Abū'l-Ṣalt Umayya is the name given to Umayya ibn 'Abd al-'Azīz ibn Abī'l-Ṣalt (1068-1134).[4] He was born at Denia in Al-Andalus but migrated to Egypt in 1096, where he rose to high esteem with the Fāṭimid khalifs until falling into disfavour, he was flung into prison. In 1112 he retired to Al-Mahdiyya, where his learning brought him the patronage of the Zairids. Ibn Khallikān says that he "possessed superior information in the different branches of general literature . . . skilled in philosophy . . . deeply versed in the sciences of the Ancients."[5] Ibn Abī Uṣaibi'a informs us that Abū'l-Ṣalt excelled in the science of music (*mūsīqī*) and that he was a performer on the *'ūd*.[6] He was the author of a *Risāla fī'l-mūsīqī* (Treatise on Music),[7] which appears to have been an important work since it was translated into Hebrew, and a passage from it is quoted by Profiat Duran in his *Ma'aseh Efod* (written in 1403),[8] hence perhaps, as Steinschneider says,[9] the work was supposed to exist in

[1] Erroneously termed a *dulcimer* by De Slane (Ibn Khallikān, *Biog. Dict.*, ii, 64). A *dulcimer* is also referred to in another place by De Slane (i, 186) where no such instrument is mentioned in the text.

[2] Ḥājjī Khalīfa, i, 367. Here he is called Ibn Bāqīyā. Ibn Khallikān, *Biog. Dict.*, ii, 64. *Wafayāt*, i, 376.

[3] Ibn Abī Uṣaibi'a, ii, 50.

[4] Collangettes (*Jour. Asiat.*, 1904, p. 382) calls him Ibn al-Zalt ibn 'Abd al-'Azīz al-Umarī. Rouanet (Lavignac's *Encyclopédie de la musique*, v, 2680) says the same.

[5] Ibn Khallikān, *Biog. Dict.*, i, 228-31.

[6] Ibn Abī Uṣaibi'a, ii, 52-62.

[7] Ahlwardt, *Verz.*, No. 5536, 5.

[8] *Grammar* (Vienna, 1863), p. 37.

[9] Steinschneider, *Jewish Literature*, 337.

the Oratory.[1] As a composer, the influence of Abū'l-Ṣalt Umayya on North African music appears to have been considerable.[2]

Ibn Bājja (Avenpace), is the more popular cognomen of Abū Bakr Muḥammad ibn Yaḥyā ibn al-Ṣaigh (d. 1138). He was born at Saragossa towards the end of the eleventh century, and practised as a physician in his native city, but after the fall of Saragossa (1118) to the Christians, he resided at Seville and Xativa. Later he went to Fez in Morocco, where he was *wazīr* at the Murāwid court. Here he was poisoned at the instigation of an enemy. He was a voluminous writer and no fewer than twenty-four of his works on medicine, philosophy, and natural science have come down to us. Besides his unrivalled gifts in these sciences, he was " skilled in the art of music (*mūsīqī*), and was a clever performer on the *'ūd* (lute)," as we are informed by Ibn Abī Uṣaibi'a.[3] Ibn Khaldūn assures us that his music (*talḥīn*) was well-known,[4] and Ibn Sa'īd al-Maghribī (d. 1274 or 1286) says that Ibn Bājja gave his name to a collection of melodies the items of which were very popular.[5] That he was " a skilful musician " is testified by his enemy Al-Fatḥ ibn Khāqān (d. 1134 or 1140). His reputation as a musical theorist appears to have been considerable since Ibn Sa'īd al-Maghribī informs us that his book on music (*mūsīqī*) enjoyed the same reputation in the West as that of Al-Fārābī in the East.[6] Indeed, after Al-Fārābī, " there was no man like Ibn Bājja for the elevated manner in which he wrote and spoke on the sciences." " Where," says another Andalusian, " are those that can be compared to Ibn Bājja for the acquirements in the science of music and philosophy ? " Unfortunately we do not possess any of the writings on music of this great author and thinker.[7]

[1] Wolf, *Bib. Heb.*, ii, 331.
[2] Al-Maqqarī, *Anal.*, i, 530.
[3] Ibn Abī Uṣaibi'a, ii, 62.
[4] Ibn Khaldūn, *Prol.*, iii, 393.
[5] Al-Maqqarī, *Anal.*, ii, 125.
[6] Al-Maqqarī, *Anal.*, ii, 125.
[7] The *Sharḥ kitāb al-samā' al-ṭabī'ī li-Arisṭūṭālīs* is not a " Commentary on the Treatise on Sound by Aristotle," as Gayangos said (*Moh. Dyn.*) i, Append. A. iii., but a " Commentary on the *Physics* (φυσικὴ ἀκρόασις)." See my *Facts for the Arabian Musical Influence*, appendix 33.

Abū'l-Ḥakam al-Bāhilī, or Abū'l-Ḥakam 'Ubaidallāh (or 'Abdallāh) ibn al-Muẓaffar ibn 'Abdallāh al-Bāhilī (1093-1155), was born at Almeria in Al-Andalus.[1] Before the year 1122 he migrated to the East, and taught at a school which he himself opened at Baghdād. Later, he was a physician in the camp-hospital of the 'Irāqian Saljūqid sulṭān Maḥmūd (1117-31). Finally, he settled at Damascus, where he was highly esteemed as a physician, mathematician, *littérateur*, and musician. Al-Maqqarī says,—" Abū'l-Ḥakam excelled in the philosophical sciences, and was skilled in medicine and fine wit. . . . He played the *'ūd* (lute) and his work on music is well-known." Ibn Abī Uṣaibi'a also testifies to his musical talents, and both these writers, as well as Ibn Khallikān, praise his " dīwān of excellent poetry."[2]

Muḥammad ibn al-Ḥaddād, or in full Abū 'Abdallāh Muḥammad ibn Aḥmad ibn al-Ḥaddād (d. 1165) was another Andalusian, and the author of a work entitled by Casiri,—*Musices Disciplina* (Musical Instruction).[3] No other information appears to be available concerning this theorist, although Ḥājjī Khalīfa mentions a Muḥammad ibn Aḥmad ibn 'Uthmān al-Andalusī, who is also called Ibn al-Ḥaddād. The latter however is said to have died in 1087.[4]

Ibn al-Naqqāsh al-Baghdādī, or Muhadhdhab al-Dīn Abū'l-Ḥasan 'Alī . . . ibn 'Īsā (d. 1178), was a renowned mathematician and music theorist at Damascus. He was personal physician to Nūr al-Dīn the Zangid *atābag* (1146-63) and was also employed at the Nūrī hospital. We know of him specially as the tutor of Abū Zakariyyā al-Bayāsī and Aḥmad ibn al-Ḥājib.[5]

Abū Zakariyyā Yaḥyā al-Bayāsī was an Andalusian who migrated to the East and lived most of his time in Egypt and Syria. He was a physician, mathematician, and musician, and was one of the medical men at the court

[1] Ibn Khallikān says Al-Yaman, whilst Bar Hebræus says Murcia.

[2] Al-Maqqarī, *Anal.*, i, 548. Ibn Abī Uṣaibi'a, ii, 144. Ibn Khallikān, *Biog. Dict.*, ii, 82.

[3] Casiri, ii, 73. The Arabic title of this work is not given by Casiri.

[4] Ḥājjī Khalīfa, iii, 245.

[5] Ibn Abī Uṣaibi'a, ii, 162, 181.

of Salāḥ al-Dīn the Ayyūbid sulṭān (1171-93). He was a pupil of Ibn al-Naqqāsh in the science of music, and Ibn Abī Uṣaibi'a says,—" Abū Zakariyyā . . . made for Ibn al-Naqqāsh many instruments of a composite nature, which he derived from engineering (*handasa*),[1] . . . was an excellent player on the '*ūd* (lute), and he constructed an organ (*urghan*), and sought by artful contrivance the playing of it."[2]

Abū'l-Majd Muḥammad ibn Abī'l-Ḥakam (d. 1180) was a son of Abū'l-Ḥakam al-Bāhilī already mentioned, and was a noted physician, mathematician, astrologer, and musician. Whilst in the service of the Zangid *atābag* Nūr al-Dīn (1146-63) at Damascus, he had charge of his hospitals. Ibn Abī Uṣaibi'a says of him,—" Abū'l-Majd had knowledge of the science of music (*mūsīqī*) and played the '*ūd* (lute); excelled in the song (*ghinā'*), the rhythms (*īqā'*[*āt*]), the *zamr* (reed-pipe), and other instruments. And he constructed an organ (*urghan*) in which he attained perfection."[3]

Abū Naṣr As'ad ibn al-Yās ibn Jirjis al-Maṭrān (d. 1191) was born at Damascus of a Christian family. He studied medicine and the sciences at Baghdād, and was a pupil of Ibn al-Naqqāsh. For some time he was in the service of Salāḥ al-Dīn, and amassed a library of ten thousand volumes.[4] Besides being the author of a number of medical works, a *Risālat al-adwār* (Treatise on the Musical Modes) is said to have been written by him.[5]

Kamāl al-Dīn ibn Man'a, or Abū'l-Fatḥ Mūsā ibn Yūnus ibn Muḥammad ibn Man'a (b. 1156) was born at Al-Mauṣil. At the Niẓāmiyya college at Baghdād he won high honours, and, returning to his native town, he became noted as a teacher of mathematics, and was later the Principal of several colleges. Ibn Khallikān

[1] Or " *geometry*."
[2] Ibn Abī Uṣaibi'a, ii, 163.
[3] Ibn Abī Uṣaibi'a, ii, 155.
[4] Ibn Abī Uṣaibi'a, ii, 175.
[5] Ahlwardt, *Verz.*, No. 5536, 25. I have not been able to verify this statement elsewhere. The only work bearing a similar title in Ibn Abī Uṣaibi'a, is a *Risālat al-adwār* entitled by Leclerc (*Hist. de la Méd. arabe.*, ii, 45),—" *Un recueil des Périodes des Chaldéens*," and by Wüstenfeld (*Gesch. d. Arab. aerzte*, 101),—" Compendium libri mansionum Ibn Wahschijjae."

says of him: "In the mathematical sciences he was particularly distinguished. . . . He knew physics . . . was acquainted with all the parts of mathematical science explained by Euklid, astronomy, conics . . . music, and mensuration. In all these sciences he was without a rival."[1]

Yaḥyā [ibn] al-Khudujj al-Mursī, also called Yaḥyā ibn al-Khudujj al-A'lam, was, as his name tells us, a native of Murcia. Al-Maqqarī informs us that he was the author of a *Kitāb al-aghānī* written in imitation of the work of Abū'l-Faraj [al-Iṣfahānī][2]. He belonged, it would seem, to the twelfth century.

Ibn Rushd (Averroës), or Abū'l-Walīd ibn Aḥmad ibn Muḥammad ibn Rushd (1126-98), the famous Andalusian philosopher, has been claimed by several writers as the author of a "Commentary on Music."[3] Renan has pointed out that this is probably an error due to the ambiguity of a Hebrew word, and that the work which these writers had in mind was Ibn Rushd's Paraphrase of Aristotle's *Poetics* and *Rhetoric*.[4] At the same time it is not unlikely, if a mistake has been made, that such a work as his *Sharḥ al-samā' al-ṭabī'ī*[5] might have misled these authors, since the above could be understood to refer to a commentary on the nature of sound.[6]

'Alam al-Dīn Qaiṣar ibn Abī'l-Qāsim (1178-1251) was born at Afsūn in Upper Egypt and died at Damascus. "In Egypt and Damascus," says Ibn Khallikān, "he was looked upon as the great master of the age in all the mathematical sciences." He had Kamāl al-Dīn ibn Man'a as his teacher, and he relates the following story of his first interview with this savant. "He [Kamāl al-Dīn] asked me by what science I wished to begin. 'By [the theory of] music,' said I. 'That happens very

[1] Ibn Khallikān, *Biog. Dict.*, iii, 467-68. Ibn Abī Uṣaibi'a, i, 306.

[2] Al-Maqqarī, *Anal.*, ii, 125. Gayangos, in his *Mohammedan Dynasties*, i, 198 (cf. 480), names him Yaḥyā ibn al-Ḥaddāj (*variants*, —al-Ḥudj and al-Khurj).

[3] Labbe, *Nova Bibl. MSS.*, 116 (quoted by Renan); Wolf, *Bib. Heb.*, i, 20; and De Rossi, *Cod. Heb.*, ii, 9-10.

[4] Renan, *Averroes*, 63. See Wenrich, *De auct. Graec.*, 152.

[5] Called *Talkhīṣ kitāb al-samā' al-ṭabī'ī li-Arisṭūṭālīs* by Ibn Abī Uṣaibi'a.

[6] Ibn Abī Uṣaibi'a, ii, 75. See Al-Maqqarī, *Moh. Dyn.*, i, Append. A, iv.

well,' he said, 'for it is a long time since anyone studied it under me, and I wished to converse with some person on that science so as to renew my acquaintance with it.' I then commenced [the theory of] music, after which I passed successively to other sciences, and, in about the space of six months, I went over more than forty works under his tuition. I was already acquainted with [the theory of] music, but I wished to be enabled to say that I had studied that science under him." Ḥasan ibn 'Umar says that 'Alam al-Dīn was particularly distinguished for his profound knowledge of music.[1]

Ibn Sab'īn, or Abū Muḥammad 'Abd al-Ḥaqq ibn Ibrāhīm ibn Muḥammad al-Ishbīlī (d. 1269) was a native of Murcia and died at Mecca. He became famous for his *Kitāb al-ajwiba 'an* [?*min*] *al-as'ula* (Answers to Questions) written at the command of the Muwaḥḥid sulṭān 'Abd al-Wāḥid al-Rashīd (1232-42) in reply to certain philosophical questions set by the Emperor Frederick II of Hohenstaufen.[2] He was also the author of a *Kitāb al-adwār al-mansūb* (Book of the Related Musical Modes), the solitary copy of which is in the library of Aḥmad Taimūr Bāshā.[3]

Abū Ja'far Naṣīr al-Dīn al-Ṭūsī (1201-74) was born at Ṭūs in Khurāsān. He was the most celebrated scientist of his day, and was especially noted for his mathematical and astronomical works. As court astrologer to Hūlāgū, the Mughal sulṭān, he accompanied the conqueror on his campaigns, and was able to amass a library of 400,000 books, pillaged from the collections of Baghdād, Syria and Mesopotamia.[4] He was a most productive author and among his mathematical works is a tract on the *'ilm al-mūsīqī* (science of music), a copy of which is preserved in the Paris Bibliothèque Nationale.[5] The Turks attribute to him, it would seem, the invention

[1] Ibn Khallikān, *Biog. Dict.*, iii, 471-3. Abū'l-Fidā', *Annal. Musl.* iv, 479, 529.

[2] Al-Kutubī, *Fawāt al-wafayāt*, i, 247.

[3] *Hilāl*, xxviii, 214.

[4] Bar Hebræus *Hist. Orient.*, 358. Abū'l-Fidā', *Annal. Musl.*, v, 37.

[5] De Slane's *Catalogue*, No. 2466. In the library of King's College, Cambridge, there is a Persian work on music entitled the *Kanz al-tuḥaf*, which is attributed to Naṣīr al-Dīn al-Ṭūsī. (*J.R.A.S.*, June, 1867, p. 118). The work may belong to another author.

of the flute called *mahtar dūdūk*[1]. His greatest pupil was Quṭb al-Dīn al-Shīrāzī (1236-1310), the author of the *Durrat al-tāj*, one of the most authoritative works on the "Systematist" theory of music.

Abū Bakr Muḥammad ibn Aḥmad al-Raqūṭī was a thirteenth century savant of Murcia, distinguished for his abilities in music, mathematics and medicine. When the Christians took Murcia (13th century), their king retained Al-Raqūṭī to teach in the schools which he founded. He died in Granada.[2]

Ṣafī al-Dīn 'Abd al-Mu'min (ibn Yūsuf) ibn Fākhir al-Urmawī al-Baghdādī was probably born at Baghdād in the early years of the thirteenth century, although his father (or grandfather) evidently came from Urmia, a town in Adharbaijān.[3] We find him at Baghdād in the service of the last 'Abbāsid khalif Al-Musta'ṣim (1243-58) as his chief court minstrel, boon companion, caligraphist, and librarian.[4] He was on very intimate terms with the khalif, who allowed him a pension of 5,000 golden pieces a year. Ṣafī al-Dīn was in Baghdād when it was sacked by Hūlāgū in 1258, and Ḥājjī Khalīfa recounts a story which is taken from the *Ḥabīb al-siyar*,[5] which relates that when the city was given over to the Mughal hordes for slaughter and pillage the great musician, by reason of his musical reputation, managed to gain access to Hūlāgū, and so charmed the conqueror by his performances on the *'ūd* that Hūlāgū ordered that Ṣafī al-Dīn, his family and property, should be spared in the general devastation.[6] Entering Hūlāgū's service, his pension was doubled to 10,000 pieces of gold, which was paid out of the revenues of Baghdād. He then became tutor of the sons of the Mughal *wazīr* or *ṣāḥib dīwān* Shams al-Dīn Muḥammad ibn Muḥammad al-Juwainī,[7] who, with his brother 'Aṭā Malik, the author of the *Ta'rīkh-i jahān gushā*, appointed the famous

1 Evliyā Chelebī, *Narrative of Travels*, i, ii, 237.
2 Casiri, ii, 81-82.
3 De Sacy, *Chrest. arab.*, i, 70.
4 *Fakhrī*, 572.
5 *Habīb al-siyar*, iii, 1, 61.
6 Ḥājjī Khalīfa, iii, 413.
7 Cf. Carra de Vaux, *Le Traité des Rapports musicaux*, p. 4.

musician to the head of the Correspondence Bureau (*dīwān-i inshā*) at Baghdād.

Ṣafī al-Dīn's two pupils, Bahā' al-Dīn Muḥammad (1240-79) and Sharaf al-Dīn Hārūn (d. 1286), the sons of the *wazīr* were extremely kind to him.[1] It was for the latter that the great musician wrote his famous treatise, the *Risālat al-Sharafiyya* (Sharafian Treatise). The former took Ṣafī al-Dīn with him to Iṣfahān when he was appointed governor of Al-'Irāq and 'Irāq 'Ajamī in 1265. On the death of Bahā' al-Dīn (1279) and the fall of the family of Al-Juwainī (1284), the savant *virtuoso* lost his protectors, and finally fell on evil days, being imprisoned for a debt of 300 pieces of gold. Yet, when he had plenty he spent money lavishly, and could indulge in fruits and perfumes costing 4,000 pieces of silver, for the benefit of his friends. Yet this man, whose textbooks were the standard authority among music theorists for centuries, and are even quoted to-day, died in a debtors' prison.[2]

Ṣafī al-Dīn 'Abd al-Mu'min was a man of wide culture. Mīrzā Muḥammad says that he was "especially celebrated for his skill in music and caligraphy." In the former art, Ibn Taghrībirdī declares him to have been excelled by none since the days of Isḥāq al-Mauṣilī, the boon companion of Hārūn al-Rashīd, whilst in the latter he is placed on a level with such masters of the art as Yāqūt and Ibn Muqla. Besides being the inventor of two stringed instruments—the *mughnī*, an arch-lute, which he devised during his stay in Iṣfahān, as well as the *nuzha*, a new type of psaltery,[3] Ṣafī al-Dīn was the author of two important treatises on the theory of music—the *Kitāb al-adwār* (Book of Musical Modes), and the *Risālat al-Sharafiyya* (Sharafian Treatise). The former work,

[1] In music, philosophy, and *belles lettres*, Bahā al-Dīn stood heads above many of his contemporaries. D'Ohsson, *Histoire des Mongols*, iv, 11-12. Sharaf al-Dīn was also "one of the most accomplished men of his day," and a *dīwān* of his poems is preserved in the British Museum (Or. 3647). See *Ta'rīkh-i jahān gushā*, xlviii.

[2] For full life of Ṣafī al-Dīn see authorities quoted by Mīrzā Muḥammad in his introduction to the *Ta'rīkh-i jahān gushā*, li.

[3] *Kanz al-tuḥaf*, Brit. Mus. MS., Or. 2361, fol. 263 v, 264 v. See my *Studies in Oriental Musical Instruments*, pp. 12-15.

which is probably the earlier and was probably written in 1252, is perhaps the better known to the theorists. Manuscripts of this work may be found in the Bodleian Library,[1] the British Museum,[2] and other collections. All sorts of commentaries (*shurūḥ*) have been written on this work, and three are to be found in the British Museum.[3] The *Risālat al-sharafiyya* is more familiar to European readers on account of a *résumé* of the work having been published by Baron Carra de Vaux.[4] Manuscripts of the work are to be found in the Bodleian Library,[5] Berlin,[6] Paris,[7] Vienna,[8] and elsewhere,[9] as well as an epitome at Cairo. It is said to have been written in 1267,[10] and we have a manuscript (Berlin) dating from 1276. At the Bodleian there is another work by Ṣafī al-Dīn entitled *Fī 'ulūm al-'arūḍ wa'l-qawāfī wa'l-badī'*, a work which deals with prosody, rhyme, and rhetoric, not with "rhythm" as has been recently stated.[11] The great repute of Ṣafī al-Dīn is that he was the pioneer of a school which propagated the "Systematist Theory."

Ibn al-Qifṭī, the more general name by which we know Abū'l-Ḥasan 'Alī ibn Yūsuf al-Qifṭī (1172-1248), is included here because he is such a valuable source of information concerning writers on the theory of music. Born at Qifṭ (the ancient Koptos) he was educated at Cairo, but spent nearly his whole life in Palestine and Syria. Although fulfilling the duties of *wazīr* at Aleppo, he devoted himself to literary studies.[12] His greatest

[1] *Bodleian Library*, Marsh 521 (two copies), Marsh 161 (two copies). See my *Arabic Musical MSS. in the Bodleian Library*.

[2] *British Museum*, Or. 136, and Or. 2361. See Ḥājjī Khalīfa, iii, 361.

[3] Or. 2361.

[4] *Le Traité des rapports musicaux ou l'épître à Scharaf ed-Dîn* (Paris, 1891).

[5] *Bodleian Library*, Marsh 115, and Marsh 521.

[6] *Berlin MS.*, Ahlwardt, *Verz.*, 5506.

[7] *Paris MS.*, De Slane, *Cat.*, 2479.

[8] *Vienna* MS. Flügel, 1515.

[9] *Journal, American Oriental Society*, i, p. 174.

[10] *Ibid.*, p. 174.

[11] *Grove's Dictionary of Music* (3rd Edit.), iv, 498. The slip is evidently due to the Latin title, *De scientiis prosodiae, rhythmorum et dictionis figuratae*, given in the Bodleian catalogue. Several erroneous statements are made in the former work concerning Ṣafī al-Dīn.

[12] Yāqūt, *Irshād*, v, 477.

work appears to have been a *Kitāb ikhbār al-'ulamā'*, which has come down to us in a synopsis made by Al-Zauzanī entitled (or at least known as) the *Ta'rīkh al-ḥukamā'* (History of the Learned), a work quoted frequently in the foregoing pages.[1]

Ibn Abī Uṣaibi'a or Muwaffaq al-Dīn Abū'l-'Anbās ibn Abī Uṣaibi'a (1202-1270) is another writer in the same category. Born at Damascus, he completed his medical education at the Nāṣirī hospital in Cairo. He was appointed to the charge of one of Salāḥ al-Dīn's hospitals in this city, and later became personal physician to the *amīr* 'Izz al-Dīn in Ṣarkhad.[2] His chief literary production, the *'Uyūn al-anbā'*, a history of physicians, is another work used in these pages for information concerning music theorists.[3]

[1] The Arabic text was edited by Lippert (Leipsic, 1903).
[2] *Travaux du VIe Congrès intern. des Orientalistes à Leide*, ii, 259.
[3] A. Müller published the text (Königsberg, 1884).

BIBLIOGRAPHY

(1) PRINTED BOOKS.

This list contains the works mentioned in the footnote references. Where several editions of the same work are given, the one marked with an asterisk is the authority quoted, although the others have generally been consulted.

J.A.—*Journal Asiatique.*

J.R.A.S.—*Journal of the Royal Asiatic Society.*

Abū'l-Fidā', *Annales moslemici, arabice et latine. Opera et studiis Jo. Jacobi Reiskii.* 5 vols. Hafniae, 1789-94.

— *Abulfedae historia Anteislamica, arabice. Edidit, vers. lat. H. O. Fleischer.* Leipsic, 1831.

Abū Tammām, *Dīwān.* Beyrout, 1889.

Al-Aghānī. See Iṣfahānī.

Ahlwardt (W.), *The divans of the six ancient Arabic poets. Edited by W. Ahlwardt.* London, 1870.

— *Verzeichniss der arabischen Handschriften der königl. Bibliothek zu Berlin.* 10 vols. Berlin, 1887-99.

Al-Akfānī, *Irshād al-qāṣid.* [Bibliotheca Indiça.] Calcutta, 1849.

Alf laila wa laila. See Macnaghten, Lane, Burton.

'Alī Bey, *Travels of Ali Bey, between the years 1803 and 1807.* 2 vols. London, 1816.

Aljoxani, *Historia de los jueces de Córdoba por Aljoxanī. Texto árabe y traducción española por Julián Ribera.* Madrid, 1914.

Amedroz (H. F.) and Margoliouth (D. S.), *The eclipse of the 'Abbāsid Caliphate. Original chronicles of the fourth Islamic century. Edited by H. F. Amedroz and D. S. Margoliouth.* 7 vols. Oxford, 1920-21.

Aumer (J.), *Die arab. Handschriften der königl. Hof- und Staatsbibl. in München.* Munich, 1866.

Al-Badā'ūnī ('Abd al-Qādir ibn Mulūk Shāh), *Muntakhabu-t-tawārīkh, by 'Abdu-l-Qādir ibn-i-mulūk-shāh, known as Al-Badāonī. Translated from the original Persian by G. S. A. Ranking.* [Bibliotheca Indica.] Vol. I., Calcutta, 1898.

Baeumker (C), *Alfarabi über den Ursprung der Wissenschaften (De ortu scientiarum). Heraus. von Clement Baeumker.* [Beit. z. Geschichte der Phil. d. Mittelalters, xix.] Münster i. W., 1916.

Al-Balādhurī, *Liber expugnationis regionum. Edidit M. J. de Goeje.* Leyden, 1866.

Banū Mūsā, *Al-ālat illatī tuzammir binafsihā.* [Al-Mashriq, xvi.] Beyrout.

Barbier de Meynard, *Ibrahim fils de Mehdi.* [Journal Asiatique, 1884.] Paris, 1884.

Bar Hebraeus (Abū'l-Faraj), *Historia orientalis. Arabice edita, et latine versa, ab Edvardo Pocockio.* Oxford, 1672.

Bartholomaeus, *Bertholomeus de proprietatibus rerum.* London, 1535.

Berlin MSS. See Ahlwardt.

Beth o'çar haṣṣpharoth. Edited by Eisig Gräber. Year I. Przemysl, 1886.

Bevan (A. A.), *The Nakā'id of Jarīr and Al-Farazdaq. Edited by A. A. Bevan.* 3 vols. Leyden, 1905-12.

Bibliotheca geographorum arabicorum. Edidit M. J. de Goeje. 8 vols. Leyden, 1870-94.

Bodleian MSS. See Uri and Nichol, Sachau and Ethé, Farmer.

British Museum MSS. See *Catalogus cod. MSS. orient.*, and Rieu.

Browne (E. G.), *A literary history of Persia from the earliest times until Firdawsī.* [vol. i.] London, 1902.

— *A literary history of Persia from Firdawsī to Sa'dī.* [vol. ii.] London, 1906.

— *The sources of Dawlatshāh, and an excursus on Bārbad and Rūdagī.* [J.R.A.S., 1899.] London, 1899.

Brockelmann (K.), *Geschichte der arabischen Litteratur.* 2 vols. Weimar u. Berlin, 1898-1902.

Al-Buḥturī, *Dīwān.* 2 vols. Constantinople, 1883.

Al-Bukhārī (Muḥ. ibn Ismā'īl), *Kitāb ṣaḥīḥ.* 4 vols. Cairo, 1888.

Burckhardt (J. L.), *Notes on the Bedouins and Wahābys.* 2 vols. London, 1830.

Burhān-i qaṭi'. Boorhani qatiu, a dictionary of the Persian language, by Moohummad Ḥoosuen ibni Khuluf oot-Tubreezee, to which is added an appendix by Thos. Roebuck. Calcutta, 1818.

Burton (R. F.), *Arabian Nights. Lady [Isobel] Burton's edition. Prepared for household reading by J. H. McCarthy.* 6 vols., London, 1886.

Caetani (L.), *Annali dell' Islam.* In progress. Milan, 1905, *et seq.*

Cajori (F.), *A history of mathematics.* 2nd edit. New York, 1919.

Carra de Vaux (Baron), *Le traité des rapports musicaux ou l'épître à Scharaf ed-Dīn, par Safi ed-Dīn 'Abd el-Mumin Albaghdādī, par M. le Baron Carra de Vaux.* Paris, 1891.

Casiri (M.), *Bibliotheca arabico-hispana Escurialensis . . . recensio et explanatio opera et studio Michaelis Casiri.* Madrid, 1760-70.

Catalogus codicum orientalium Bibliothecae Academiae Lugduno Batavae. 6 vols. Leyden, 1851-77.

Catalogus cod. MSS. orient. qui in Museo Brit. asservantur. London, 1838-71.

Caussin de Perceval (A. P.), *Essai sur l'histoire des Arabes avant l'Islamisme.* 3 vols. Paris, 1847-8.

— *Notices anecdotiques sur les principaux musiciens arabes des trois premiers siècles de l'Islamisme.* [J. A., 1873.] Paris, 1873.

Chenery (T.), *The assemblies of Al-Harīrī. Translated by T. Chenery.* London, 1867.

Christianowitsch (A.), *Esquisse historique de la musique arabe aux temps anciens.* Cologne, 1863.

Collangettes (M.), *Etude sur la musique arabe.* [J. A., 1904, 1906.] Paris, 1904, 1906.

Corpus inscriptionum Semiticarum. Paris, 1881 *et seq.*

Dalton (O. M.), *The treasures of the Oxus with other examples of early oriental metal-work.* 2nd edit., London, 1926.

Darwīsh Muḥammad, *Kitāb ṣafā' al-awqāt fī 'ilm al-naghamāt.* Cairo, 1910.

Delphin (G.) and Guin (L.), *Notes sur la poésie et la musique arabes dans le Maghreb algérien.* Paris, 1886.

Derenbourg (H.), *Les manuscrits arabes de l'Escurial.* [Ecole des langues orientales vivantes, ii. sér., x, xi.] Paris, 1884-1903.

De Slane (Mac Guckin), *Catalogue des MSS. arabes de la Bibliothèque Nationale.* 1883-95. Paris.

Dieterici (F.), *Die Propaedeutic der Araber im zehnten Jahrhundert.* Berlin, 1865.

D'Ohsson (A. C. Mouradja), *Histoire des Mongols depuis Tchinguiz-Khan jusqu'à Timour Bey ou Tamerlan.* 4 vols. The Hague, Amsterdam, 1834-5.

D'Ohsson (J. Mouradja), *Tableau général de l'empire othoman.* 7 vols. Paris, 1788-1824.

Doughty (C. M.), *Travels in Arabia Deserta.* Cambridge, 1888.

Dozy (R. P. A.), *Glossaire dēs mots espagnols et portugais dérivés de l'arabe, par R. Dozy et W. H. Engelmann.* Leyden, 1869.

— *Historia Abbadidarum, praemissis scriptorum Arabum de ea dynastica locis nunc primum editis.* (*Scriptorum Arabum loci de Abbadidio*). 2 vols. Leyden, 1846-52.

— *Histoire des Musulmans d'Espagne, jusqu'à la conquête de l'Andalousie par les Almoravides.* 4 vols. Leyden, 1861.

— *Supplément aux dictionnaires arabes.* 2 vols. Leyden, 1877.

Eclipse of the 'Abbāsid Caliphate, The. See Amedroz and Margoliouth.

Encyclopaedia of Islām, The. A dictionary of the geography, ethnography and biography of the Muḥammadan peoples. Leyden, London, 1908 *et seq.*

Encyclopaedia of religion and ethics, The. See Hastings.

Escorial MSS. See Casiri, Derenbourg.

Evliyyā Chelebī. See Evliyyā Efendī.

*Evliyyā Efendī, *Narrative of travels in Europe, Asia, and Africa in the seventeenth century by Evliya Efendi. Translated from the Turkish by J. von Hammer.* London, 1846-50.

— [Evliyyā Chelebī], *Siyāhat-nāma.* 6 vols. Constantinople, 1896-1900.

Fakhrī. See Ibn al-Ṭiqṭaqā.

Al-Fārābī, *Iḥṣā al-'ulūm. Edited by Muḥammad Riḍā.* [Al-Irfan, vol. vi.] Saida, Syria, 1921.

Al-Farazdaq. See Bevan.

Farmer (H. G.), *The music and musical instruments of the Arab, by F. Salvador-Daniel. Edited by Henry George Farmer.* London, 1915.

— *The Arabian influence on musical theory.* London, 1925.

— *The Arabic musical MSS. in the Bodleian Library.* London, 1925.

— *The influence of music: From Arabic sources. A lecture delivered before The Musical Association.* London, 1926.

— *Studies in oriental musical instruments.* [To be published shortly.]

— *Facts for the Arabian musical influence.* [To be published shortly.]

— *The organ of the ancients. From eastern sources.* [To be published shortly.]

Fihrist. See Al-Warrāq.

Flandrin (E.-N.), and Coste (P.), *Voyage en Perse de MM. Eugène Flandrin et Pascal Coste pendant les années* 1840 *et* 1841. 7 vols. Paris, 1843-54.

Flügel (G.), *Die arab., pers., und türkischen Handschriften der k.k. Hofbibliothek zu Wien.* 3 vols. Vienna, 1865-67.

Forbes (D.), *A Dictionary, Hindustani and English: Accompanied by a reversed dictionary, English and Hindustani.* 2 pts. London, 1866.

Freytag (G. W. F.), *Arabum proverbia vocalibus instruxit.* Bonn, 1838-43.

*Al-Ghazālī, *Emotional religion in Islām as affected by music and singing. Being a translation of a book of the Iḥyā 'ulūm ad-dīn of Al-Ghazzālī* By D. B. Macdonald. [J.R.A.S., 1901-02.]

— *Iḥyā 'ulūm al-dīn.* 4 vols. Būlāq, 1891.

Al-Ghuzūlī, *Maṭāli' al-budūr.* 2 vols. Cairo, 1882-3.

Goldziher (I.), *Muhammedanische Studien.* 2 pts. Halle, 1888-90.

Ḥājjī Khalīfa, *Kashf al-ẓunūn. Lexicon bibliographicum et encyclopaedicum. Edid. G. Flügel.* Leipsic, London, 1835-58.

Al-Hamadhānī (Ibn al-Faqīq), *Kitāb al-buldān.* [Bibl. Geog. Arab., v.] Leyden, 1885.

Al-Ḥarīrī. See Chenery, Steingass.

Hartmann (M.), *Das Muwaššaḥ.* Weimar, 1897.

Haskins (C. H.), *Studies in the history of mediaeval science.* Cambridge (U.S.A.), 1924.

Hastings (J.), *Encyclopaedia of religion and ethics. Edit. by J. Hastings, with the assistance of J. A. Selbie.* Edinburgh, 1908-26.

Hauser (F.), *Ueber das kitāb al ḥijāl der Benū Mūsā.* Erlangen, 1922.

**Hidāya. The Hidayah with its commentary called the Kifayah.* Published by Hukeem Moulvee Abdool Mujeed. 4 vols. [Calcutta] 1831-4.

— *The Hedaya or Guide: A commentary on Mussulman laws. Translated by C. Hamilton,* 4 vols. London, 1791.

Hirschfeld (H.). *New Researches into the Composition and Exegesis of the Qoran.* London, 1902.

Homenaje á D. Francisco Codera en su jubilación del profesorado. Estudios de erudición oriental. Saragossa, 1904.

Hommel (F.), *The ancient Hebrew traditions as illustrated by monuments.* London, 1897.

Howorth (H. H.), *History of the Mongols. From the 9th to the 19th Century.* 4 vols. London, 1876-88.

Huart (C.), *A history of Arabic literature.* London, 1903.

— *Histoire des arabes.* 2 vols. Paris, 1912-13.

Al-Hujwīrī ('Alī ibn 'Uthmān), *The Kashf al-maḥjūb, the oldest Persian treatise on Ṣūfism. Translated by R. A. Nicholson.* London, 1911.

Ibn al-Abbār (Abū 'Abdallāh), *Kitāb al-takmila. Edit. D. F. Codera.* Madrid, 1889.

Ibn 'Abd Rabbihi, *'Iqd al-farīd.* 3 vols Cairo, 1887-8.

Ibn 'Abdūn, *Commentaire historique sur le poème d'Ibn Abdoun, par Ibn Badroun, publié par R. P. A. Dozy.* Leyden, 1846.

Ibn Abī Uṣaibi'a, *'Uyūn al-anbā' fī ṭabaqāt al-aṭibbā'.* 2 vols. Königsberg, 1882-4.

Ibn al-Athīr ('Alī ibn Muḥammad), *Al-kāmil fī al-ta'rīkh.* 12 vols. Cairo, 1884-5.

— *Usd al-ghāba.* 5 vols. Cairo, 1869-71.

Ibn al-Athīr (Naṣr Allāh), *Al-mathal al-sā'ir. Edited by Muḥammad al-Ṣabbāgh.* Būlāq, 1865.

Ibn Badrūn. See Ibn 'Abdūn.

Ibn al-Faqīq. See al-Hamadhānī.

Ibn Ḥajar, *Iṣāba fī tamyīz al-ṣaḥāba. Edit. by Sprenger.* 4 vols. Calcutta, 1856-73.

Ibn Hishām ('Abd al-Malik), *Kitāb sīra rasūl Allāh. Das Leben Muhammads nach Muhammad ibn Isḥāk, bearbeitet von Abd al-Malik ibn Hischam. Heraus. von F. Wüstenfeld.* 2 vols. Göttingen, 1859-60.

*Ibn Khaldūn, *Muqaddima. Texte arabe publié par M. Quatremère.* [Notices et extraits des manuscrits de la Bibl. du Roi, xvi, xvii, xviii (=i, ii, iii.] Paris, 1858.

— *Prolégomènes historiques d'Ebn Khaldoun.* [Notices et extraits, xix, xx, xxi.] Paris, 1862-68.

— *Extraits d'Ibn Khaledoun. De la musique. Par M. de Hammer.* [Mines de l'Orient, vi.] Vienna, 1818.

*Ibn Khallikān, *Biographical Dictionary, trans. from the Arabic by Baron Mac Guckin de Slane.* 4 vols. Paris, London, 1843-71.

— *Wafayāt al-a'yān.* 2 vols. Būlāq, 1882.

Ibn al-Qifṭī, *Ta'rīkh al-ḥukamā'. Edit. Lippert.* Leipsic, 1903.

Ibn Sīda, *Kitāb al-mukhaṣṣaṣ. Edit. by Muḥammad Maḥmūd al-Shanqīṭī and others.* Būlāq, 1898-1903.

*Ibn al-Ṭiqṭaqā, *Elfachri. Geschichte der islamischen Reiche, von Ibn etthiqthaqa. Arabisch heraus. von W. Ahlwardt.* Gotha, 1860.

— *Al-Fakhrī. Histoire des dynasties musulmanes par Ibn aṭ-Tiqṭaqā. Traduit de l'Arabe par Emile Amar.* [Archives Marocaines, xvi.] Paris, 1910.

Al-Ibshīhī (Muḥammad ibn Aḥmad), *Al-mustaṭraf.* Cairo, 1896-7.

*Ikhwān al-Ṣafā', *Kitāb Ikhwān al-Ṣafā'. Edit. by Aḥmad ibn 'Abdallāh.* 4 vols. Bombay, 1887-9.

— *Rasā'il Ikhwān al-Ṣafā'.* Cairo, 1366.

— *Die Abhandlungen der Ichwān es-Safā in Auswahl. Heraus. von Dr. Fr. Dieterici.* Leipsic, 1886.

India Office MSS. See Loth.

'Iqd al-farīd. See Ibn 'Abd Rabbihi.

*Al-Iṣfahānī (Abū'l-Faraj), *Kitāb al-aghānī.* 20 vols. Būlāq, 1869.

— *The twenty-first volume of the Kitāb al-aghānī, being a collection of biographies not contained in the Būlāq edition.* Leyden, 1888.

— *Tables alphabétiques du Kitāb al-aghānī. Rédigées par I. Guidi.* Leyden, 1900.

— *Kitāb al-aghānī.* [Sāsī edit.] 21 vols. Cairo, 1905-6.

— *Taṣḥīḥ kitāb al-aghānī.* Cairo, 1916.

Jaussen (A. J.) and Savignac, *Mission archéologique en Arabie.* 2 vols. Paris, 1909-20.

Al-Jundī ('Uthmān ibn Muḥammad), *Risāla rauḍ al-masarrāt.* Cairo, 1895.

Jurjī Zaidān, *Umayyads and 'Abbāsids, being the fourth part of Jurjī Zaidān's History of Islamic civilisation. Translated by D. S. Margoliouth.* London, 1907.

Al-Juwainī, *The Ta'rīkh-i-jahān-gushā of 'Alā'u'd-Dīn 'Aṭā Malik-i-Juwaynī. Edited by Mīrzā Muḥammad.* 2 vols. London, 1912-16.

Kāmil. See Al-Mubarrad.

Kashf al-maḥjūb. See Al-Hujwīrī.

Kay (H. C.), *Yaman, Its early mediaeval history, by Najm ad-Din 'Omārah al-Ḥakami. The original texts, with translation, by H. C. Kay.* London, 1892.

Kiesewetter (R. G.), *Die Musik der Araber.* Leipsic, 1842.

King (L. W.), *A History of Babylon from the Foundation of the Monarchy to the Persian Conquest.* London, 1915.

Kosegarten (J. G. L.), *Alii Ispahanensis liber cantilenarum magnus Arabice editus adjectaque translatione adnotationibusque illustratus ab J. G. L. Kosegarten.* Gripesvoldiae, 1840, *et seq.*

— *Die moslemischen Schriftsteller über die Theorie der Musik.* [Zeit. f.d. Kunde des Morgenlandes, v.] Bonn, 1844.

Kremer (A. von), *Culturgeschichtliche Streifzüge auf dem Gebiete des Islams.* Leipsic, 1873.

Al-Kutubī (Muḥammad ibn Shākir), *Fawāt al-wafayāt. Edited by Naṣr al-Hūrīnī.* 2 vols. Būlāq, 1866.

L'abrégé des merveilles. Traduit de l'Arabe, par Carra de Vaux. Paris, 1898.

Lammens (P. H.), *Etudes sur le règne du Calife Omaiyade Mo'āwia Ier.* [Mélanges de la Faculté Orientale. Université Saint-Joseph, Beyrouth, i.-iii.] Beyrout, 1906-8.

Land (J. P. N.), *Recherches sur l'histoire de la gamme arabe.* [Actes du Sixième Congrès International des Orientalists tenu en 1883 à Leide]. Leyden, 1883.

— *Remarks on the earliest development of Arabic music.* [Trans. of the Ninth Congress of Orientalists, 1892, vol. ii.] London, 1893.

— *Tonschriftversuche und Melodieproben aus dem muhammedanischen Mittelalter.* [Vierteljahrsschrift für Musikwissenschaft, ii]. Leipsic, 1886.

Lane (E. W.), *Madd al-qāmūs, an Arabic-English lexicon, by E. W. Lane.* London, 1863-93.

— *The Thousand and one Nights, commonly called The Arabian Nights' Entertainment. A new translation from the Arabic, by E. W. Lane. A new edition by Edward Stanley Poole.* 3 vols. London, 1883.

— *An account of the manners and customs of the modern Egyptians, in the years* 1825-28. 5th edit. London, 1860.

Lane-Poole, (S.), *A history of Egypt in the Middle Ages.* London, 1901.

— *The Moors in Spain. With the collaboration of Arthur Gilman.* 4th edit. London, 1890.

Lavignac (A.), *Encyclopédie de la musique et dictionnaire du Conservatoire. Histoire de la musique.* 5 vols. Paris, 1913-22.

Leclerc (L.), *Histoire de la Médecine arabe. Exposé complet des traductions du Grec. Les sciences en Orient, leur transmission à L'Occident par les traductions latines.* 2 vols. Paris, 1876.

Le Strange (Guy), *Baghdad during the Abbasid Caliphate. From contemporary Arabic and Persian sources.* Oxford, 1900.

Leyden MSS. See *Catalogus Codicum.*

Lichtenthal (P.), *Dizionario e bibliographia della Musica.* 4 vols. Milan, 1826.

Loth (O.), *Catalogue of the Arabic MSS. in the library of the India Office.* London, 1877.

Löwenthal (A.), *Honein Ibn Ishāk, Sinnsprüche der Philosophen. Nach der hebräischen Uebersetzung Charisi's ins Deutsche übertragen und erläutert von A. Löwenthal.* Berlin, 1896.

Lyall (C. J.), *The Mufaḍḍaliyyāt: An anthology of ancient Arabian odes, compiled by Al-Mufaḍḍal. Edited by C. J. Lyall.* 2 vols. Oxford, 1918-21.

— *Translations of ancient Arabian poetry, chiefly Prae-Islamic.* London, 1885.

Macnaghten (W. H.), *The Alif Laila or Book of the Thousand Nights and One Night, in the original Arabic. Edited by W. H. Macnaghten.* 4 vols. Calcutta, 1839-42.

Madrid MSS. See Robles.

Mafātīḥ al-ʻulūm. See Van Vloten.

Al-Maidānī. See Freytag.

Malter (H.), *Saadia Gaon, His life and works.* Philadelphia, 1921.

Al-Maqqarī, *Analectes sur histoire et la littérature des Arabes d'Espagne par Al-Makkari.* [*Texte arabe.*] *Publiés par MM. Dozy, Dugat, Krehl et Wright.* 2 vols. Leyden, 1855-61.

— *The history of the Mohammedan dynasties in Spain. By Al-Makkarī. Translated by Pascual de Gayangos.* 2 vols. London, 1840-3.

Al-Maqrīzi, *Al-mawāʻiẓ wa'l-iʻtibār. Edited by Muḥammad Quṭṭa al-ʻAdawī.* 2 vols. Būlāq, 1853.

Margoliouth (D. S.), *The Letters of Abu'l-ʻAlā of Maʻarrat Al-Nuʻmān. Edited by D. S. Margoliouth* [Anecdota Oxoniensia.] Oxford, 1898.

Al-Marrākushī (Abd al-Wāḥid), *The history of the Almohades, by Abdo-'l-Wāhid al-Marrēkoshī. Edited by R. Dozy.* Leyden, 1881.

Al-Masʻūdī. *Les prairies d'or. Texte et traduction par Barbier de Meynard et Pavet de Courteil.* 9 vols. Paris, 1861-77.

— *Le livre de l'avertissement et de la revision. Trad. par B. Carra de Vaux.* Paris, 1896.

— *Kitāb al-tanbīh wa'l-ischraf.* [Bibl. Geog. Arab., viii.] Leyden, 1894.

Migne (J. P.), *Patrologiae cursus completus; Accurante J.-P. Migne.* Paris, v.d.

Milan MSS. See Von Hammer-Purgstall.

Minhāj-i-Sarāj. *Ṭabaqāt-i-nāsirī: by The Maulana, Minhāj-ud-Dīn. Translated from the original Persian by H. G. Raverty.* [Bibliotheca Indica.] 2 vols. London, 1881.

Mīr Khwānd, *The Rauzat-us-safa; or Garden of Purity. . . . by Mirkhond. Translated from the original Persian by E. Rehatsek.* 5 vols. London, 1891-4.

Mitjana (R.), *L'Orientalisme musical et la Musique arabe.* [Le Monde Oriental, 1906.] Uppsala, 1906.

Mu'allaqāt. See Ahlwardt, *The divans.*

Al-Mubarrad, *The Kāmil of El-Mubarrad. Edit. by W. Wright*. Leipsic, 1874-92.

Mufaḍḍaliyyāt. See Lyall.

Muir (W.), *The life of Moḥammad from original sources. A new edition by T. H. Weir*. Edinburgh, 1923.

— *The Caliphate. Its rise, decline, and fall. From original sources. A new edition by T. H. Weir*. Edinburgh, 1915.

Munich MSS. See Aumer.

Munk (S.), *Mélanges de philosophie juive et arabe*. Paris, 1859.

Mūrisṭus, *'Amal al-ālat illatī ittakhadhahā Mūrisṭus yadhhabu ṣautuhā sittīn mīlan*. [Al-Mashriq, ix.] Beyrout.

— *Ṣan'at al-urghan al-jāmi' li-jamī' al-aṣwāt*. [Al-Mashriq, ix.]. Beyrout.

— *Kitāb ṣan'at al-juljul*. [Al-Mashriq, ix.] Beyrout

Mustaṭraf. See Al-Ibshīhī.

Myers (C. S.). See Tylor.

Nāṣir-i Khusrau, *Sefer nameh* [*Safar nāma*]. *Relation du voyage de Nassiri Khosrau . . . pendant les années de l'Hégire* 437-444 (1035-1042). *Trad. par C. Schefer*. [Ecole des langues orientales vivantes, iie sér.] Paris, 1881.

*Al-Nawawī, *Minhadj at-talibin, Texte arabe, avec traduction et annotations par L. W. C. van den Berg*. 3 vols. Batavia, 1882.

— *Minhaj et talibin: A manual of Muhammadan law according to the school of Shafii. Translated into English from the French edition of L. W. C. van den Berg, by E. C. Howard*. London, 1914.

Nicholson (R. A.), *A literary history of the Arabs*. London, 1907.

— *The Risālat al-ghufrān by Abu'l-'Alā al-Ma'arrī* [J. R. A. S., 1902.] London, 1902.

Nihāyat al-arab. See Al-Nuwairī.

Nöldeke (T.), *Geschichte des Qorans*. Göttingen, 1860.

Al-Nuwairī, *Nihāyat al-arab*. 5 vols. Cairo, 1925.

Owen (J.), *The skeptics of the Italian Renaissance*. London, 1893.

Paris MSS. See De Slane.
Parisot (J.), *Musique Orientale*. Paris, 1898.
Perron (A.), *Femmes arabes avant et depuis l'Islamisme*. Paris, Algiers, 1858.

Al-Qaswīnī (Zakariyyā), *Āthar al-bilād. Heraus. von F. Wüstenfeld*. Göttingen, 1847.
Quatremère (E. M.), *Histoire des Mongols de la Perse, écrite en Persan par Rashid-Eldin. Trad. par M. Quatremère*. Paris, 1836.
Rawlinson (G.), *History of Phoenicia*. London, 1889.
Reinach (T.), *La Musique grecque*. Paris, 1926.
Renan (E.), *Averroès et l'Averroïsme: Essai historique*. *2me edit*. Paris, 1861.
Ribera (J.), *La Ensenañza entre los Musulmanes Españoles*. (*Discurso leido en la Universidad de Zaragoza*). Saragossa, 1893.
— *La música de las cantigas. Estudio sobre su origen y naturaleza*. Madrid, 1922.
Rieu (C.), *Catalogue of the Persian MSS. in the British Museum*. 3 vols. London, 1879-83.
— *Supplement to the catalogue of the Arabic MSS. in the British Museum*. London, 1894.
Robles (F. Guillen), *Catálogo de los manuscritos árabes existentes en la Biblioteca Nacional de Madrid*. Madrid, 1889.
Sachau (E.) and Ethé (H.), *Catalogue of the Persian, Turkish, Hindustani, and Pushtu MSS. in the Bodleian Library*. Oxford, 1889.
Sale (G.), *The Koran. Translated into English from the original Arabic*. London, 1857.
Salvador-Daniel (F.), *La Musique arabe, ses rapports avec la Musique grecque et le chant gregorien* [2me edit.] Algiers, 1879.
See Farmer.
Sayyid Aḥmad Khān, *Essay on the manners and customs of the Pre-Islamic Arabians. By Syed Ahmed Khan Bahador*. London, 1870.
Sayyid Amīr 'Alī, *The life and teachings of Mohammed, or the spirit of Islam*. London, 1891.
— *A short history of the Saracens*. London, 1899.
Schrader (E.), *Keilinschriftliche Bibliothek*. Berlin, 1889, *et seq*.
Al-Shīrāzī (Ibrāhīm ibn 'Alī), *Jus Shafiticum. At-Tanbīh. Edit. A. W. T. Juynboll*. Leyden, 1879.

Sismondi (J. C. L. S. de), *Historical view of the literature of the south of Europe. Trans. by T. Roscoe.* 2 vols. London, 1846.

Soriano Fuertes (M.), *Historia de la música Española desde la venida de los Fenicios hasta el año de* 1850. 4 vols. Madrid, 1855-59.

Steiner (H.), *Die Mütaziliten, oder die Freidenker im Islam* Leipsic, 1865.

Steingass (F. J.), *The Assemblies of Al Ḥarīrī. Translated from the Arabic. By F. Steingass.* London, 1898.

Steinschneider (M.), *Jewish literature from the eighth to eighteenth century. From the German.* London, 1857.

— *Die Arabischen Uebersetzungen aus dem Griechischen.* [1. Beihefte zum Centralblatt f. Bibliothekswesen, v, xii, Leipsic, 1889-93. 2. Archiv f. Pathologie, cxxiv. 1891. 3. Zeitschrift f. Mathematik, Sect. hist.-lit., xxxi, 1886. 4. Zeitschrift d. deutschen morg. Gesellschaft, 1, 1896.]

— *Al-Farabi (Alpharabius), des arabischen philosophen Leben u. Schriften.* St. Petersburg, 1869.

— *Die europäischen Uebersetzungen aus dem Arabischen bis Mitte des* 17 *Jahrhunderts.* [Sitz. Akad. d. Wiss. Wien. cxlix, cli (=i, ii).] Vienna, 1904-5.

Suter (H.), *Die Mathematiker und Astronomen der Araber und ihre Werke.* [Abhand. z. Gesch. d. Mathematik, x, xiv.] Leipsic, 1900-1902.

Al-Suyūṭī, *Al-muzhir fī 'ulūm al-lugha.* 2 vols. Būlāq, 1865-6.

Syed Ahmed Khan. See Sayyid Aḥmad Khān.

Syed Ameer Ali. See Sayyid Amīr 'Alī.

Ṭabaqāt al-naṣirī. See Minhāj-i-Sarāj.

*Al-Ṭabarī, *Annales quos scripsit Abu Djafar Mohammed Ibn Djarir At-Tabari. Edit. M. J. de Goeje.* 15 vols. Leyden, 1879-1901.

— *Chronique de Tabari, trad. sur la version persane d'Abou-'Ali Mohammed Bel'ami, par M. Hermann Zotenberg.* 4 vols. Paris, 1867-74.

Ta'rīkh-i-jahān-gushā. See Al-Juwainī.

Al-Tibrīzī, *A commentary on the ten ancient Arabic poems. Edited by C. J. Lyall.* [Bibliotheca Indica.] Calcutta, 1894.

Al-Tirmidhī, *Al-ṣaḥīḥ.* 2 vols. Cairo, 1875.

Toderini (G. B.), *Letteratura turchesca.* 3 vols. Venice, 1787.

Tripodo (P.), *Lo stato degli studii sulla musica degli Arabi.* Rome, 1904.

Tylor (E. B.), *Anthropological essays presented to Edward Burnett Tylor in honour of his 75th birthday.* Oxford, 1907.

Uri (J.) and Nicoll (A.), *Catalogus. cod. MSS. Orient. bibl. Bodleyanae.* 2 pts. Oxford, 1787, 1835.

Usd al-ghāba. See Ibn al-Athīr.

Van Vloten, *Liber mafātīh al-olūm, auctore Abū Abdallah Mohammed ibn Ahmed ibn Jūsof, al-Khowarezmi. Edidit. G. van Vloten.* Leyden, 1895.

Vienna MSS. See Flügel.

Von Hammer-Purgstall, *Catalogo dei cod. arabi, pers. e turchi, della Bibl. Ambrosiani.* [Bibl. Italiana, xciv.] Milan, 1839.

Von Hammer-Purgstall, *Literaturgeschichte der Araber* 7 vols. Vienna, 1850-56.

Von Schack (A. F.), *Poesie und Kunst der Araber in Spanien und Sizilien.* 2 vols. Stuttgart, 1877.

Al-Wāqidī, *Muhammad in Medina. Das ist, Vakidi's Kitab al-Maghazi in verkürzter deutscher Wiedergabe heraus. von J. Wellhausen.* Berlin, 1882.

Al-Warrāq, *Kitāb al-fihrist mit Anmerkungen heraus. von G. Flügel, J. Rödiger, A. Müller.* 2 vols. Leipsic, 1871-2.

Wead (C. K.), *Contribution to the history of musical scales.* [Smithsonian Institution.] Washington, 1902.

Wenrich (J. G.), *De auctorum Graecorum versionibus et commentariis Syriacis, Arabicis, Armeniacis, Persicisque commentatio.* Leipsic, 1842.

Wiedemann (E.), *Ueber Musikautomaten bei den Arabern.* [Centenario della Nascita di M. Amari, Bd. 2.]

Wüstenfeld (H. F.), *Geschichte der arabischen Aerzte und Naturforscher.* Göttingen, 1840.

— *Geschichte der Fatimiden-Chalifen, nach arabischen Quellen.* [Abhand. Gesell. Wiss. Göttingen. xxvi, xxviii. 1880–81].

Yafil (E.), *Majmū' al-aghānī wa'l-alḥān min kalām al-andalus*. Algiers, 1904.
Yafil (E. N.) and Rouanet (J.), *Répertoire de Musique arabe et maure. Collection d'Ouvertures, Mélodies, Noubat, Chansons, Préludes, Danses, etc.* 25 pts Algiers, 1904, *et seq*.

Zākī Bāshā (Aḥmad), *L'aviation chez les Musulmans*. Cairo, 1912.

(2) MANUSCRIPTS.

1. 'Abd al-Mu'min ibn Ṣafī al-Dīn, *Bahjat al-rūḥ*. Bodleian MSS. *Ouseley*, 117.
2. Al-Amūlī (Muḥammad ibn Aḥmad), *Nafā'is al-funūn*. British Museum MS. *Add*. 16827. fols. 429-45.
*3. Al-Fārābi, *Kitāb al-mūsīqī*. Leyden MS. *Cod*. 651 *Warn*.
4. Al-Fārābī, *Kitāb al-mūsīqī*. Madrid MS. 602 (Robles).
5. Al-Fārābī, *Iḥṣā' al-'ulūm*. Escorial MS. 646. fols. 27-45.
6. Ḥunain ibn Isḥāq, *Ijtimā'āt al-falāsifa*. Munich MS. *Cod. Mon. arab*. 651.
7. Ibn Ghaibī ('Abd al-Qādir), *Jāmi' al-alḥān*. Bodleian MS. *Marsh* 828
8. Ibn Khurdādhbih [*Title not given*]. Berlin MS. *Pm*. 173, fol. 1.
9. Ibn Sīnā, *Dānish nāma: dar 'ilm mūsīqī*. Brit. Mus. MS. *Or*. 2361, fols. 157-161v.
10. Ibn Sīnā, *Dānish nāma: dar 'ilm mūsīqī*. Brit. Mus. MS. *Add*. 16659, fols. 333-337v.
*11. Ibn Sīnā. *Kitāb al-najāt*. Bodleian MS. *Marsh*, 521. fols. 159-170v.
12. Ibn Sīnā, *Kitāb al-najāt*. Bodleian MS. *Marsh* 161. fols. 1-9v.
*13. Ibn Sīnā. *Kitāb al-shifā'*. India Office MS. 1811. fols. 152v.-174v.
14. Ibn Sīnā, *Kitāb al-shifā'*. Royal Asiatic Society MS. 58.

15. Ibn Sīnā, *Kitāb al-shifā'*. Bodleian MS. *Pocock* 250, fols. 74-93v.
16. Ibn Sīnā, *Kitāb al-shifā'*. Bodleian MS. *Pocock* 109, fols. 74v.-308v.
17. Ibn Zaila (Abū Manṣūr Al-Ḥusain), *Kitāb al-kāfī fi'l-mūsīqī*. Brit. Mus. MS., *Or*. 2361. fols. 220-36v.
18. Ikhwān al-Ṣafā', *Rasā'il*. Bodleian MS. *Hunt* 296, fols. 23-38.
19. Ikhwān al-Ṣafā', *Rasā'il*. Bodleian MS. *Marsh* 189, fols. 25v-41v.
20. *Kanz al-tuḥaf*. Brit. Mus. MS. *Or*. 2361, fols. 247-69.
21. *Kanz al-tuḥaf*. Leyden MS. *Cod*. 271 (2) *Warn*.
22. Al-Kindī, *Risāla fī khubr ta'līf al-alḥān*. Brit. Mus. MS. *Or*. 2361, fols. 165-8.
23. Al-Kindī, *Risāla fi'l-luḥūn*. Berlin MS. *We*. 1240. fols. 22-24v.
24. Al-Kindī (?) [*Title not given*]. Berlin MS. *We*. 1240. fols. 25-31.
25. Al-Kindī, *Risāla fī ijzā' khabariyya al-mūsīqī*. Berlin MS. *We*. 1240. fols. 31v.-35v.
26. Al-Lādhiqī ('Abd al-Ḥamīd), *Fatḥiyya fī 'ilm al-mūsīqī*. Brit. Mus. MS. *Or*. 6629.
27. Lisān al-Dīn (Ibn al-Khaṭīb) (?), [*Title not given*], Madrid MS. 334 (3) (Robles).
28. *Ma'rifat al-naghamāt al-thamān* (sic). Madrid MS. 334 (2) (Robles).
29. *Muḥammad ibn Murād MS*. Brit. Mus. MS. *Or*. 2361, fols. 168v-219v.
30. Mūrisṭus, *Ṣan'at al-juljul*. Brit. Mus. MS. *Or*. 9649. fols. 11v.-13.
31. Mūrisṭus, *Ṣan'at al-urghīn al-zamrī*. Brit. Mus. MS. *Or*. 9649, fols. 6v-11.
32. Mūrisṭus, *Ṣan'at al-urghīn al-būqī*. Brit. Mus MS. *Or*. 9649, fols. 1v-5.
33. Al-Rāzī (Fakhr al-Dīn), *Jāmi' al-'ulūm*. Brit. Mus. MS. *Or*. 2972.
34. Al-Rāzī (Fakhr al-Dīn), *Jāmi' al-'ulūm*. Brit. Mus. MS. *Or*. 3308.
*35. Ṣafī al-Dīn 'Abd al-Mu'min, *Kitāb al-adwār*. Brit. Mus. MS. *Or*. 136. fols. 1-39v.
36. Ṣafī al-Dīn 'Abd al-Mu'min, *Kitāb al-adwār*. Brit. Mus. MS. *Or*. 2361. fols. 18v-32.
37. Ṣafī al-Dīn 'Abd al-Mu'min, [*Kitāb al-adwār*]. Bodleian MS. *Marsh* 161. fols. 10-42v.

38. Ṣafī al-Dīn 'Abd al-Mu'min, *Kitāb al-adwār*. Bodleian MS. *Marsh* 161. fols. 43-83.
39. Ṣafī al-Dīn 'Abd al-Mu'min, *Kitāb al-adwār*. Bodleian MS. *Marsh* 521. fols. 1-32v.
40. Ṣafī al-Dīn 'Abd al-Mu'min, *Kitāb al-adwār*. Bodleian MS. *Marsh* 521. fols. 118-58.
41. Ṣafī al-Dīn 'Abd al-Mu'min, [*Kitāb al-adwār*]. Paris MS. *Arabe* 2865. fols. 6-23v.
42. Ṣafī al-Dīn 'Abd al-Mu'min, *Risālat al-sharafiyya*. Bodleian MS. *Marsh* 115. fols. 2-55v.
43 Ṣafī al-Dīn 'Abd al-Mu'min, [*Risālat al-sharafiyya*] Bodleian MS. *Marsh* 521. fols. 34v.-116.
44. *Sharḥ al-adwār*. Brit. Mus. MS. *Or*. 2361. fol. 33v. *et seq*.
45. *Sharḥ Maulānā Mubārakshāh*. Brit. Mus. MS. *Or*. 2361.
46. [Al-Shalāhī], *Kitāb al-imtā' wa'l-intifā'*. Madrid MS. 603 (Robles).
47. Al-Shīrāzī (Kuṭb al-Dīn), *Durrat al-tāj*. Brit. Mus. MS. Add. 7694.
48. Al-Ṭūsī (Naṣīr al-Dīn) [*Title not given*]. Paris MS. *Arabe* 2466. fols. 197v-198.
49. Yaḥyā ibn 'Alī ibn Yaḥyā, *Risāla fī'l-mūsīqī*. Brit. Mus. MS. *Or*. 2361. fols. 236v-238v.

INDEX TO PERSONS

SUBJECT AND GEOGRAPHICAL INDEX